146

CONNECTING MATHEMATICS FOR ELEMENTARY TEACHERS

David Feikes
Purdue University North Central

Keith Schwingendorf
Purdue University North Central

Jeff Gregg
Purdue University Calumet

PEARSON

Addison
Wesley

Boston San Francisco New York
London Toronto Sydney Tokyo Singapore Madrid
Mexico City Munich Paris Cape Town Hong Kong Montreal

Reproduced by Pearson Addison-Wesley from electronic files supplied by the author.

ISBN-13: 978-0-321-54266-3
ISBN-10: 0-321-54266-5

5 6 BB 10 09

The Connecting Mathematics for Elementary Teachers Project was funded by the National Science Foundation, grants DUE 0341217 and DUE 0126882. Opinions expressed are those of the authors and not necessarily those of the National Science Foundation.

Dedication

This book is dedicated to children, that they might understand mathematics and to future teachers, that they might understand how children understand mathematics.

Contents

Introduction

To the student[1]:

Connecting Mathematics for Elementary Teachers (CMET) materials are designed to be a supplement for a variety of elementary mathematics education courses including content, methods, and graduate courses. These materials have been designed to help you connect **your own learning of mathematics** with **how children understand and learn mathematics**. In addition, the CMET Supplement attempts to show how children's learning of mathematics in elementary school is connected to more advanced mathematics in middle and high school. Consequently, this supplement primarily focuses on how children learn and understand

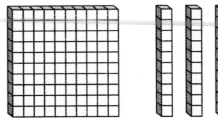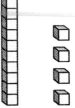

mathematics and not on how to teach mathematics. While this supplement is not designed to teach you how to teach mathematics to children, we believe that learning how children think mathematically will be helpful in your teaching of mathematics to children.

Every child is different. Our descriptions of how many or most children learn are not a guarantee of how every child thinks mathematically. The best way to find out what a child is thinking is to ask him/her. The CMET Supplement attempts to provide general descriptions of children's learning. These descriptions are intended to help you understand how children approach mathematics differently than adults. By helping you connect children's thinking to your own learning, we hope that this will improve your understanding of both mathematics and children thereby enhance your ability to teach mathematics to children.

As you use this supplement, try to consider how you learned mathematics, how children learn mathematics, and how you will teach mathematics to children. The more you understand mathematics and how children think about mathematics, the better teacher you will be. Our advice is:

- Read the supplement along with your textbook,
- Do the Problems and Exercises, and
- Try to understand how children learn mathematics.

---

[1] Note: Throughout the supplement, **student** refers to you, a preservice elementary teacher or graduate student, and **child** refers to an elementary school student.

Organization

Each section contains insights and examples of how children come to understand mathematics. Many of the descriptions of how children learn are based on research, but some are based on the authors' personal experiences with helping children learn mathematics. We have attempted to use our own knowledge and experiences along with research to present descriptions of how children understand the mathematics. We have also attempted to describe the "why" behind the mathematics that you will be teaching to children because, as a teacher, you should be able to explain the mathematics to children. Key underlying, mathematical concepts are presented and discussed. Manipulatives are discussed in relationship to the mathematics children are learning. As a teacher, it is important to understand the mathematics that a manipulative represents or embodies. Occasionally, a few class activities are included to help you see how children think mathematically. Connections are made to children's later developments in mathematics, which might include the mathematics that children will learn in later grades or even middle or high school. In summary, the CMET Supplement attempts to connect the mathematics you are learning with the mathematics you will be teaching children.

At the end of each section are "**Problems and Exercises**" for you to solve. These problems and exercises are different than the problems in your mathematics textbook in that they are specifically designed to help you learn how children learn mathematics. Many of these questions are from the National Assessment of Educational Progress (NAEP) and the Third International Mathematics and Science Study (TIMSS). The NAEP tests are only given in the United States and are used to measure national achievement. The TIMSS tests are given in the United States and internationally and used primarily to compare mathematics achievement in the United States with other countries. Both these tests are normally given every two to four years and are used to measure the educational achievement in mathematics in grades 4, 8, and 12. The test questions along with the performance data of children on the test questions are available at the following websites:

NAEP: http://nces.ed.gov/nationsreportcard/itmrls/
TIMSS: http://timss.bc.edu/timss2003i/released.html
             http://timss.bc.edu/timss1999i/timss_test.html
             http://timss.bc.edu/timss1995i/Items.html

NAEP
National Assessment of Educational Progress

Another key feature of this supplement is "**Children's Solutions and Discussion of Problems and Exercises**" section.   Here we present both children's solutions and errors or a discussion for some of the "**Problems and Exercises**". With the NAEP and TIMSS questions, we give the percentage of children who had the correct solution. With some NAEP questions we also give children's actual solutions. All the data we present may not be indicative of how a particular child or class will perform on the problem. The data is intended to provide a general idea on how many children perform on similar problems.

Before looking at the "**Children's Solutions and Discussion of Problems and Exercises,**" be sure to do the problems first and then see how children attempted them. Especially consider what mathematics you will need to understand in order to understand and facilitate children's growth in learning mathematics. To help you reflect on these connections and understandings, each section also has "**Questions for Discussion**". These are general questions for you to discuss, write about, or reflect upon.

We sincerely hope that you enjoy using our supplement and find it useful in your learning of mathematics. More importantly, we hope that this supplement allows you to make important connections to the ways that children learn and think about mathematics.

Preface to the Instructor

Connecting Mathematics for Elementary Teachers, (CMET) is designed to be used with any course and textbook for the mathematical content or methods courses for elementary teachers. We have developed alignment tables that show how CMET is aligned with the most widely used textbooks in mathematics education. The tables for textbooks published by Pearson can be found in the CMET Instructors Guide and all available tables can be found on our website: http://www.cmetonline.com.

Purpose of CMET

CMET is not specifically designed to teach mathematics, but to help preservice teachers connect the mathematics they are learning with how children learn and understand mathematics. The intent is that this will enhance preservice teachers' understanding of mathematics and consequently improve their future teaching of mathematics to children. Students are more motivated to learn when they can see the connection between their learning and their future profession.

Using CMET

We have two main suggestions in effectively using CMET. First, having students read CMET is essential; consider assigning the reading of the CMET section along with the corresponding section that you are covering in the mathematics content textbook. You may assign some or all of the **Problems and Exercises** at the end of each section. These problems are designed for children; some are eighth grade problems so a few may be a bit more challenging. Most answers are in the back of the book. Encourage students to solve these problems first. However, the key is the **Children's Solutions and Discussion of Problems and Exercises. So,** the second main suggestion is to, whenever possible, discuss or cover the data and children's solutions from this section with your students. The data and solutions are designed to provide insights into how children understand mathematics. The **Questions for Discussion** may be more useful in a methods or graduate course in mathematics education.

These are a few suggestions for using CMET. We would be interested in learning how others have used our book, especially in methods and graduate mathematics education courses. You can email your comments and suggestions to dfeikes@pnc.edu.

CMET and Students

Most students in mathematical content courses for elementary teachers are apprehensive about learning mathematics. Our hope is that preservice teachers not only learn mathematics, but that they begin to develop an understanding of how children think about mathematics, learn to appreciate mathematics, and enjoy teaching it.

With CMET, students should never say, "Where will I ever use this?"

Acknowledgements

We would first like to thank our wives, Julie (Feikes) and Lisa (Schwingendorf). We could not have written this book without their support and encouragement. Second, our own children, Jaime, Mike, Katie, Andrew, Aaron (Feikes), and Jessica, Ryan, Jeff, and Karen Teller (Schwingendorf) who helped us learn how children think. We acknowledge their contribution to our understanding of how children learn and come to understand mathematical concepts.

Many have contributed to this book - some in small ways and some in large ways. We would like to thank research consultants David Tall and Grayson Wheatley for their insightful comments and encouragement and Mary Jane Eisenhauer, Michelle Stephan and Marcela Perlwitz for their contributions, as well as David Pratt and Sarah Hough for their extensive evaluation and help in refining the book, and Teresa Henning for her thoughtful editing of the manuscript.

We would also like to thank Anne Brown, Carol Steiner, Carol Castellon, Barbara O'Donnell, Ann Taylor, and Danny Breidenbach for piloting our materials; Nancy Brinklow, Sara Sightes, and Diane Kilkenny for their reading of the materials; Nadine Kost for the creation of our first cover logo, and our secretaries Gwen Vernich, Stephanie Jimenez, and Kay Toll for their help in the preparation of the manuscript.

Many undergraduates have helped in the collection of data included in the book including: Melanie Hoffman, Deana Sommers, Carol Kurmis, Jaime Smith, Salina Thomason, Julie Crawford, Tara Sobecki, Sarah Sims, Amy Hardesty-Asher, Stephanie Koehl, Tamara Trajkovski, Sarah Briggs, Camellia Dabagia, Dana Lippelt, Kristen Pawlik, Susanna Rownd, Crystal Ridley, Alyssa Buechley, Samanatha Babb, Ray Callahan, Chris Goodwin, Julie Hanaway, Kim Holt, Jill Posiadlik, Kristin Richardson, Abby Vanlaningham, David Demmon, Becky Welter, Ian Pappas, Becky Lane, Carrie Miller, Kelly Harmon, Moniqua Neal, Maria Yovino, Brett Parks, LouAnn Tuttle, Heather Walters and Ashley Davis.

Finally, we would like to thank the editorial staff at Pearson for their hard work and dedication to detail. CMET would not have come to fruition without the expertise of Joe Vetere and his graphical wizardry. Thanks for sticking with us from the beginning, Joe. Marnie Greenhut, our editor who came on board and re-energized the project. Joanne Dill for helping to turn our project from a lot of files and paper into real book, and Becky Anderson, our marketing manager, without whose help our book would just be sitting on the shelves of friends and family.

Chapter 1: Problem Solving

Educators, parents, and children frequently attribute different meanings to the term 'problem solving.' Some educators hold the view that children learn and understand mathematics through solving problems. Further mathematics should be a sense making activity—that is learning mathematics should make sense. Real understanding comes from solving problems. The purpose of this chapter is to explore various views of problem solving as well as your own understandings of problem solving. The discussions and exercises in this chapter explore why problem solving is important, encourage reflection on your own learning and future teaching of problem solving, and most importantly, describe how children solve problems.

1.1   An Introduction to Problem Solving

What is Problem Solving?

Before considering how children solve problems, it is important to first consider what problem solving is and the different meanings held by educators, parents, and children:

- "General problem solving" is the practice of engaging students in working on challenging, non-routine problems (not necessarily word or story problems). The intent of such general problem solving sessions is to help students develop a repertoire of problem-solving strategies, which are sometimes called heuristics. Examples of heuristics would be 'guess and check' and 'work backwards'.
- The term "problem solving" may be used as a label for certain teaching practices encouraged by current reform efforts in mathematics education. In this case, we speak of "a problem solving approach" to teaching, "problem-centered learning" (PCL), or an "inquiry approach." A problem solving approach is characterized by a significant amount of small-group work and by whole-class discussions in which children explain their thinking, justify their solutions, and question each other. The teacher orchestrates the discussions by asking questions, challenging children's ideas, and offering guidance, however, the teacher largely refrains from the traditional practice of showing children a single procedure for solving a certain type of problem and then having a child spend a great deal of time practicing that procedure. Most all mathematical topics, including addition, subtraction, multiplication, division, concepts of fractions, spatial reasoning, and the notion of area, may be taught with such a problem solving approach.
- Many textbooks label routine tasks and exercises, word or story problems, as problem solving. These word problems often contain the same operation as the previous set of computation tasks. Typically, a heavy emphasis is placed on using key or clue words.

Some elementary-level mathematics textbooks include "general problem solving" and sometimes may include several sections on problem solving. However, reform-oriented curriculums (e.g., Everyday Mathematics, Math Trailblazers, Investigations in Number, Data, and Space), integrate a "problem solving approach" throughout the text and attempt to teach all topics through such an approach. More information on these reform textbooks is available at the Alternatives for

Rebuilding Curricula Center website:
http://www.comap.com/elementary/project/arc/curricul.html.

Whichever elementary mathematics textbook you use once you become a teacher, you will be teaching some form of problem solving to children. Also, the children you will be teaching will need to be good problem solvers in order to be successful in high school, college, and life applications.

Since problem solving will be an important term in your life as a teacher and in the lives of the children you will be teaching, it is important that you begin to reflect on what this term means to you and others. When encountering this term, you might ask yourself, "What does 'problem solving' mean to these authors?" For the most part, this section on problem solving uses a "general problem solving" definition, but you will also find references to a "problem solving approach" to teaching.

Why do Problem Solving?

Some educators believe learning to solve problems (i.e., problem solving) is the primary reason for studying mathematics. According to this view, mathematics education includes more than simply becoming proficient at adding, subtracting, multiplying, and dividing. Such an education requires the development of mathematical understandings of these operations and other mathematical concepts in order to solve problems. Understanding mathematics implies knowing how and why mathematics works and not the rote following of set steps and procedures.

Another reason problem solving is important is the fact that in an appropriate classroom environment, problem solving may help students improve their self-image in relation to mathematics. That means that students may become more confident and comfortable with mathematics; they may even learn to enjoy math. Further, a problem-solving approach has been shown to help students develop a better and richer understanding of mathematics (Cobb, Wood, & Yackel 1991; Carpenter, Fenema, & Franke, 1996; Kamii & Housman, 1999).

Problem solving helps children construct mathematical relationships. Practice in problem solving also encourages children to develop their own strategies and processes for solving problems. The traditional textbook approach of using story problems and teaching key words often fails to capture the essence of problem solving because this approach does not always engage children in an inquiry process with mathematically challenging activities. Wheatley characterizes many traditional textbooks' approach to teaching problem solving as "the solving of well-defined questions based on certain information provided, frequently with the method specified" (Wheatley & Reynolds, 1999).

Wheatley's characterization suggests that often children and teachers view mathematics as a collection of facts and rules and not as a sense-making activity. While thinking of Wheatley's characterization and your own views of mathematics instruction, consider how the following excerpt from a pre-service teacher compares with your own views of mathematics and the point Wheatley is making.

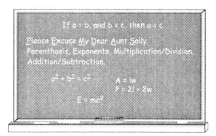

Each following year another layer of rules was added to the preceding year. This layer effect continued until one graduated from high school. Mathematics became a stumbling stone by the time I reached ninth grade algebra. In that freshmen algebra class I became convinced that I was not a "math student."

Because this student did not have a sense making understanding of mathematics and because she could not memorize all the facts and rules of algebra, she was not able to succeed. Notice that her beliefs about mathematics not only impacted her ability to do well in the class, but they also negatively impacted her self-esteem. By learning how to employ a problem solving approach to teaching, this student and others like her can learn to change such beliefs and as a result, become better teachers who are more self-confident in their mathematical abilities.

This next excerpt from another pre-service teacher reveals how common it is to not view mathematics as a sense making activity. She states:

> I was taught to memorize rules and was tested with drills. It is common to teach in the same manner you were taught... I was ... very rule oriented in my thinking about math. It is a hard habit to break. I can remember thinking I just want to know the rule when learning math.

An essential question is how to break this recurring cycle of teachers teaching the way they were taught and emphasizing the memorization of rules. Memorizing rules without understanding does not serve students well when they need to apply mathematics to solve problems outside of school or when they need to apply their knowledge to learn more advanced mathematics. The NCTM Standards (1989, 1991, 2000) call for:

> The creation of a curriculum and an environment, in which teaching and learning are to occur, that are very different from much of the current practice ... The kind of teaching envisioned in these standards is significantly different from what teachers themselves have experienced in mathematics classes. (pp 1-2, NCTM, 1991)

This statement suggests that pre-service teachers need to be prepared to learn how to teach mathematics differently from the way that they may have been taught. Throughout this chapter and the ones that follow, mathematics is presented as more than a collection of facts and procedures. Mathematics is and should be a sense making activity.

Learning to Teach Problem Solving

What is the best way to learn how to teach problem solving? The best way is to experience problem solving. Since learning to teach problem solving well requires one to experience the act of problem solving, the activities in this chapter are designed to allow you to experience problem solving both from your own and a child's perspective. As you solve the problems in your textbook and in this supplement, try to think about how these activities might relate to the problems that you will be doing with children someday. Three questions that you might ask yourself, not just when solving problems, but throughout this course are:

- How might children solve this type of problem?
- What might children learn from working on this problem?
- Do I understand the mathematics in the problem well enough to teach children?

What is a (Mathematical) Problem for Children?

When considering the many definitions of a problem, it is important to ask: "What is a problem for children?" Two second-grade classrooms, one rural and one urban, were asked this very question: "What is a problem?"   For the children in the rural setting, an example of a problem was "if you miss the bus." The students were asked how they would solve this problem, and they responded that they would call their mom and ask her to take them to school. In the urban

school, problems given by the children were "if you do not have enough to eat" or "there are gunshots at night." The problems offered by the urban students are not as easily solved as the problems offered by the rural students. In this course you will be solving problems like missing the bus—problems that you can readily solve. In real life not all problems can be solved.

Often when children and teachers are asked to think of problem solving they think of word or story problems. However, for young children who cannot yet read or who have not been introduced to story problems, the world is full of problems to be solved. Many situations that arise naturally in the classroom lend themselves to the creation of mathematical problems. For instance, sharing materials such as markers or blocks offers children the chance to think about the ways in which groups of materials can be divided equally. It is important to remember that problem solving is not limited to solving word problems.

The effective practice of having children work together when they are problem solving can even become a problem solving activity in and of itself. For example, suppose that a teacher has decided to have children work in pairs. The teacher has the class count off beginning at 1. She tells them that 1 will pair with 2, 3 with 4, 5 with 6, and so on. (As you get to know your children better, one method is to pair students of like ability or alternatively, of different

abilities.) What if child number 17 raises his hand and asks, "Who is my partner?" If we are going to teach using a problem-solving approach and if we want our students to really do problem solving, then we cannot tell the children how to solve this problem. We must try to find a way to help <u>them</u> construct their own solution to the problem. Since it is likely that if number 17 does not know who his partner is, other children do not know who their partners are either.

Involving the whole class in solving this problem together can be a productive activity for everyone.

In response to this problem of pairing children, students in other mathematical content classes have suggested telling the children that the person on their right is their partner. However, this solution does not account for that fact that some partners are sitting front-to-back and others maybe on the child's left. Another suggested solution to this problem is to tell the children that if they are an odd number they should go to the next higher number. This solution will work, but in a first or second grade classroom student number 17 might respond, "I don't know if I am even or odd." How might a child determine if a number is even or odd? A common response is that they could divide their number by 2, but most first and second graders don't know how to divide by 2. Another suggestion is to redo the counting and count 1,2; 1,2; etc., but the teacher may not want to repeat the counting off process, as the teacher's goal may be to solve the problem without starting over.

How would you help the child number 17 and the other children in the class figure out who their partners are without telling them? *What makes this situation a problem for children? How does this problem compare to the textbook problems given to children? How is this particular problem similar or different from those problems?*

Children's Beliefs about Solving Problems

When preparing to teach problem solving to children, it is important to understand what beliefs children already possess when it comes to problem solving. While it is not possible to characterize the beliefs that every individual child may have regarding problem solving, we do know that many children have the following beliefs about solving problems:
- There is one right way to solve a problem.
- Mathematics is a set of rules and procedures.
- Learning mathematics is mostly memorizing.
- Elementary school mathematics is computation.
- Mathematics problems should be solved quickly.
- The goal of mathematics is to obtain "right answers."
- The teacher and the textbook are the mathematical authority (Cai, 2003; Frank, 1991).

Now that you have a sense of what children believe about problem solving, it is important to ask yourself some important questions about these beliefs. Before reading the next section, try to answer these questions:
- How do these children's beliefs compare to my own beliefs about problem solving?
- In what ways might my beliefs both help and interfere with my ability to teach children to problem solve?
- In what ways might these children's beliefs both help and interfere with my ability to teach children to problem solve?
- How do my own beliefs and those of children both support and interfere with the understanding that mathematics is more than a collection of facts; it is a sense making activity?

How Children Solve Problems

Children in the early primary grades are more likely to use a 'guess and check' strategy when solving problems. As children progress in their development of problem solving ability (often a gradual process), they begin to use the error of each guess to adjust their next guess and come closer to the solution. For example, consider how a child would solve this problem:

If a pencil and eraser cost 40¢ and the pencil costs 10¢ more than the eraser, how much does each cost?

A child may guess 20¢ for the pencil and 10¢ for the eraser, but realizing that the total is not enough (30¢), she may increase her guesses. She may now guess 30¢ for the pencil and 20¢ for the eraser, but when she realizes that her total is now too much (50¢), she may adjust her guesses to the middle of her guesses. In this instance, her guess for the pencil would be 25¢, and her guess for the eraser would be 15¢ which would give her the desired total of 40¢. By using each guess to adjust her next guess, this child is demonstrating more sophisticated thinking than just giving random guesses.

Children are also much more likely to act out or model problems than are adults. Adults tend to try to solve problems in their heads first through abstract thinking. However, sometimes children's methods are more productive than adults' methods. Children are also more likely to use "trial and error" than are adults. Studies of expert and novice (which would include most children) problem solvers indicate that novice problem solvers tend to focus on the superficial information of the problem (National Research Council, 1985).

The following example occurred in a fourth-grade urban classroom with two girls who were working together on word problems. One of the problems asked:

How many pieces of candy could one buy for 72 cents if each piece costs 6 cents?

Initially, the two girls were stumped. However, with a great deal of thought and discussion, they made 72 (7 strips of 10 and 2 ones) with their counting cubes and then divided the 72 into groups of six. They then counted the strips of 6 to arrive at their answer. Notice how the girls physically modeled the problem with manipulatives in order to solve it.

Problem Solving Steps

Almost every American elementary mathematics textbook uses Polya's four-step problem solving process, or a variation thereof, to help children become better problem solvers. His four steps are:

- Understand the Problem,
- Devise a Plan,
- Carry Out the Plan, and
- Look Back.

Several elementary mathematics textbooks directly teach Polya's four step process and some even require children to demonstrate how they followed that process. Keep in mind that this approach is only one way to approach problem solving. If it helps, then it is a good way but there are other ways.

Research is beginning to show that the four-step approach is not how mathematicians and scientists really think about a problem (Sfard, 1994). They say that they rarely understand a problem until after it is solved. And their "plan" could not be called a real plan but perhaps a hunch or intuition. Experts become better problem solvers by solving many problems and by developing a repertoire of strategies or techniques that they can fall back on.

Mason, Burton and Stacey (1985) offer the following suggestions for problem solving:

- STUCK, Good! RELAX and ENJOY it!
    Now something can be learned.
- Sort out What you KNOW and What you WANT,
- SPECIALISE,
- GENERALISE,
- Make a CONJECTURE,
- Find someone to whom to explain why you are STUCK.

It is okay for children to struggle with problems. Frequently, teachers feel that as soon as a child is struggling they should jump in and tell the child what to do. Some even consider jumping in to help to be an aspect of "good teaching." But does telling the child what to do make for good learning? It is important to remember that while there is no one best approach for teaching problem solving, it is very important to let children experience problem solving for themselves. As you both teach problem solving and solve problems on your own, be sure to use the steps that help you, and encourage children to use the steps that help them!

Problem Solving Strategies - Heuristics

To help you understand the variety of strategies that may help you and children problem solve, we offer here a list of some of the most common problem-solving strategies, also called heuristics.

1	Guess and Check
2	Make a List or Table
3	Write an Equation—Use Algebraic Reasoning
4	Work Backwards
5	Break into Smaller Parts
6	Draw a Picture or Diagram
7	Act It Out or Model the Problem
8	Look for a Pattern
9	Do Something
10	Grind It Out – The Long Way
11	Take a Break and Try Again!

Children often have their own names for these heuristics and may also use heuristics that are not listed here. For instance, children will sometimes name the strategies after a method that a child in their class used. In such an instance, 'Grind It Out' might be called 'Brian's Method'. Children may also come up with strategies other than those on the list. When asked to reflect on their problem solving, children and students frequently indicate that they used combinations of two and sometimes three strategies to solve a problem.

While these strategies have proven to be powerful tools in helping children and adults solve problems (Suydam, 1987), they become less powerful when a teacher or textbook directly tell the child which heuristic to use. For instance, you may find that children's mathematics textbooks (and your own college textbooks) often tell children what strategies to use for each problem. When textbooks suggest a strategy for each problem they are treating heuristics as rules.

Wheatley (1984) emphasizes "Heuristics are not Rules!" Instead, they are **tools** that people often use when solving problems. These tools help problem solvers understand the problem and organize their thinking about it. Yet, often in textbooks, a heuristic is given or suggested for each word problem or exercise. As a result, children may end up applying known procedures to tasks without thinking about the task. Such a "hint" may make the problem easy to solve—so easy, in fact, that it is not really a problem at all—but ultimately such an approach limits children's thinking and does not help them to become good problem solvers.

When a textbook offers a "hint" as to what heuristic a student should use, the textbook may inadvertently cause the child to ignore the fact that other strategies may also help them solve the problem. In solving real-life problems, no one tells children what heuristics to use. In fact, determining what strategy to try is often a significant step in the problem solving process. Children cannot develop this skill if they are simply told what strategy to use. Using heuristics as rules is not true problem solving.

When heuristics are taught as rules, both children and their parents can become frustrated. For instance, a mother of a fourth grade child was concerned because her daughter's teacher insisted that her daughter do the problems in her mathematics textbook by using the strategy that was provided. These hints for each problem were heuristics such as 'work backwards.' However, the mother knew that these hints did not connect to the way that her daughter was thinking about each problem, and the child was becoming very frustrated. What affect do you think this teacher's approach to heuristics is likely to have on this child's attitudes and beliefs about mathematics? What would you do if you were this child's parent? What would you do if you were this child's teacher?

Another way to help children become familiar with these strategies so that they can use them readily is to ask them to solve a set of problems in any way they choose. When they are finished, the teacher can ask them to look back and determine which strategy they used on which problem. This approach will help children become familiar with these strategies and personalize these strategies to suite their unique thinking and learning styles.

As you begin to problem solve and teach problem solving, be sure to keep in mind that heuristics can be valuable tools for problem solving, but they are only tools. Children will choose the tools that they are most comfortable with and that make sense to them. Different carpenters may choose different tools to complete the same job, but they both get the job done. The better the tools that one has at his or her disposal, the better and more efficient one can be at completing the job. Hence, our goal as teachers of problem solving is to provide opportunities for children to learn and feel comfortable with a variety of tools. The goal is not just the solution to the problem. We are sometimes more interested in the problem solving process than the answer to the problem!

1.1   Problems and Exercises

Problems in set A are designed for pre-service teachers. Each problem in Set A contains comments or suggestions, in italics, for you to think about as you solve the problem. The problems in Set B are designed for both pre-service teachers and children to solve. Be sure to solve the problems first BEFORE considering the data on how children solved the problem and BEFORE looking at the children's solutions in the **Children's Solutions and Discussion of Problems and Exercises** section. As you solve the problems in Set B, consider what mathematics you may need to understand in order to facilitate children's learning of mathematics on these same problems.

Problem Set A

As you try to solve the following problems, **focus on the processes** you use to come to a solution. Also, as you solve these problems, think about how children might solve similar problems. Finally, as you work on these problems, do not forget that one of the key suggestions for teaching problem solving is to focus on the process, not the product! In these problems the processes you use are what are important. If children understand the processes then they will be able to apply or transfer what they have learned to other problems.

1. Find the sum: $1 + 2 + 3 + ... + 998 + 999 + 1{,}000 = ?$

    How did you attempt to solve this problem? What patterns did you find? Did you find a pattern of a pattern? If you tried to use a formula, what formula did you use? Do you really understand how and why the formula works? Could you explain the formula to someone else?

2. A protractor and a compass cost $3.00. If the protractor costs $.80 more than the compass, how much does each cost?

    How many different ways might pre-service students solve this problem? A fourth- or fifth-grade class might also come up with these same ways except for an algebra solution. Do you understand how and why these different ways work?

3. Looking in my backyard one day I saw some boys and dogs. I counted 24 heads and 72 feet. How many boys and how many dogs were in my backyard?

    How did you solve this problem? How might children solve this problem with a picture?

4. There are four volumes of Charles Dickens's collected works on a shelf. The volumes are in order from left to right. The pages of each volume are exactly 2 inches thick. The covers of each volume are exactly 1/6 inch thick. A bookworm started eating at page 1 of Volume I and ate to the last page of Volume IV. What is the distance the bookworm traveled?

A common method when solving this problem is to draw a picture and come up with the following solution: 4 sets of pages x 2 in. per set = 8 in. and 6 covers x 1/6 in. per cover = 1 in. so the total distance is 8 + 1 = 9 inches. This is a common solution given by other pre-service teachers, but it is not how far the bookworm traveled. Some students interpret the cover to be a total of 1/6 in. for the entire book and they come up with 8 + 6 x 1/12 = 8 1/2 inches thick, which also is not how far the bookworm traveled. How far did the bookworm travel?

5. How many fence posts will it take to fence a rectangular field 250 feet by 300 feet if the fence posts are exactly 5 feet apart?

   Some students find the perimeter and divide by 5; other students find the perimeter, divide by 5, and then subtract 4 because they believe they have counted the corners twice; still other students make the rectangle into a line, divide the length of the line by 5, and then subtract 1. How can we check to see which method works?

6. If a snail is at the bottom of a well that is 100 feet deep and he climbs up 8 feet each day but slips back 5 feet each night, how long will it take him to climb out of the well?

   Some students may divide 100 by 3 as the first step to find the solution. How can we determine if this step will help?

7. Which number does not belong?

   15   23   20   25

   Is there only one correct answer here?

8. How many rectangles are in this figure?

   What is a rectangle? How can you help children make sure they get all the rectangles? Some children do not find it natural to classify a square as a rectangle since they tend to classify objects into separate categories. Initially, for many children, a shape cannot be both a square and a rectangle—it is one or the other.

Problem Set B

Solve the problems first and then consider some data on how children solved the problems found in the **Children's Solutions and Discussion of Problems and Exercises** section.

1. Looking in my backyard one day I saw some horses and turkeys. I counted 18 heads and 48 feet. How many horses and how many turkeys were in my backyard?

2. A pencil and a pen cost 40¢ together. If the pen costs 10¢ more than the pencil, how much does each cost?

3. A grandfather clock strikes once at one o'clock, twice at two o'clock and so on. How many times does the clock strike in one day? What if the clock also struck once every 15, 30, and 45 minutes after the hour? How many times would it strike in a day?

4. Nathan takes a number, adds 2 to it, and then multiplies the result by 3. He ends up with 24. What was his original number?

5. If there are 57 third-grade students at Lincoln School and each student needs one pencil for the state test, how many pencils should the principal buy if the pencils come in packages of 12?

6. Mrs. Johnson has 25 children in her class. They are in a line for recess. Mary is number 9 in line and Sam is number 21. How many students are between Mary and Sam?

7. Which number does not belong? How might second grade children explain which number does not belong?

            6   10   12   15

8. The rule for the table is that numbers in each row and column must add up to the same number. What number goes in the center of the table? (TIMSS, 2003).

4	11	6
9		5
8	3	10

    a.   1
    b.   2
    c.   7
    d.   12

1.1   Questions for Discussion

1.   Find at least two problems in the supplement or in your textbook where you used each of the problem solving strategies listed in this chapter.
2.   What do you think of when you hear the term, "Problem Solving?"
3.   Why study problem solving?
4.   How are your own personal experiences learning mathematics in school like or unlike the experiences of the students quoted in this chapter?
5.   What might you do so that problems really are problems for children and not routine tasks?
6.   How do children solve problems differently than adults?
7.   What does it mean to focus on the process when teaching mathematics? Give some specific examples.
8.   Describe one of your solution methods for a problem in this supplement or your textbook of which you were particularly proud.
9.   What is the best way to solve a problem?
10.   What should a teacher do when a child is stuck?
11.   How might you introduce problem-solving strategies, heuristics, to children?
12.   Were Polya's four steps useful to you in solving problems? Would you teach them to children? Why or why not?
13.   What would you do as a teacher if the elementary mathematics textbook gives a problem solving strategy for each problem and requires children to use Polya's four step process?

1.1   Children's Solutions and Discussion of Problems and Exercises for Set B

1.   Many fourth and fifth grade children who got the problem correct drew 18 heads and put 2 feet under each head and then added 2 more feet to the heads until all the feet were used up. "I put 18 heads and I put 2 feet under every head until I got 48." The most common error was to add the two numbers $(18 + 48 = 66)$.
2.   In one fourth grade class 40% (8 out of 20) had the correct solution. Of those eight, four used guess and check. This problem was too difficult for second graders; no one was able to solve it.
3.   In a fifth grade class 30% (7 out of 23) had the first part of the problem correct. Each of these students had written out the first 12 hours and then doubled the answer. Only one student solved the second part correctly.
4.   Sixty-five percent of fourth and fifth graders (35 out of 54) had a correct solution to this problem.
5.   Seventy-one percent of fourth and fifth grade children (72 out of 102) had a correct solution for this problem. A few children gave 4½ boxes as their solution. Some children used tally marks and circled 12 tally marks to make a box.
6.   Only 36% (16 out of 45) of third graders had this problem correct. Several children subtracted, $21 − 9$, and came up with the incorrect solution of 12 However, many of the children who wrote out the numbers or used a number line, still had an incorrect solution. Three children added all the numbers $(25 + 9 + 21)$.

7.   Of 53 second graders, 40% said 6 did not belong, 4% said 10 did not belong, 4% said 12 did not belong, 49 % said 15 did not belong and one did not answer the question, he added all the numbers. Some reasons for 6 not belonging were: "it does not have 1 in front of it; it is to far away from the other numbers; it's too small; the other numbers are teens; 6 is not a teens[sic]." In giving a reason for why 15 did not belong, one child said, "I skip counted by 2 and 15 wasn't in the skip count."

8.   Internationally 61.1% of fourth graders had this problem correct and 58.3% of children in the United States had this problem correct (TIMSS 2003).

1.2   Patterns

Most of mathematics involves finding patterns. A formula is a generalization of a mathematical pattern that someone has created or discovered. For a right triangle with sides of length 'a' and 'b' and hypotenuse 'c', the Pythagorean theorem, $a^2 + b^2 = c^2$, is a generalization of a pattern that was discovered about the relationship between the lengths of the sides of right triangles. Children will not be asked to find patterns this complex, but they will be finding simpler numerical and geometric patterns to prepare them for finding more complex patterns in future life and mathematic applications.

A major change in elementary textbooks is the increased emphasis on pattern finding. Recent reforms efforts have called for the introduction of algebraic reasoning in elementary school mathematics. **Finding patterns can be classified as algebraic reasoning** because it is an activity that involves generalization and abstraction. New elementary mathematics textbooks will have even more pattern-finding activities because of this increased emphasis on algebraic reasoning.

Patterning is one of the first activities that kindergarten students do in school. A great source of pattern activities can be found in *Mathematics Their Way (MTW)* by Mary Baratta-Lorton (1976). MTW offers a hands-on, activity-based approach to teaching children mathematics in Kindergarten through second grade. An example of an MTW activity from an urban kindergarten class involved the teacher making an AB pattern with two colors of Unifix Cubes— green, red, green, red, green, red, etc. She gave each child 10 cubes, 5 cubes of one color and 5 cubes of another color, and asked them to make her pattern with their cubes. Many children did, but one little boy had an AB<u>AABB</u>AB arrangement but said that it was an AB pattern. Patterning of this type may be obvious for adults, but it can be challenging for young children.

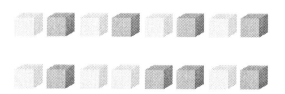

Another example from MTW is for the children to snap and clap. The teacher may snap and clap twice (an ABB pattern) and then ask the class to repeat the pattern. As children get better at finding patterns it is suggested that the teacher make patterns throughout the day and ask children to name or continue the pattern. For example, she could line the class for dismissal by boy, girl, boy, girl and then either ask the class what her pattern is or ask the class to finish lining up by this pattern. The brilliance of this type of pattern finding is that children are not looking at symbols on a page but are actively engaged in acting out and finding the patterns. Patterning activities can eventually be extended to three items, to growing patterns (e.g., ABABBABBBA), and to numbers.

As children progress to higher grades, their sophistication in finding patterns will also progress. They will be asked to find numerical and geometric patterns. An example of a numerical pattern-finding activity is the following:

___, 4, 7, ___, 13, ___, ___

How can you describe this pattern? _____

A common error children make in completing patterns like this one is that they make the first number 3, because the pattern goes up by three.

Children will also be asked to find geometric patterns and generalize their thinking. For older students, problems like the one below help develop the rudiments of algebraic thinking. These problems ask them to describe, extend, and make predictions about the numerical aspects of geometric patterns. Children may be asked to generalize a pattern and describe it symbolically. This type of problem introduces students to one of the primary uses of algebra—describing numerical relationships in a generalized form. Generalizing arithmetic is the basis for algebraic thinking.

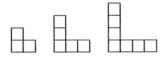

Draw the next three figures in the sequence. How many tiles are needed for the 10th figure in the sequence?; the 20th figure?; the 100th figure?; the nth figure?

1.2   Problems and Exercises

Solve these problems first and then consider the data on how children solved the problems found in the **Children's Solutions and Discussion of Problems and Exercises** section

Continue and describe (i.e., AB) each pattern.

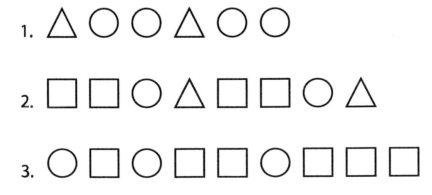

1. △ ○ ○ △ ○ ○

2. ☐ ☐ ○ △ ☐ ☐ ○ △

3. ○ ☐ ○ ☐ ☐ ○ ☐ ☐ ☐

4. ___ 5 ___ 11 ___ 17 ___ ___ 26 ___

5.   If you double the sides of a rectangle, what happens to its perimeter?

6.   If you double the sides of a rectangle, what happens to its area?

7.   Complete row 6 and row 7 for the following pattern:

$$
\begin{array}{ccccccccc}
 & & & & 1 & & & & \\
 & & & 1 & & 1 & & & \\
 & & 1 & & 2 & & 1 & & \\
 & 1 & & 3 & & 3 & & 1 & \\
1 & & 4 & & 6 & & 4 & & 1 \\
\end{array}
$$

8.   Find the next three numbers for the following pattern:

2, 7, 5, 10, 8,

9.   Here is a number pattern.

100,   1,   99,   2,   98,   ☐,   ☐,   ☐,

What three numbers should go in the boxes (TIMSS, 2003)?
      a. 3, 97, 4
      b. 4, 97, 5
      c. 97, 3, 96
      d. 97, 4, 96

1.2   Questions for Discussion

1.   Describe a patterning activity that you might do in kindergarten or first grade.
2.   Other than the Pythagorean Theorem, what are some other mathematical patterns?
3.   Describe a pattern you found in solving problems from this supplement or the textbook.
4.   Why do some say that mathematics is about finding patterns?

1.2   Children's Solutions and Discussion of Problems and Exercises

1&2.   In one first grade class 89% (17 out of 19) children were able to continue the two patterns successfully. However, several children only put the next shape in the pattern and did not continue it.

3.   In the same first grade class, only one-third of the children (6 out of 18) could complete this growing pattern correctly. This pattern is more difficult because the number of squares increases.

4.   Children may say that the first number should be 3 because the numbers in the pattern increase by 3. In one third grade class 36% (10 out of 28) filled in the blanks correctly and 50% gave the correct rule, 'Add 3.' Some of these students had all the numbers correct except they had a 3 in the first blank.

5&6.   Children may say that both the perimeter and area would double.

7.   Notice how starting with the second row each row in the pattern is related to the coefficients of $(X + 1)^1$, $(X + 1)^2$; $(X + 1)^3$, etc.

8.   In the same third-grade class as #4, 65% (17 out of 26) gave the correct pattern, '+5, -2').

9.   In the United States 92.5% of girls and 88.8% of boys in fourth grade had this problem correct, internationally 68.7% of children in fourth grade had the problem correct (TIMSS 2003).

1.3   Mathematical Reasoning

Deductive and Inductive Reasoning

Your college mathematics textbook may discuss inductive and deductive reasoning. These types of reasoning are powerful tools for mathematical thinking. However, children may not be able to characterize their mathematical thinking as following either line of reasoning (Reid, 2002). This fact is consistent with Piaget's assertion that young children are not capable of reflecting on their thinking at a level that would allow them to make such distinctions. Thus, in elementary school, the goal is not to teach inductive and deductive reasoning as if they were topics that must be covered.

Most elementary school children are not ready to understand deductive reasoning—reasoning from the general to the specific. For example, a rectangle can be defined as: A quadrilateral (4 sides) with 4 right angles. However, many children will say that a square is not a rectangle.

In this instance, children are unable to reason from a general definition to a specific case. In secondary school, geometry is premised on deductive reasoning. However, even in high school, most students still do not understand the formal deductive reasoning that is typically presented in proofs.

In contrast, children are frequently able to apply inductive principles—reasoning from the specific to the general. However, they, like secondary students, are typically unable to apply formal inductive reasoning to test a hypothesis. At most, they rely on counterexamples to disprove their hypothesis. Sometimes their inductive reasoning is correct but they are unable to show why it is correct. For example, a child may add several pairs of odd numbers and surmise that the sum of any two odd numbers is even (1 + 3 = 4, 3 + 7 = 10, etc.). Here the child's assumption is correct but he cannot prove it is correct except by giving more examples. A child may make an incorrect assumption by working from examples such as in subtraction one always subtracts the smaller number from the larger number or multiplication makes numbers bigger. However, counterexamples disprove these conjectures, for example, 2 − 3 = -1 and 6 x ½ = 3. Despite the fact that they are sometimes wrong, children's conjectures may prove mathematically rich and should be encouraged.

Sense-Making

While children are not usually capable of deductive reasoning, children still should be encouraged to develop their mathematical reasoning (NCTM 2000). So what does that mean? Foremost, it means that mathematics should be a **sense-making activity**! That is, mathematics should not involve students blindly following rules that they do not understand. The mathematics children engage in should make sense to them. When it does, they will begin to see mathematical relationships and how mathematics grows and interconnected. This sense-making does not just happen during a designated "mathematics" time. As children are presented with situations in the classroom, teachers can "mathematize" the world to help them make these connections. In primary classrooms, creating natural opportunities for children to think about mathematics can occur while counting out teacups in dramatic play, building with blocks in explorative play, or playing games with rules like Hi Ho Cherry Oh! or Chutes and Ladders. Mathematical reasoning is promoted when children are asked to explain their mathematical thinking, to attempt to make sense of others' thinking, and to endeavor to resolve conflicting viewpoints that arise during discussions of mathematics.

As an illustration of this kind of thinking, can you explain why each of the numbers in problem #7 in Section 1.1 (15, 23, 20, 25) does not belong? Can you explain why verbally? In writing? On the other problems in this supplement or your textbook, did another student use a different method than yours? Did it make sense to you? Can you reconcile the two methods so that they both make sense? Often children will present their own way of solving problem different from your way and the textbook. To teach mathematical reasoning you must try to make sense of children's explanations, and more importantly, you must try to help the class make sense of these explanations as well. What questions might you ask the class to help them make sense of apparently different solution methods that may be the same? As you try to answer these questions, consider examples from your experiences in this class.

An example of a child who is making sense of mathematics is the first grader who solves the problem, 3 + 4 = ? by reasoning: "I know that 3 + 3 = 6 and since 4 is 1 more than 3; the answer must be 1 more than 6, which is 7." Here the child is utilizing mathematical relationships that can be extended to other problems. For such a child, **mathematics is a sense-making activity**! This kind of sense making may eventually give him or her far greater mathematical power.

Key Words

It is important for children to reason mathematically. Numerous examples illustrate that children are not reasoning mathematically and are not making sense of the mathematics. In fact, some instructional strategies may actually encourage children **not** to reason. Teaching children to only look for key or cue words, a common practice when teaching word problems, can encourage children not to think. For example, when learning to read word problems, children are sometimes taught that "altogether" means add and "left" means subtract. What do you think children who have been taught key words will do on the following problem: "Johnny walked 9 blocks. Then he turned left and walked 5 blocks. How many blocks did Johnny walk?" Children taught key words will often subtract (i.e., 9-5) and give 4 as their answer. The answer 4 makes no sense in this problem; it is not a reasonable answer given that at the start of the problem Johnny has already walked 9 blocks.

Many children try to directly translate the word problem to arithmetic operations. That is they look for two numbers and an operation without giving meaning to the problem or think about what the problem is asking. Children using key words also tend to struggle with problems that involve more than one step, such as a problem where both addition and subtraction are required. Children who are more successful learn to transform the problems into a physical, representational, or mental model (Pape, 2004). To get a clear sense of why a sense making approach to mathematics is so important and how transforming problems can be useful, consider the next problem and its discussion.

 Mary checked out 6 books from the library. The next week she returned 2 books and checked out 4 new books. How many books does she have checked out from the library?

This problem can be classified as a multi-step problem, and it is a problem where focusing on key words will typically not help in children to solve the problem. However, modeling the problem may help children derive a solution. Here are some possible ways to model the problem.

- A physical model of the problem could involve using actual books or cubes to represent the books.
- A representational model might involve using tally marks or pictures to represent the books.
- A mental model might involve mentally thinking about the physical action of checking out and returning books.

For children who try to solve problems by looking for key words, **mathematics is not a sense-making activity!**

Incorporating Writing and Mathematics

Integrating writing and mathematics is becoming very popular. Asking children to write about how they went about solving a particular problem can be one way to promote and explore children's mathematical reasoning. In addition, writing activities provide another means of assessing children's learning. More importantly, writing about mathematics also encourages children to reflect on their mathematical thinking and make their mathematical ideas more precise and communicable. These activities also provide opportunities for children to practice their writing.

1.3   Problems and Exercises

Solve the problems first and then consider the data on how children solved the problems found in the **Children's Solutions and Discussion of Problems and Exercises** section.

1.   Mary's team defeated Larry's team by 15 points. If Mary's team scored 24 points, how many points did Larry's team score?

   In this problem, children have difficulty deciding who won the game.

2.   Sam walked home from school. He walked 8 blocks, turned left, and walked 5 blocks. How many blocks did he walk?

3.   How might a third grade class that was first given 100 + 100 = 200; mentally find: 99 + 99 = _____?

4.   A special checkerboard has 6 squares on each side. How many squares are on the checkerboard?

5.   Mary had 9 white mice. She gave her brother 4 white mice. The next day one of her mice had 7 babies and another mouse had 3 babies. How many mice does she have now?

6.   John's best time to run 100 m. is 17 seconds. How long will it take him to run 1 km (Vershaffel, De Corte, & Lasure, 1994)?

7.   Steve has bought [sic] 4 planks of 2.5 m each. How many 1 m. planks can he saw out of these planks (Vershaffel, De Corte, & Lasure, 1994)?

8.   There are 450 soldiers to be bused to their training site. Each bus can hold 36 soldiers. How many buses are needed (Vershaffel, De Corte, & Lasure, 1994)?

1.3   Questions for Discussion

1.   Do you think elementary students, even fifth graders, are capable of understanding deductive reasoning? Explain why or why not.

2.   What does the statement, "**mathematics should be a sense-making activity**," mean?

3.   In your schooling, did mathematics always make sense? Describe a case where it did or did not.

4.   Would you teach a "key" word approach to children? Why or why not?

5.   Do you believe that mathematics should always be a sense-making activity? Why or why not?

6.   How can we help children use their real world knowledge when solving problems like Problem #7 in this exercise set? Children may say John will have 10 boards, 1 foot long!

7.   Should children ever be given mathematical problems that do not have a solution? Why or why not?

1.3   Children's Solutions and Discussion of Problems and Exercises

1.   In one third grade class 6 out of 16 children added, 24 + 15 = 39; the other 10 children correctly solved the problem.

2.   Some children may indicate the answer is 3.

3.   In a third-grade class discussion, one child said, 'since 100 plus 100 is 200 you just have to take away 2'. A second child lined up numbers in her head and carried. She did it correctly. A third child in the class indicated he took 1 from one of the 99's, added it to the other 99 to get 100, and then added 100 and 98. Another child said the answer 1,818 but she couldn't explain how she got it. How do you think she arrived at 1,818?

4.   In one fourth grade class, 65% (13 out of 20) were unable to solve this problem. Six children drew a checkerboard putting 6 squares on each side but none in the center. Five added 6 + 6.

5.   In one fourth-grade class 33% (7 out of 21) had an incorrect solution. Of these, one child added the 'one' mentioned in the problem and came up with 16 mice.

6.   In a study of fifth graders in Belgium only 3% (2 out of 75) gave a realistic solution (Vershaffel, De Corte, & Lasure, 1994).

7.   In a study of fifth graders in Belgium only 13% (10 out of 75) gave a realistic solution (Vershaffel, De Corte, & Lasure, 1994).

8.   In a study of fifth graders in Belgium only 49% (37 out of 75) gave a realistic solution (Vershaffel, De Corte, & Lasure, 1994). One wrote, "They will need 12 buses and probably some additional cars."

Chapter 1: References

Baratta-Lorton, M. (1976). *Mathematics Their Way.* Menlo Park: Addison-Wesley.

Cai, J. (2003. What research tells us about teaching mathematics through problem solving. In F. Lester (Ed.), *Teaching mathematics through problem solving.* Reston, VA: NCTM.

Cobb, P., Wood, T., & Yackel. E. (1991). A constructivist approach to second grade mathematics. In E. von Glasersfeld (Ed.), *Constructivism in Mathematics Education.* Dordrecht, Holland: Reidel.

Carpenter, T. P., Fennema, E. & Franke, M. L. (1996). Cognitively guided instruction: A knowledge base for reform in primary mathematics instruction. *Elementary School Journal, 97,* 3-20.

Frank, M. (1988). Problem solving and mathematical beliefs. *Arithmetic Teacher, 35,* 32-34.

Kamii, C. & Housman, L. (1999). *Young children reinvent arithmetic: Implications of Piaget's theory* 2nd ed.). New York: Teachers College Press.

Mason, J., Stacey, K., & Burton, L. (1985). *Thinking mathematically revised edition.* London. Prentice Hall.

National Council of Teachers of Mathematics. (1989). *Curriculum and evaluation standards for school mathematics.* Reston, VA: NCTM.

National Council of Teachers of Mathematics. (1991). *Professional standards for teaching mathematics.* Reston, VA: NCTM.

National Council of Teachers of Mathematics (2000). *Principles and standards for school mathematics.* Reston, VA: NCTM.

National Research Council (CRMSTE) (1985). *Mathematics, science, and technology education: A research agenda.* Washington, DC.

Pape, S. J. (2004). Middle school children's problem solving behavior: A cognitive analysis forma reading comprehension perspective. *Journal for Research in Mathematics Education, 35*(3), 187-219.

Reid, D. A. (2002). Conjectures and refutations in grade 5 mathematics. *Journal for Research in Mathematics Education, 33*(1), 5-29.

Sfard, A. (1994). Reification as the birth of metaphor. *For the Learning of Mathematics, 14*(1) 44-55.

Suydam, M. (1987). Indications from research on problem solving. In F. Curcio (ed.) *Teaching and learning: A problems solving focus.* Reston, VA: NCTM.

Verschaffel, L., De Corte, E. & Lasure, S. (1994). Realistic considerations in mathematical modeling of school arithmetic word problems. *Learning and Instruction, 4*(4), 273-294.

Verschaffel, L., De Corte, E., & Vierstraete, H. (1999). Upper elementary school pupils' difficulties in modeling and solving nonstandard additive word problems involving ordinal numbers. *Journal for Research in Mathematics Education, 30*(3), 265-285.

Wheatley, G. & Reynolds, A. (1999). *Coming to Know Number.* Tallahassee: Mathematics Learning.

Wheatley, G. (1984). *Problem solving in school mathematics.* Technical paper 84.01R. West Lafayette: Purdue University.

Chapter 2: Sets

The first section in this chapter gives a historical account of set theory and why it is studied in many mathematical content courses for elementary teachers. The second part of this section considers how children develop number and then looks at the ways set theory can be used to define number and the four basic mathematical operations. The second section in this chapter describes Venn diagrams and how they may be used to organize information in mathematics as well as in other subjects.

The rationale for studying set theory is that it allows one to define the concept of number and the four basic operations associated with number (addition, subtraction, multiplication, and division). Set theory is also one of the foundations of higher mathematics.

2.1   Set Theory

From a child's point of view **sets** are just collections or groups of objects. However, mathematicians have created a branch of mathematics based on the notions of groups of objects known as set theory. Why is it important to study set theory? Set theory is a common topic in mathematics textbooks for elementary teachers. However, it is rarely addressed explicitly in elementary mathematics textbooks except in discussions of fractions of a set.

<u>A Historical Perspective</u>

In 1957 the Russians launched Sputnik, the first satellite to orbit the earth. This event created the "space race" and served as a catalyst for reforming mathematics and science education in the United States. To address the crisis of confidence brought on by the launch of Sputnik, prominent mathematicians and scientists were consulted in order to improve K-12 education. They developed "New Math," which included set theory. Set theory was included because they believed that children could understand it and because set theory describes the fundamental structure of mathematics. From a mathematical standpoint, set theory provides the fundamental building blocks of our number system. The problem with presenting set theory in elementary school, as we later discovered through the works of Piaget and others, was that this is not how children learn mathematics. For the most part, "New Math" is no longer taught in elementary schools.

What is Number?

In order to understand why we study set theory, consider the following problem: Define **the number 7**? Try to use the rules for defining words. For example, you should not use the words you are trying to define in the definition. Hence, neither the word "number" nor the word "seven" should be used. In addition, the definition should not contain circular reasoning. For example, you should not define 7 as 1 more than 6 because now 6 and 1 must also be defined.

Number is difficult to define, and in mathematics, set theory is used to define it. More importantly, number is a difficult concept that we expect 4 and 5 year-olds to master. If we cannot define number well, or we use higher-level mathematics to define number, how can we expect 4 and 5 year-olds to understand number, let alone start adding and subtracting numbers? Numbers are not properties of objects. For instance, given this set of asterisks, * * * *, we may say that there are four asterisks, but one cannot actually see four. Four is a creation of our mind; the number four is a mental construct of our mind!

How do Children Develop the Concept of Number?

In order for children to develop or understand the concept of number they must first understand counting and one-to-one correspondence. Let us examine what each of these concepts mean from a child's perspective.

Counting

"One, two, three, four, six, seven, eleven!" To a young child, this exclamation may make perfect sense. Counting is a string of number words in arbitrary order. As children learn this sequence of words, they have not yet attached meaning to each word. "Three" is simply something that is said after two and before four; it does not necessarily suggest a quantity to the young child.

As a child develops, he or she learns to recite "one, two, three, four, five, six, seven" with consistent success. This is a milestone for a child! He or she has mastered an important piece of social knowledge. However, reciting numbers in order does not guarantee that the child understands what "seven" means. Learning to recite numbers in their correct order is like learning the alphabet. Knowing the alphabet does not mean one knows how to read, but it is a necessary foundation for reading. Likewise correctly reciting numbers in order does not guarantee that the child will connect the spoken word "seven" to the written symbol "7." A child's understanding of the written symbol will come later. The child must still conquer the task of figuring out "how many" are in a collection. Gaining an understanding how many are in a collection is the difference between "counting by rote and counting with numerical meaning" (Kamii, 1982).

As a child's understanding continues to develop, counting tells the child *how many* are in a collection. Knowing and, most importantly, using the counting sequence to figure out "how many" is an important foundation to understanding the concept of number. (Clements, 2004; Kamii, 1982; Baratta-Lorton, 1976).

One-to-one Correspondence

Once the child has command of oral counting, she must connect each word with an object in the collection to determine "how many." For example, using a set of seven keys, the child must match each number word ("one," "two," "three," etc.) to each key, counting with <u>one-to-one correspondence</u>. Typically, the child will point to each key or move the counted keys to the side to create some order. The child who does not have one-to-one correspondence will randomly point to the keys while reciting the memorized sequence of number words. He or she may skip over a key or count a key twice, resulting in an incorrect count. "There are six keys!" he may exclaim.

Recognizing Small Numbers

Young, preschool age children may be able to recognize small numbers without counting. When asked to name or select small numbers, for example, a child shown 3 blocks may indicate that there are 3 blocks without counting the blocks. They are able to take into account all the elements of the set at once rather than counting them one by one, Children are more likely to recognize the numbers 1, 2 and 3 without counting and less occasionally they are likely to recognize 4 without counting (Bruce & Threlfall, 2004). Children are not always consistent in this skill; sometimes they will recognize three objects without counting and other times they will count out the 3 objects. However, some educators do believe that the recognition of small numbers may help children understand counting and the concept of number (Baroody, Tilikainen, & Tai, 2006)

Cardinal and Ordinal Numbers

Preschool age children tend to understand cardinal numbers (an indication of quantity or how many) better than ordinal numbers (an indication of order). For example, children are more likely to be able to select 6 objects from a collection (cardinal), than to indicate the sixth object (ordinal) in a set. Children first learn ordinal numbers, such as first, second and third, from everyday experiences. They may likely learn larger ordinal numbers such as fourth, fifth and sixth by adding a 'th' to the cardinal number words i.e., four, five and six (Fuson & Hall, 1983). Preschool children benefit from experiences naming ordinal numbers e.g., first, second, third, fourth, fifth (Bruce & Threlfall, 2004).

Set Theory and Basic Operations

The intertwining of their counting ability and their intuitive notions about sets (collections of objects) forms the foundation not only for children's construction of a concept of number, but also for their development of an understanding of the basic operations with numbers. Set theory can complement children's developing understanding of these operations. Consider, for instance, how set theory can be used to define the four basic operations. For instance, "2 + 3" involves combining two sets, "7 – 4" involves removing objects from a set or comparing two sets, "2 x 4" can be viewed as two sets of four, and "12 ÷ 3" asks how many sets of three there are in 12 or if 12 were divided into three sets, how many would be in each set. Notice how these descriptions might be useful in explaining addition, subtraction, multiplication, and division to children.

Reasons for Studying Set Theory

The preceding discussion suggests the following reasons why it is important for prospective teachers to study set theory:

- Set theory provides a context for mathematicians to define number and the four basic operations on numbers.
- Studying set theory may provide insights into the structure of our number system and higher-level mathematics.
- It is important for future teachers to understand the basis for the mathematics that will be taught to children.
- Much of children's mathematics is based on their intuitive notions about sets of objects.

Children do explore some of the fundamental aspects of set theory without using the formal language and notation of set theory. For membership in a set, children will likely know that "Tuesday" is not part of the set or group 'spring, summer, winter, fall". Likewise, classes often self divide themselves into boys and girls which is a partitioning of a set. The formality is missing but not the fundamental ideas of set theory.

2.1   Problems and Exercises

Solve the problems first and then consider some data on how children solved the problems found in the **Children's Solutions and Discussion of Problems and Exercises** section.

1.   A child counting seven objects says, "One, two, three, four, five, six, seven." When he says "five" in the sequence, what does that mean?

2.   A child counts out 8 marbles from a bag. When asked to put 3 marbles back into the bag, he counts, "one, two, three" and puts only the marble that he pointed to when he said three back in the bag. Why?

3.   Why would a child say that each row of paperclips has the same number? What mathematical concept might this problem illustrate?

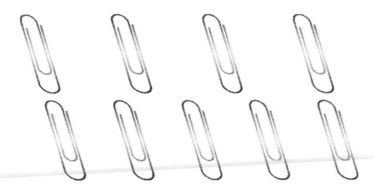

4.   Explain what "4 x 6" means.
5.   How many floors are there between the third floor and the twelfth floor of a downtown office building?

2.1   Questions for Discussion

1.   Why is it important to study set theory?
2.   Why is number so difficult to define?
3.   How do children first come to understand number?
4.   How are cardinal and ordinal numbers used in problem #5?
5.   How is recognizing small numbers related to a child's need to count?   Is being able to recognize small numbers an indication of 1-1 correspondence? Why or why not?

2.1   Children's Solutions and Discussion of Problems and Exercises

1.   Is 'five' the word after 'four' and before 'six' or does 'five' signify that at that point the child has counted five objects?
2.   This problem illustrates the difficulty that children have in distinguishing "cardinal' from "ordinal."
3.   This problem is an example of one of Piaget's conservation tasks which he uses as an indication of the developmental level of the child but not as something that needs to be taught to the child.
4.   A third grader wrote, "The first number is how many groups there are. The second one is how many are in the group." In one third grade class over half the class (16/24) drew a picture to explain what '4 x 6' meant, most others explained it in words or with numbers.
5.   In a third grade class 22% (6/27) had the correct solution. The most common error was $12 - 3 = 9$.

2.2   Venn Diagrams

Venn diagrams are drawings representing the relationship between sets. They are not necessarily pictures of sets! They are a representation of the relationship of sets. They are sometimes used in the elementary school to help children organize and reflect on their thinking. They can be a powerful tool for classification. An example of the use of a Venn diagram that occurred in a second-grade classroom involved children's siblings. Two intersecting circles in a rectangle were drawn on a poster board. The circles were labeled "Brothers" and "Sisters," respectively. The children put their names in the appropriate section according to whether they had brothers only, sisters only, brothers and sisters, or had no brothers and sisters. The intersection of the two circles was for those who had both brothers and sisters, the rest of the Brothers circle was for those who had brothers only, the rest of the Sisters circle was for those who had sisters only, and the space outside both circles was for children with no brothers or sisters. This poster remained on the bulletin board for several months. A valuable learning experience occurred when one student had a new baby in the family and moved his name to another region of the diagram. This was a nice activity because it related directly to the children. Furthermore, because the teacher left the Venn diagram on the bulletin board for several months, children had the opportunity to reflect on the Venn diagram and the use of sets throughout the school year. This Venn diagram activity was not just one-day, but an experience that offered continuous learning opportunities!

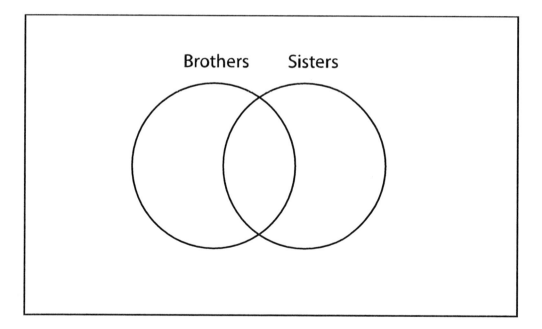

At a more advanced level, Venn diagrams can be used to solve problems involving three intersecting sets. Consider the examples from your college textbook. These problems would be very difficult to solve without using Venn diagrams.

2.2 Problems and Exercises

Solve the problems first and then consider some data on how children solved the problems found in the **Children's Solutions and Discussion of Problems and Exercises** section.

1. Fill in the Venn diagram by listing the activities associated with each group.

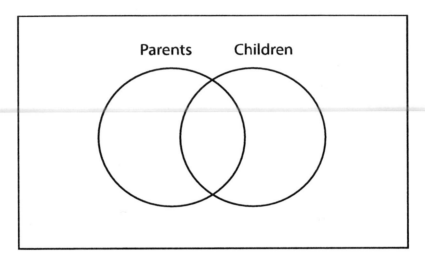

2. Where would you place the following numbers in the Venn diagram:

    15, 18, 20?

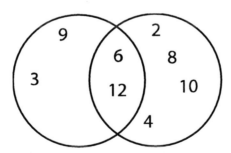

3. For this Venn Diagram, follow the directions and answer the questions that come after.

Lightly color the circle on the left yellow. Lightly color the circle on the right blue.

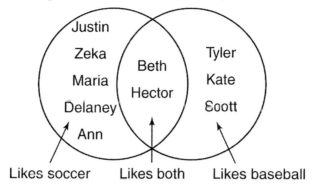

Do you like soccer, or baseball, or both?

Likes soccer   Likes both   Likes baseball

a. What does the yellow circle show?
b. How many children like soccer?
c. What does the blue circle show?
d. How many children like baseball?
e. What do you notice about Beth and Hector?

4. Consider this figure and answer the question that comes after it.

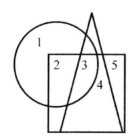

Which number is in the square and the circle but is NOT in the triangle (TIMSS, 1995).

a. 2
b. 3
c. 4
d. 5

2.2   Questions for Discussion

1. How can using Venn diagrams help children organize their thinking?
2. Why don't Venn diagrams necessarily represent sets?
3. How might you use a Venn diagram in teaching science to children?
4. Can you come up with another Venn diagram activity like the brother/sister activity described here that children could relate to on a daily basis? What would that activity be?

2.2   Children's Solutions and Discussion of Problems and Exercises

1.   Here are some responses from a third grade class.

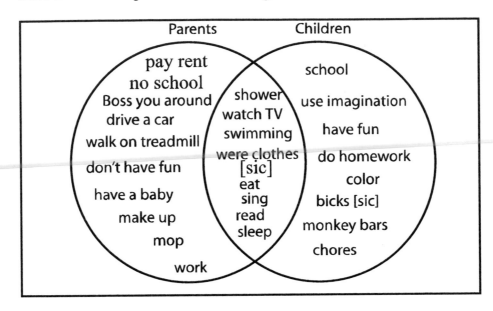

2.   A problem similar to this was given on a state mathematics achievement test.

3.   A third grader, working with his father, lightly colored only the left half portion of the left circle yellow. When asked why he colored the left circle as he did, the child paused briefly and then colored the common portion of the two circles yellow. He then proceeded to lightly color entire right circle blue, coloring the blue over the yellow. The third grader's final answers to five questions about the diagram above are given below for this activity. He correctly answered question 1. However, he incorrectly answered 5 for question 2. When asked to think about his answer to question 2, he then changed his answer to 7. When asked why he changed to 7, the child said "There were two students who liked both soccer and baseball and 5 plus 2 is 7." He correctly answered questions 3-5 as shown below. When asked why he answered 5 for question 4, he stated that "Two students liked both soccer and baseball and 3 students liked only baseball and 2 plus 3 is 5."

1. What does the yellow circle show?

   They all like soccer.

2. How many children like soccer? __7__

3. What does the blue circle show?

   They all like baseball.

4. How many children like baseball? __5__

5. What do you notice about Beth and Hector?

   They both like soccer and baseball.

4. On the 1995 TIMSS international test, 55% of third graders and 65% of fourth graders selected the correct answer.

Chapter 2   References

Baratta-Lorton, M. (1976). *Mathematics their way.* Menlo Park: Addison-Wesley.

Baroody, A. J., Tiilikainen, S. H. & Tai, Y. (2006). The application and development of an addition goal sketch. *Cognition and Instruction, 24*(1), 124-170.

Bruce, B. & Threlfall, J. (2004). One, two, three and counting. *Educational Studies in Mathematics, 55*, 3-26.

Clements, D. (2004). In D. Clements & J Sarama (Eds.) *Engaging young children in mathematics: Standards for early childhood education.* NJ: Lawrence Erlbaum Associates.

Fuson K. C. & Hall, J. W. (1983). The acquisition of early number word meanings: a conceptual analysis and review, In H. P. Ginsburg (Ed.) *The Development of Mathematical Thinking.* New York: Academic Press.

Kamii, C. (1982). *Number in preschool & kindergarten: Educational implications of Piaget's theory.* Washington: National Association for the Education of Young Children.

Chapter 3: Whole Numbers

Chapter 3 is at the heart of CMET and at the heart of what many consider to be elementary school mathematics: addition, subtraction, multiplication and division. There is also a great deal of research which describes how children think about these four basic operations. As a result, this chapter is longer than all the others and is rich with descriptions of children's mathematical thinking. The first section describes some manipulative models of our number system. Section two describes how addition and subtraction are counting activities for children. Section three describes how children come to know multiplication and division. Section four describes how children understand the basic properties of numbers such as commutative and associative. Section five gives many examples of how children may develop their own self-generated algorithms as well as describing ways to help children understand the standard algorithms. For example, we describe how children come to understand the standard algorithm of long division. The issue of whether children should be encouraged to develop their own algorithms is very controversial! Our intent is to present descriptions and examples of children's thinking and let the reader develop his or her own position on this issue. The last section describes how children estimate and use mental math.

3.1 Numeration Systems

A common unit in third and fourth grade is the study of ancient number systems such as Egyptian or Mayan systems. As future elementary teachers, you will study these systems because you may teach them to children. Other ancient number systems include Roman and Babylonian systems. The Roman Numeral System also has everyday uses. In your college course, you may study all or some of these systems to learn about their advantages and disadvantages. More importantly, by studying these systems the intent is to learn how they relate to our system of numbers, the Hindu-Arabic System.

The Need for Numbers

Several years ago a two-part PBS series featured a primitive, nomadic tribe, which gathered sweet potatoes in jungles of Papua, New Guinea. Their numbering system consisted of **one, two, and many**. One, two, and many were their only numbers. Why didn't they have more numbers? They had no need for other numbers. In their daily lives, they could talk about one sweet potato, two sweet potatoes, or many sweet potatoes! As society evolved the need arose to count or keep track of how many of a thing, like sweet potatoes, one has or does not have.

Some would argue that numbers arose out of a need; such a case could certainly be made for zero and negative numbers! When children start counting, like the tribe in Papua, New Guinea, they start with one, not zero. Zero was also one of the last numbers developed by man. Zero is used as both a placeholder and a quantity (nothing) on which operations can be performed. The first person that balanced a checkbook probably had a need for negative numbers!

Models of Our Number System

This section describes some common manipulatives such as Unifix cubes and Base Ten Blocks that are used to help children develop number concepts.

Unifix Cubes (a brand name also known as linker cubes, multi-links etc.)

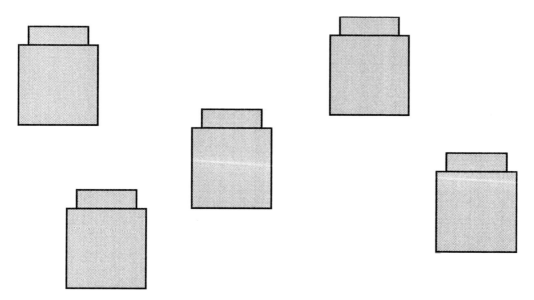

Unifix cubes are an especially good model for young children. They may help children make sense of regrouping which may be called trading, borrowing, or carrying in the standard addition and subtraction algorithms. Consider the process of carrying or trading in 27 + 38.

$$\begin{array}{r} {\scriptstyle 1} \\ 27 \\ +38 \\ \hline 5 \end{array}$$

A child may represent 27 with two strips of ten cubes and seven loose cubes and 38 with three strips of ten cubes and eight loose cubes. Then, ten of the loose cubes may be stacked together to form another strip of ten. In other words, the child puts ten ones together to make one ten. Thus, the child has 3 + 2 + 1 tens (strips) and 5 ones (individual cubes). One advantage of Unifix cubes over other manipulatives is that they allow children to physically stack ten ones together to make one ten. Or, in the case of re-grouping in subtraction, children may break a ten into ten ones. **The experiences of "making" a ten and "breaking" a ten into ones are crucial in helping children come to see ten as <u>both</u> ten individual units and as a unit itself (which is composed of ten smaller units).** For young children, the key to understanding place value is the ability to move flexibly back and forth between these two conceptions of ten. Therefore, a strip of ten Unifix Cubes is a good manipulative because it can be thought of as ten cubes or as one strip of ten.

Base Ten or Dienes Blocks

Base Ten Blocks consist of the following:

1. A unit represents 1.
2. A long represents 10.
3. A flat represents 100.
4. A block represents 1,000.

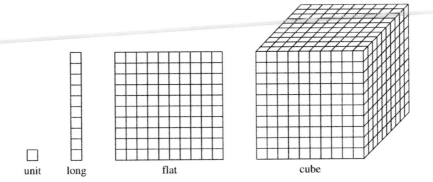

Three considerations before using or disadvantages of Base Ten Blocks are:

- First and foremost, the units are very small and young children may swallow them. Base Ten Blocks are also too small for young children to manipulate easily.

- Next, consider the block, which is supposed to represent 1,000. What is a common misconception that children have about this manipulative? Often, children conceptualize the block as representing 600 because it has 6 faces of 100 each. They cannot visualize the center flats. (The new plastic Base Ten Blocks that Velcro together may be helpful for this, but few schools will have this newer, more expensive version of the manipulative.) In one classroom, a group of fourth graders was trying to convince a classmate that the block represented 1,000, but he could not see it and insisted the block was 600. More often than not, the teacher will quickly go over the values of the manipulatives and then spend more time illustrating computation problems with them, not realizing that there may be a few children who are confused with the illustration because they are thinking the blocks represent 600.

- Finally, while Base Ten Blocks are very common in elementary schools, the teacher will rarely have enough for the entire class to use. Thus, it is often the case that Base Ten Blocks are used by the teacher as a physical model, but they are not used as manipulatives. **A manipulative is something that a child manipulates.**

Some advantages of Base Ten Blocks are:

- Base Ten Blocks may be useful as a remediation tool with a smaller group of students.
- Base Ten Blocks may be beneficial in helping children make sense of multi-digit addition and subtraction problems, borrowing and carrying, and place value.

Expanded Notation

Changing numbers back and forth between standard notation and expanded notation is a common activity in elementary textbooks from third grade on up. Here's an example:

$$576 = (5 \times 100) + (7 \times 10) + (6 \times 1)$$

Why are children asked to do this? Children are asked to do this activity in hopes that they might learn what the five, the seven, and the six represent in the number 576. However, children may just complete the task of expanded notation, following the pattern, without developing a real understanding of place value.

A type of questioning that might help children construct a viable understanding of place value is to ask, "How many tens are in 576?" Questions such as this one focus more on the meaning of the digits than simply asking, "What digit is in the tens' place?" Understanding place value involves more than just memorizing that the location of a digit in a number represents a certain value, i.e., the seven in 576 represents seven tens. Understanding place values also includes realizing that there are also 57 tens in 576! Children, typically, spend a great deal of time learning the names for the location of the digits, yet many children do not understand place value because they just memorize the locations and the value of each place. As we have previously stated, the concept of ten is the key to understanding place value and we will return to this concept in several of the upcoming sections.

3.1   Problems and Exercises

Solve the problems first and then consider some data on how children solved the problems found in the **Children's Solutions and Discussion of Problems and Exercises** section.

1.   A **palindrome** is a word or number that is the same forwards and backwards, such as Bob, mom, dad, pop, level, racecar, radar, etc. What are some other words that are palindromes? Is "I" a palindrome? Some numbers that are palindromes are: 121, 22, and 48,284. Is "7" a palindrome?

Consider the following assertion: every number can eventually be made into a palindrome by the process of reversing the digits, adding the original and new number, and repeating if necessary. For example, 23 is not a palindrome, but if the digits are reversed and added, 23 + 32 = 55, you get a palindrome. For twenty-three, the process was only completed once. Try 37. Reverse the digits and add, 37 + 73 = 110. The sum, 110, is not a palindrome, but if the process is repeated, 110 + 011 = 121, you get a palindrome. So, making 37 into a palindrome requires that the process be completed twice.

Try to make 98 into a palindrome.

2.   a. What number is in the tens place for 5,437?
      b. How many tens are in 5,437?
      c. Which question, 2a or 2b, might encourage children to think more about place value? Why?

3.   A sixth grader indicated he believed that the flat in Base Ten blocks represented 240. How do you think he developed this conception?

4.   Draw pictures to show how you would first use Unifix Cubes and then Base Ten Blocks to illustrate how to add 27 + 35.

5.   Which number is equal to eight tens plus nine tens?
    a.   17
    b.   170
    c.   1700
    d.   17000 (TIMSS, 2003)

6.   Each small square, □, is equal to 1. There are 10 small squares in each strip. There are 100 small squares in each large square.

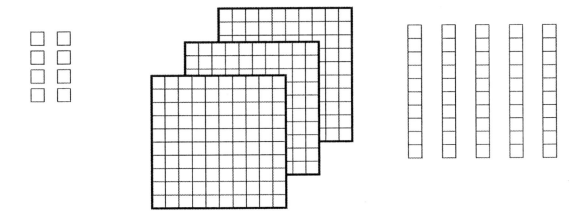

What number is shown (TIMSS, 2003)?
    a. 16
    b. 358
    c. 538
    d. 835

7.   In which pairs of numbers is the second number 100 more than the first number (TIMSS, 1995)?
    a.   199 and 209
    b.   4236 and 4246
    c.   9635 and 9735
    d.   51 863 and 52 863

3.1   Questions for Discussion

1.   What are some examples of everyday uses of Roman Numerals?

2.   Why do we have base ten rather than base eight? In all likelihood, if aliens from outer space came to this planet and had 8 fingers, they would use base eight or sixteen, not ten!

3.   Why did you and why do children study ancient number systems such as the Egyptian number system?

4.   Why do you think the tribe described in Papua, New Guinea, only had numbers for 1, 2, and many? What implications does this fact have for number systems we use?

5.   Are Unifix Cubes a good model of our number system? Why or why not?

6.   Would you use Base Ten Blocks, and if so, what would you be looking for as children worked with them?

7.   With any manipulative that represents a mathematical concept, is the mathematics in the manipulative or does the manipulative embody the mathematics? Explain this difference.

8,   Why is a child's ability to write numbers in expanded notation not a guarantee of understanding place value?

3.1   Children's Solutions and Discussion of Problems and Exercises

1.   Turning the number 98 into a palindrome requires repeating the described process somewhere between 20 and 30 times. As a result, turning 98 into a palindrome is a great problem to give to fifth and sixth graders to practice addition. They can start the problem with a calculator but the calculator soon is ineffective, as the numbers grow to be more than the number of digits possible to enter on the calculator. Hence, children are practicing their computation, while problem solving.

2.   In a fifth grade class, 86% (18/21) had a correct solution, but 11 of the 21 thought that the solution to b. was also 3. Only 38% (8/21) indicated that there were 543 tens in the number. A way to rephrase the question in terms of a context children can relate to is to ask: 'How many 10-dollar bills would it take to make $5,437?'

3.   The class had been talking about the number of 'squares' on a long and a flat in their descriptions of how many each manipulative represented, rather than the number of cubes in a long and a flat.

4.   Which model would be more meaningful to a first-grader?

5.   On the 2003 TIMSS international test, 64.7% of fourth graders gave the correct response.

6.   Eighty-nine percent of fourth graders gave the correct solution (TIMSS, 2003).

7.   Internationally only 33% of third graders and 49% of fourth graders answered this question correctly on the 1995 TIMSS test given to both third and fourth grade children.

3.2   Addition and Subtraction

Addition and subtraction can be defined in terms of set theory, but as we demonstrate in Chapter Two, children do not think about these concepts in this fashion. If young children do not use set theory to understand addition, how might children in kindergarten or first grade, who do not know the fact directly, solve 3 + 4?

Children will initially count.
*   They may count using Unifix cubes or counters.
*   They may count on their fingers
*   They may count in their heads.
In all these cases they are *counting*.

How will the same children solve 7-5? They will *count*!

Since both addition and subtraction are counting activities for many young children, it may **not** be necessary to separate problems into addition and subtraction as many elementary textbooks do.

Eventually, children start to learn facts, such as doubles (e.g., 2 + 2, 5 + 5, etc.), and use them to help solve addition problems. Likewise, they learn that subtraction is the opposite of addition and use their known addition facts to solve subtraction problems. But, it is important to emphasize that when children are first learning to add and subtract, they *count*.

Some college textbooks attempt to classify addition into different categories, such as adding measures and adding sets. However, most young children will solve both types of problems by counting.

One Child's Perspective of Addition

The next example illustrates how one child thought of addition. A college student, in a mathematics methods course for elementary teachers, told this story of how she interpreted her teacher's instructions for addition. She said that addition was explained to her as the operation of combining or putting things together. To solve 3 plus 4 she thought of a strip of 3 and a strip of 4. How do young children physically combine things? They might use paste. If you use paste, you would overlap one of the squares of the 3 and the 4, which would give you 6. As a child this college student thought of addition in exactly this manner. The class asked her why she didn't always get the wrong answer and know that something was not right. She said that she knew her answer was always 1 less than what the teacher wanted so she always added 1 to her answer.

This student's example illustrates the importance of asking children to explain their thinking regardless of whether their answers are correct or incorrect. How would a teacher ever know that a child was thinking this way unless she asked the student how she solved the problems?

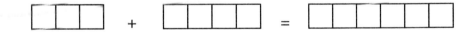

Counting Types

Repeated observation has shown that most children pass through similar levels of development in their use of counting, although they do not all progress at the same rate. After children have developed the concept of number, (see Chapter 2), five different levels of development, or five different "counting types," have been identified. They are:

- Perceptual
- Motor
- Verbal
- Abstract
- Part/Whole (Steffe, von Glasersfeld, Richards, & Cobb, 1983)

In this section, we will define and discuss each of these levels.

Perceptual Counters

Children at the perceptual counting stage need to <u>see and touch objects</u> in order to count them. They cannot count hidden objects. For example, they would be unable to solve a problem like that below where they are shown some squares, told that three more are hidden under the piece of cloth, and asked how many there are altogether.

Perceptual counters cannot count abstract objects. In other words, when perceptual counters use their fingers to count, their fingers are the objects they are counting. The number words they say refer to their fingers. They cannot use their fingers to keep track of the counting of abstract objects (e.g., imagined squares, days of the week, etc.)

Motor Counters

Like perceptual counters, motor counters have to "make" a number. A number is not real for them until they count it. However, motor counters do not have to touch objects in order to count them, and they can count hidden objects, but <u>they must point with their fingers or use some type of sensori-motor action to count.</u> Motor counters can solve the problem with visible and hidden squares described above, but they must start counting at 1 in order to make the 6. Then they will count the three hidden squares by pointing at three imagined squares.

If the above problem were changed so that children were told that there were some squares hidden under the cloth and that altogether there were 9 squares, motor counters would not be able to determine the number of hidden squares. This type of problem, called a "missing addend" problem, is conceptually more difficult.

Verbal Counters

Verbal counters are very similar to motor counters in their developing abilities. The primary difference is that verbal counters do not need to make a motor action as they are counting. However, they still need to count from 1 and they cannot do missing addend problems. The most sophisticated problem they can do is one such as 9 – 4. They will put up 9 fingers, counting as they do so, and then take four away. In other words, children at this level can make collections and take away from them by counting. Then, in general, they will count to determine how many are left. Like perceptual and motor counters, verbal counters do not have an abstract concept of number. For them, a number is meaningful only when it refers to a specific collection of objects they have counted. They cannot just put the number 7 in their heads and think that it represents 7 objects of some kind. They need to think of actual objects and count "One, two, three, four, five, six, seven." This kind of conceptualizing is what we mean when we say that they need to "make" a number.

Summary and Discussion of Pre-Abstract Counting Types; Perceptual, Motor, and Verbal

Perceptual: must actually see objects in order to count them

Motor: can count hidden objects; points at them with finger

Verbal: can count hidden objects; does not need to point

- cannot do missing addend problems
- always begin counting at 1
- do not have an abstract concept of number, i.e., a number is not real until they make it by counting actual objects

It is important to realize that children at these levels are developing normally. In kindergarten, most all children are perceptual, motor, or verbal counters. About one-half of beginning first graders are at one of these levels and a few second graders may be also. Most students move beyond verbal counting during first grade. Instruction for children at these pre-abstract levels needs to include activities involving manipulatives, spatial number patterns (e.g., dot patterns, finger patterns, ten frames), and counting. Such activities will give children opportunity to reflect upon and understand the concepts of addition and subtraction.

Finger Counting

A related issue that arises in the early grades is the use of finger counting. Should teachers discourage finger counting? For children at these pre-abstract levels, counting objects is the only way they have of solving problems involving numbers. If finger counting is prohibited and no other manipulatives are available, some students may use their toes or the numbers on a clock, but those who don't figure out such clever ways will be lost. Thus, it is preferable to keep finger counting out in the open. The teacher needs to see what methods children are using. Identifying a child's methods can help a teacher determine the level at which a child is operating. Knowing a child's level of understanding is important for teaching because it enables the teacher to select developmentally appropriate activities. Drill-and-practice on the basic facts and banning finger counting will be detrimental to children at these pre-abstract counting levels. Instead, these children need activities that will permit counting while simultaneously challenging them to develop more sophisticated means of thinking about number.

Abstract Counters

The ability to solve missing addend problems (e.g., 9 visible squares, some hidden, 13 in all, how many are hidden?) is evidence that children have reached the abstract counting level. Typically, they solve such problems by counting on. For the above problem, they might count "nine … ten, eleven, twelve, thirteen," putting up one finger for each number. Abstract counters can also solve subtraction problems by counting backwards. For 14 – 5, they might count "fourteen …

thirteen, twelve, eleven, ten, nine," again putting up one finger for each number. There are two important differences between this type of counting and that evidenced by pre-abstract counters. First, abstract counters can <u>put a number (at least a relatively small number) in their heads</u> and work with it meaningfully. They do not have to count it out starting at 1. Second, in the missing addend problem, the child says "ten, eleven, twelve, thirteen" while putting up 4 fingers and uses this to determine that the answer is 4. This approach indicates that the child is <u>using her fingers to keep track or as a record of her counting</u>. She is not counting her fingers as objects, as a pre-abstract counter does, but instead is using her fingers to keep track of the counting of abstract objects.

Part/Whole Counters

Part/Whole counters move one step beyond abstract counters in that they can solve subtraction problems in two different ways. Not only can they count backwards to solve subtraction problems, as abstract counters do, but they can also "close the gap." In other words, they can solve a problem such as 16 – 13 by counting "thirteen … fourteen, fifteen, sixteen," putting up one finger each for 14, 15, and 16 to determine that the answer is 3. This capability indicates that part/whole counters see a relationship between addition and subtraction. It also means that they are beginning to form an understanding of part/whole relations. In order to be able to close the gap in the above problem, a child must view 13 as part of the whole collection of 16 and then the child counts on to find the missing part.

Children at the part/whole level will still count back to solve subtraction problems when it is more efficient to do so. For example, given the problems 17 – 6 and 21 – 16, a part/whole counter would count back to solve the first one and close the gap, (count on), to solve the second one. At an earlier stage a child may count back for both of these problems.

Children at the abstract and part/whole counting levels need activities that will help them move beyond counting and develop thinking strategies (discussed in the next section). They are beginning to learn some of the "basic facts." Part/Whole Counters have or are in the process of developing the concept of ten.

Counting Based Strategies

The ways in which children develop counting based strategies can also be categorized into levels. These levels have been adapted from the work of Baroody, Tiilikian, and Tai (2006).

Count-All

For 3 + 4, the child counts three objects (can be fingers), counts four objects, and then counts all the objects together starting at 1.

Count-All with some short-cuts

For 3 + 4, the child holds up three fingers for 3 and four fingers for 4. The child then counts all the objects starting with 1. The child can only use this strategy with small numbers less than ten.

Count-All from the first number

For 3 + 4, the child counts, 'one, two, three' for the first number and then continues on with 'four, five, six, seven.' The child does not count the first number twice. The child may also learn to start from the larger number. This ability is sometimes considered as a separate developmental level.

Count-On

For 3 + 4, the child says, 'three' and then counts on saying, 'four, five, six, seven."

Count-On from the larger number

For 3 + 4, the child says, "four' and then counts on, 'five, six, seven.'
This characterization is the more widely used view in describing children's counting. Nevertheless, these counting based strategies are very similar and in many ways parallel the first four stages of the counting types: Perceptual, Motor, Verbal, and Abstract.

Concept of Ten and Place Value

Children initially view 10 as ten separate units. Children who conceptualize 10 this way can only solve a problem like 25 + 16 by counting on from 25 by ones. They have difficulty coordinating the counting of tens and ones because they do not see numbers as made up of tens and ones, even when presented with physical models that represent tens and ones. That is, they do not think of 25 as 2 tens and 5 ones. They see ten as 10 individual units.

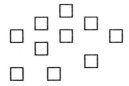

10 as ten small units

Next, children come to see 10 as either ten separate units or one single unit, but not both at the same time. In other words, they cannot coordinate these two different ways of thinking about 10. Children at this level can count by tens, but they cannot count on by ten from a given number unless that number is 20, 30, 40, 50, etc. Thus, it is as if children at this level see two separate units, big units (tens) and little units (ones), but they do not see them as related to each other. We could illustrate their two distinct <u>mental</u> representations of 10 at this level by the figure that follows.

10 as ten small units   10 as one big unit

At the next level, children come to see 10 as a unit that is composed of ten smaller units. This understanding is a part/whole conception of 10. These children can think of numbers as made up of tens and ones. As a result, they can count on <u>by 10</u> from a number such as 38. Children at this level can coordinate the counting of tens and ones and can switch flexibly between the two. We could illustrate their <u>mental</u> representation of 10 by the following figure.

10 as a unit composed of ten smaller units

The concept of ten is one of the most important concepts that we hope children learn by the end of second grade but not all third graders have this concept.

To develop this part/whole concept of 10, children need experience building and "unbuilding" tens. One way to do this is by using manipulatives such as Unifix cubes or Multilinks that allow children to put individual cubes together to form bars of 10 and to break bars of 10 into individual cubes (ones). Note that base 10 blocks and activities using money do not provide the opportunity for students to physically make and break apart tens. This is not to say that such materials are not useful, but for some children the experience of actually building "a ten" with the cubes may be especially significant.

Thinking Strategies and Learning "Basic Facts"

Once children reach the abstract counting level, they are ready for activities that will help them move beyond counting and develop <u>thinking strategies</u>. A thinking strategy involves using a known result to figure out an unknown result. For example, a child might say: I know that $5 + 5 = 10$, so $5 + 6 = 11$.

Children tend to learn "doubles" such as $2 + 2$, $5 + 5$, etc. first, so their initial use of thinking strategies tends to build off of these known results. Problems can be sequenced to promote the development of these strategies, and teacher questioning may also encourage students to relate problems and thus develop thinking strategies. Note that when children use the strategies above, they are no longer counting by ones to solve problems.

Developing thinking strategies helps children move beyond counting and facilitates the learning of the basic facts or number combinations because the use of thinking strategies involves constructing relationships among the basic facts. These relationships make the facts easier to learn because children see the facts as related to each other rather than as isolated bits of information. In addition, if a child does forget a fact, being able to apply thinking strategies will enable that child to figure it out instead of simply not knowing. Elementary school textbooks frequently encourage and organize their content to encourage children's development of thinking strategies.

Five types of thinking strategies that children often use are the following:

1.   Doubles Plus One (Can be extended to doubles plus 2)
      Example: I know 5 + 5 = 10, so 5 + 6 = 11.
2.   Doubles Minus One (Can be extended to doubles minus 2)
      Example: I know 5 + 5 = 10, so 5 + 4 = 9.
3.   Compensation (Moving 1 from one number to another)
      Example: I know 6 + 6 = 12, so 5 + 7 = 12.
4.   Inverse Relationship:
      Example: I know 7 + 5 = 12, so 12 – 7 = 5.
5.   Filling Up Tens:
      Example: For 8 + 5 = ___ , I took 2 from the 5 and added it to the 8 to make 10.
      Then, I had 3 left over, so I got 13.

Learning the basic facts is not just a matter of simple memorization. Children's memorization of some basic facts is not necessarily an indication of mathematical understanding. Children need extensive experience solving single-digit addition and subtraction problems, first by counting, then by using thinking strategies, before they are ready to commit these facts to memory meaningfully. These initial experiences help children build understanding of numbers and of the operations of addition and subtraction. Once such understanding is developed, children begin to commit the facts to memory through meaningful repetitive activities (i.e., practice). It is necessary for children be fluent and efficient with basic facts in order for them to construct efficient methods for calculating with two- and three-digit numbers.

In summary, the use of thinking strategies is important because they:

- help children move beyond counting toward the learning of the basic facts;
- help children construct a network of relationships among the facts;
- provide a basis for methods for adding and subtracting larger numbers;
- help children develop number sense, i.e., the ability to take numbers apart and put them back together in a different way;
- promote the belief that mathematics is a sense-making activity.

Subtraction/Take-Away

Children often refer to subtraction problems as take-away problems. When the word 'subtract' or 'minus' is used in a problem, children will frequently ask, "Do you mean 'take-away?'" Their language and their mathematical understanding are related to the physical activity they associate with the concept of subtraction.

Counting-back

In the Abstract and Part/Whole stages of development we described two methods that children might actually use to subtract or do 'take-aways:' counting-back and counting-up. When counting-back, children have an understanding of counting backwards, not just rote memorization of the number words in reverse order. How a child counts on a number line is an indication of his understanding of counting-back. To illustrate consider, 12 – 3. A child may start at 12 and then verbally or mentally count back, "one, two, three." He ends at 9; therefore, his answer is 9. This child's thinking is not an indication that he understands 'counting-back'. A child who understands the process of counting-back mentally or verbally says, "eleven, ten, nine."

Counting-up

Counting-up is a method that many children develop naturally, and it is also taught specifically in some mathematics elementary textbooks. In the previously mentioned developmental stages counting-up was described as counting-on, but counting-up often involves more than just counting by ones. To illustrate, consider the problem, 62-28. A child may add 2 to 28 to get 30, add three more tens either as three tens or a chunk of thirty to get 60, add 2 to the 60 to get 62 and then add all the numbers that were added: $2 + 30 + 2 = 34$.

Two Levels of Difficulty for Subtraction in Context

A distinction is made for subtraction in different contexts, not because of the way children solve the problems, but because one type of subtraction problem is conceptually more difficult for children. In the following two word problems, the operation and number sentence are the same: $17 - 9 = 8$.

1. Mary has 17 marbles. She gave 9 to her brother Tom. How many marbles does Mary have now?

2. Mary has 17 marbles. Her brother Tom has 9 marbles. How many more marbles does Mary have than Tom?

What is happening in each problem? That is, what is the physical action suggested? In the first problem the action is to take something away and it is classified as a **take-away** problem. In the second problem, two quantities are being compared and it is classified as a **compare** problem.

Which problem is more difficult for children, take-away or compare?

If these problems were given to second graders, they would have more trouble with the compare problem than the take-away problem. We can understand this phenomenon in terms of the counting types discussed in the previous section. Children at the Part/Whole level can solve the compare problem because they can conceptualize 9 marbles as part of the whole collection of 17 marbles and then count on to find the missing part. However, children who are not yet at this level have great difficulty making sense of the compare situation because they can only think in terms of adding to or taking away from a given amount.

These two classifications for subtraction are made because they are different for children in terms of their difficulty! This difference in difficulty exists even though children may be counting, using a thinking strategy, or a known fact to solve both types of problems.

3.2   Problems and Exercises

Solve the problems first and then consider some data on how children solved the problems found in the **Children's Solutions and Discussion of Problems and Exercises** section.

1.   Using your best judgment, classify each example of children's thinking by the counting types **Perceptual, Motor, Verbal, Abstract, and Part/Whole**.
   a. To add 9 + 7, a child adds 8 + 8.
   b. To add 9 + 7, a child takes 1 from the 7 to make 9 a 10, and adds 10 + 6.
   c. To add 9 + 7, a child counts 10, 11, 12, 13, 14, 15, 16.
   d. To add 9 + 7, a child counts out 9 Unifix cubes and 7 Unifix cubes, puts them together in a pile, and counts them all.
   e. To add 9 + 7, the child points at each Unifix cube as he is counting.
   f. To add 28 + 13, a child adds 1 and 2 and says 30; adds 8 + 3 = 11, takes the 1 ten from the 11, and adds it to 30 to get 40, and then adds 40 + 1 to get 41.

2.   Charles has 23 acorns that he found at the park. On his way home he lost 8 of them. How many does he have now? (What type of subtraction problem is this?)

3.   Nancy helped Mario on his paper route. Nancy delivered 8 papers and Mario delivered 23 papers. How many more papers did Mario deliver than Nancy? (What type of subtraction problem is this?)

4.   The difference between 85 and 53 is 32. Meredith added some number to 85 and then added the same number to 53. What would be the difference between the two new numbers (NAEP, 1990)?
   a. More than 32
   b. Less than 32
   c. 32
   d. It depends on the number added to 85 and 53.

5.   Solve: 503 – 207 = (NAEP, 1992)
   a. 206
   b. 296
   c. 304
   d. 396

6.   Subtract   6000
                      -2369   (TIMSS, 1995)

   a.   4369
   b.   3742
   c.   3631
   d.   3531

7.   Lia is practicing addition and subtraction problems. What number should Lia add to 142 to get 369? (TIMSS, 2003).

3.2   Questions for Discussion

1.   What process do children use when they first do addition? Subtraction?
2.   What are two types of subtraction problems and which one is more difficult for children? Give an example of each.
3.   What are the five counting types, and how would you use this knowledge in your teaching of children?
4.   Is it okay for children to count on their fingers? Explain your answer.
5.   Why would you not give timed tests to pre-abstract counters?

6. What is the **concept of 10**?
7. How are 'thinking strategies' related to mathematics as a 'sense-making activity' (section 1.3) in learning the basic addition and subtraction facts?
8. What is the difference between 'counting-on' and 'counting-up'?

3.2   Children's Solutions and Discussion of Problems and Exercises

2 & 3. In a first grade class 84% (16 out of 19) solved problem #2 correctly. The 3 who missed the problem made an error subtracting. Most children drew out 23 acorns or boxes to represent acorns, crossed out 8 of them and counted the rest. In problem #3, 60% (12 out of 20) solved the problem correctly. However, of the 8 who missed it, 5 added, and 3 subtracted incorrectly.

4. 19% of fourth graders gave the correct response (NAEP, 1990).
5. 53% percent of fourth graders answered this question correctly (NAEP, 1992).
6. Internationally 50% of third graders and 71% of fourth graders answered the problem correctly (TIMSS, 1995).
7. In the United States, 70.8% of fourth grade gave the correct solution and internationally the average was 61.8% (TIMSS, 2003).

3.3   Multiplication and Division

Multiplication

As children develop an understanding of place value and a part/whole conception of numbers (i.e., the ability to think of a given number as a unit which itself is made up of smaller units), they are forming a basis that will enable them to make sense of multiplication and division.

In elementary school, multiplication is typically presented as repeated addition. For example, on the balance problem below, children typically add $4 + 4 + 4 + 4 + 4 + 4$ to get 24 and are told that a "shorthand" way to write this is $6 \times 4 = 24$. Children also benefit from skip counting experiences (e.g., counting by fours: 4, 8, 12, 16, 20, 24, ...) as this provides an efficient way for them to perform repeated addition.

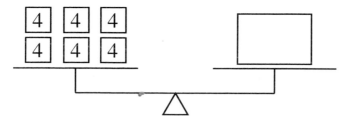

For balance problems like this one, third graders often say they multiplied, but for them that means that they added and then used a multiplication number sentence to represent their thinking. **For them multiplication is repeated addition!**

From Additive to Multiplicative Thinking

From our adult point of view, we see $6 \times 4 = 24$ as a sentence that states that 24 can be thought of as being made up of six units of four. However, research indicates that just because children can perform repeated addition (and write multiplication number sentences to describe their repeated addition) does not mean they are yet capable of multiplicative thinking. Multiplicative thinking grows out of additive thinking but is more complex.

Multiplicative thinking is the ability to count and think with units greater than one. For example, rather than counting six piles of three objects one at a time, one can count by six's and can think of 'six' as a base unit. In order to think multiplicatively, children must be able to simultaneously think about units of one and units of more than one (Clark & Kamii, 1996). Children must be able to count units of 3, units of 4, etc. Counting by units does not just mean being able to count by 3's, 4's, etc., but it also means being able to keep track of how many 3's, 4's, etc. they have counted.

To help additive thinkers become multiplicative thinkers, they need activities that will encourage them to <u>think</u> in terms of units larger than 1. Activities involving dot pattern sequences provide one approach.

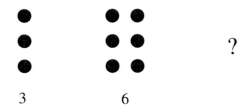

3   6

Can you keep this pattern going?

The key is to encourage children to think in units greater than one. For example, in this pattern they may be thinking in terms of <u>groups of 3</u>.

Children need to be challenged to mentally organize the arrays in units larger than one. For example, they might count the array below by three's or four's.

According to a study by Clark and Kamii (1996), about 45% of second graders and 64% of third graders exhibit some multiplicative thinking. However, only 49% of fifth graders displayed what these researchers called "solid multiplicative thinking." These statistics suggest that the ability to think multiplicatively develops slowly. Furthermore, just as asking pre-abstract counters to memorize basic addition facts may hinder their development and lead to nonsensical mathematical behavior, so too will asking additive thinkers to memorize the multiplication tables. Additive thinkers will interpret multiplicative situations additively because that is the only way they can interpret these situations. Thus, the multiplication table will not make sense to them because they cannot use known facts to figure out ones they don't know, as they can for addition facts. For example, if an additive thinker is asked to use $4 \times 4 = 16$ to help figure out 5×4, she will probably reason that the answer is 17 because 5 is one more than 4.

Problems that, from our adult perspective, might be called "division" problems can also help students think in terms of units larger than 1 (Steffe and Killion, 1989). One type of problem might be to give children a large group of blocks, say 74, and pose the question: "There are 74 blocks. Can you make the 74 blocks into stacks of ten?" After students make one stack, the teacher can ask, "How many stacks of ten could you make like that?" Another type of problem would be to ask, "If you count by 3's to 15, how many groups of 3 would you count?" These types of problems can help children move beyond the need to physically make or see the units larger than one that they are counting.

Additive thinkers must first learn the number word sequences for <u>counting</u> in units greater than one. Children first learn to count by twos, threes, fours, etc.

Children also need an opportunity to relate multiplication ideas to "real-world" contexts. Simple word problems like the following can provide such an opportunity:

> Jennifer brought cupcakes to school. She had 6 cupcakes in each box. She had 5 boxes. How many cupcakes did she bring?

Although it is important initially for children to be able to "act out" problems of this type using objects of some kind to facilitate their thinking and counting, the teacher should encourage children to figure out the total "without counting by ones."

Cartesian Products

Cartesian products are sometimes used to illustrate multiplication, but this representation is initially not viewed as illustrating multiplication by children. An example of a Cartesian product problem is: If I have 3 pairs of pants and 4 shirts, how many different outfits can I make? One third-grade teacher of 35 years noted, "They do not pick up on the idea of solving the problem by using multiplication. Third graders will make a list: pant A, shirt 1, pant A, shirt 2, etc., and then count how many options there were." Cartesian products are important later in probability and in the counting principle, but this product may not be a good way to introduce third graders to the concept of multiplication.

Multiplication Thinking Strategies and Basic Facts

As children begin to employ multiplicative thinking (counting and thinking with units greater than one), it is important to encourage them to develop thinking strategies that will facilitate their learning of the multiplication basic facts ("multiplication tables"). Learning simple facts will enable them to construct <u>a network of relationships</u> among the facts.

One example of a multiplication thinking strategy is "I know 5×5 is 25, so 6×5 must be 30 because it is just <u>one more 5</u> than 5×5." Another example is "I know 8×5 is 40, so 8×6 must be 48 because to get 8×6 you <u>add one to each of the eight fives</u> in 8×5 so 8×6 is 8 more than 8×5." In these examples children are intuitively applying the distributive property of multiplication over addition e.g., $8 \times 6 = 8(5 + 1) = (8 \times 5) + (8 \times 1) = 40 + 8$. Helping students to develop these kinds of thinking strategies solidifies their multiplicative thinking and provides a foundation for learning the basic facts. Encouraging children to develop this kind of thinking also lays a foundation for algebraic thinking, specifically applications of the distributive property. One way to promote the use of thinking strategies is to sequence problems (e.g., 2×3, 3×3, 4×3, 5×3) and encourage children to relate a given problem to a previous problem or problems.

How Young Children Divide

Your textbook may make several distinctions for division. This supplement only makes two because children who do not know their division facts and who do not yet know that multiplication is the opposite of division predominantly solve division problems in two distinct ways.

As early as second grade, children are capable of developing solution strategies for problems such as the following:

   A. Mrs. Wright has 28 children in her class. If she wants to separate her class into 4 equal groups, how many children will be in each group?

   B. Mrs. Davies has 30 children in her class. She wants to put them into groups of 5. How many groups will she have?

Initially, children solve these problems using physical materials (e.g., cubes) or pictures to model the situation. For instance, for Problem A, children might draw 4 circles and sequentially allocate tally marks to the circles (i.e., one in this group, one in this group, one in this group, and so on) until they have made 28 tally marks. Then they can count the number of tally marks in each circle.

As children's methods become more sophisticated they might allocate tallies more than one at a time. For example, they might allocate 5 to each group on the first pass, then one to each group, then one more to each group.

For Problem B, children might make 5 tally marks, circle them, make 5 more tally marks, circle them, and so on until they have made 30 tally marks. Then they can count the number of groups of 5 they have made. Alternately, students might add 5's until they get to 30 or subtract 5's until they get to zero, i.e.:

$$5 + 5 = 10, 10 + 5 = 15, 15 + 5 = 20, 20 + 5 = 25, 25 + 5 = 30 \text{ or}$$

$$30 - 5 = 25, 25 - 5 = 20, 20 - 5 = 15, 15 - 5 = 10, 10 - 5 = 5, 5 - 5 = 0.$$

Then they can count the number of 5's they added or subtracted.

The two problems above illustrate two different interpretations of division. Note that Problem A involves forming a given number of groups. The problem then is to determine the size of each group. This is called the **fair-sharing** or **partitioning** model of division.

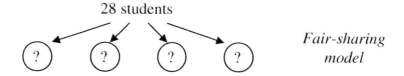

Fair-sharing model

In contrast, Problem B involves forming groups of a given size. The problem then is to determine how many groups of that size can be formed. This is called the **measurement** or **repeated operation** model of division.

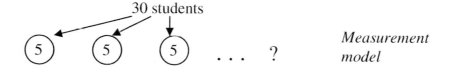

Measurement model

The reason this model is called a repeated operation model is that, as illustrated from the above solution examples, children repeatedly add or subtract the size of each group. The reason it is sometimes called a measurement model is that both the approach of repeatedly adding or subtracting 5 and the approach of making 5 tally marks, circling them, etc. are analogous to successively laying 5-unit rulers end-to-end until the entire 30 units is "measured."

Young children may at first be more comfortable with problems that fit the fair-sharing model because they are likely to be familiar with the activity of sharing. However, it is important to ensure that they have many experiences with both types of division situations. The context of the problem plays a large part in determining the method of solution that children will employ.

With experience, children's solution strategies become more sophisticated. For the problem:

> Tonight 45 parents will be visiting our school. Six parents can sit at each table. How many tables do we need?

The variety of solution strategies typically produced by second and third graders might include the following:

1) using cubes or drawing a picture to model the situation
2) using repeated subtraction (i.e., 45 – 6 = 39, 39 – 6 = 33, etc.) and keeping track of the number of 6's subtracted
3) using repeated addition to build up to 45
4) using a known multiplication fact as a shortcut and building up to 45 from there (e.g., 6 × 6 = 36, plus another 6 is 42 ⇒ 7 tables will seat 42 so altogether 8 tables are needed)

The above problem does not work out "evenly" and it is important for children to experience these types of problems because such problems are common in everyday situations and children need to think about how to deal with the "remainder." For example, in the above problem, the remainder necessitates an additional table. However, if the problem involved sharing 45 marbles among 6 children, the 3 "leftover" marbles might be ignored. And, for a problem of sharing 10 chocolate bars among 4 children, it might well be possible to split the 2 leftover chocolate bars among the 4 children so that each gets $2^1/_2$ bars. The point is that children should be encouraged to construct answers that make sense in the context of a problem. To say they need "7 remainder 3 tables" does not make sense.

Division By and With 0

Fifth graders may experience division <u>by</u> and <u>with</u> zero. Many times teachers just **tell** students that division by 0 is not possible without explaining why. We believe teachers should be able to explain division by and with 0 to fifth graders and above.

$$7 \div 0 = ? \qquad\qquad 0 \div 7 = ?$$

Most fifth-grade children know that multiplication is the opposite of division and many of them use this knowledge to solve single-digit or two-digit division problems. For example, to find $56 \div 7 = ?$, they might ask themselves, $7 \times ? = 56$.

To explain division by and with 0 to children, write out a division number sentence and underneath it write out the corresponding multiplication sentence.

$$12 \div 3 = ? \qquad 7 \div 0 = ? \qquad 0 \div 7 = ?$$
$$3 \times ? = 12 \qquad 0 \times ? = 7 \qquad 7 \times ? = 0$$

For $0 \times ? = 7$, there is nothing that you can multiply by 0 to get 7 so $7 \div 0$ is not possible or is undefined. For $7 \times ? = 0$, one can replace the "?" with 0 so this answer is 0, i.e., $0 \div 7 = 0$. Not all fifth graders may understand this explanation, but it is important that they see that there is a reason for the rules in mathematics and that math is not magic! Some children will understand this explanation.

Order of Operations

While your textbook covers order of operations, it is not likely that you will be teaching all of these rules at once to children. You are more likely to be teaching the order of operations in regards to addition and subtraction for third grade, and the order of operations in regards to multiplication and addition/subtraction for fourth and fifth grade. In fifth grade, you might also introduce grouping symbols. In the middle school grades, children often learn the order of operations through mnemonics such as: **P**lease **E**xcuse **M**y **D**ear **A**unt **S**ally which suggests that the order of operations are: **P**arenthesis, **E**xponents, **M**ultiplication, **D**ivision, **A**ddition, **S**ubtraction. One note is that some children believe that multiplication comes before division, and addition comes before subtraction.

3.3   Problems and Exercises

<u>Solve the problems first</u> and then consider some data on how children solved the problems found in the **Children's Solutions and Discussion of Problems and Exercises** section.

1. a. There are 9 rows of chairs. There are 15 chairs in each row.
        What is the total number of chairs (TIMSS, 2003)?
    b. A movie theater has 10 rows with 14 seats in each row. If 12 seats are
        empty, how many people are seated in the theater?
    c. Each student needs 8 notebooks for school. How many notebooks are
        needed for 115 students (TIMSS, 2003)?

2. How do you think second graders will solve the following problems?

    a. Mary wants to share 12 cookies fairly among her 3 friends. How many
        cookies will each friend receive?
    b. Johnny has 12 pieces of candy and the candy comes in packages of 3.
        How many packages of candy does he have?

3. For the following balance a second grade class gave the following number
    sentences to represent their thinking.

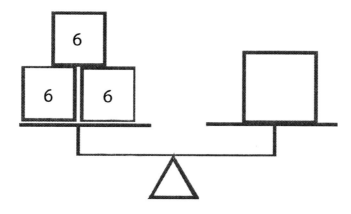

    a. 6 + 6 + 6 = 18   b. 16 + 2 = 18
    c. 3 x 6 = 18   d. 6 x 3 = 18

    How do you think the children explained each number sentence?

4. Ninety-eight children are going on a field trip to the zoo. If each school bus holds
    40 children, how many buses will they need? Circle the correct answer.
    a. 2
    b. 2 Remainder 18
    c. 2.45
    d. 3

    How do you think children will respond to this problem?

5. Describe how you would explain these two problems to a fifth grade class;

    $$5 \div 0 = ? \qquad\qquad 0 \div 5 = ?$$

6.   Three third-grade children found $5.00 on their way to school. Their teacher told them they could keep the money if no one claimed it after one week. How might they divide up the money? What do you think they might do with the extra money to be fair to everyone?

7.   Addition Fact
                        4 + 4 + 4 + 4 + 4 = 20

Write the addition fact as a multiplication fact (TIMSS, 1995).

                    ___ x ___ = ___

8.   Carl has 3 empty egg cartons and 34 eggs. If each carton holds 12 eggs, how many more eggs are needed to fill all three cartons (NAEP, 2003)?

9.   Christy has 88 photographs to put in her album. If 9 photographs will fit on each page, how many pages will she need (NAEP, 1992)?
      a. 8
      b. 9
      c. 10
      d. 12

10.   A store sells 168 tapes each week. How many tapes does it sell in 24 weeks (NAEP, 1992)?
      a. 7
      b. 192
      c. 4,032
      d. 4,172

11.   a. $204 \div 4 =$
      b.   A piece of rope 204 cm long is cut into 4 equal pieces. Which of these gives the length of each piece in centimeters (TIMSS, 2003)?
             a. $204 + 4$
             b. 204×4
             c. $204 - 4$
             d. $204 \div 4$
      c. $15 \times 9 =$

3.3   Questions for Discussion

1.   What is multiplication for children first learning it?
2.   What are the two ways that young children divide (assuming they do not yet know their multiplication or division facts)?
3.   Why would you use or not use Cartesian Products to first introduce the concept of multiplication to children?
4.   Explain what is meant by 'multiplicative thinking' and 'additive thinking'.
5.   How is a child's learning of the basic multiplication facts similar to learning the basic addition facts? What role does thinking strategies play in a child's learning the multiplication facts?
6.   Why should children be proficient in addition facts before learning their multiplication facts? Why do children who do not know their addition facts have so much trouble understanding multiplication?

3.3   Children's Solutions and Discussion of the Problems and Exercises

1. a. Sixty-six percent of fourth grades gave the correct result on the 2003 TIMSS test.

    b. This problem was given to 120 fourth and fifth grade children. 56% were able to solve the problem correctly. Some drew pictures and other just multiplied and subtracted the numbers. A common error was to multiply incorrectly. For 10 x 14, solutions given were 40, 400 and 1400.

    c. In the United States, 54.2% of fourth grade girls and 48.3% of fourth grade boys had this problem correct (TIMSS, 2003).

2. These two problems were given to a third grade class (n = 20) and over 90% of the children had the correct solution for both problems. Almost every child drew a picture.

3   a. Many children will know 6 + 6 =12 then count from twelve, "12,   13, 14, 15, 16, 17, 18."

    b. In this case, a child reasoned that "6 + 6 = 12, then if you take the 2 off and added the 6 back on you get 16, and then 16 and 2 is 18"

    c. The balance is showing 3 groups of 6.

    d. The balance is showing 6, three times.

4. This problem was given to two different classes. In the fourth grade class 20 out of 21 children chose b. In a third grade class, 16 out of 18 children chose d. Why do you think there was such discrepancy in the class's answers?

6. One child suggested buying a piece of gum with the extra 2 cents and sharing it among the three children. Another said to buy a band aid. Fairness is very important to children.

7. Internationally 63% of third graders and 77% of fourth grades gave either 5 x 4 = 20 or 4 x 5 = 20 (TIMSS, 1995)

8. Only 46% of fourth graders gave the correct answer (NAEP, 2003).

9. 37% of fourth graders gave the correct response (NAEP, 1992).

10. 55% of fourth graders gave the correct response (NAEP, 1992).

11. a. In the United States, 56.2 % of boys and 53.1% of girls answered this problem correctly.

    b. In the United Sates 75% of the boys (fourth-grade) and 64.3% of the girls (fourth grade) answered this problem correctly. More children could set the problem up correctly than could actually do the computation.

    c. Here 75.0% of the girls and 71.7% of the boys answered this problem correctly (TIMSS, 2003).

3.4   Properties of Whole-Number Operations

Even algebra students have a difficult time with tests requiring them to name the properties of whole number operations. This fact is puzzling considering that high school students intuitively know the properties when they involve numbers. They know intuitively that 3 + 4 = 4 + 3, but they have difficulty naming this property as the commutative property when it is illustrated using variables, $a + b = b + a$. Understanding how children come to know these properties can help explain this phenomenon. For children, properties are not laws but are expression of what they already know.

Commutative Property

Addition

To illustrate how children think about the commutative property of addition, try or think about the following activity called "Target." In elementary school, Target is a common mental math activity. At this level, the purpose of the activity is to practice computation where children have opportunities to provide a variety of solutions. In the activity of Target, children are to give two numbers that create the target number. In the version of Target described here, children may only use one operation, addition. In constructing your answers, pretend you are a first or second grade child. **The target number is 10, give pairs of numbers whose sum is 10.**

Did your class give both 7 + 3 and 3 + 7? Would first and second graders give the reversed pairs of numbers?

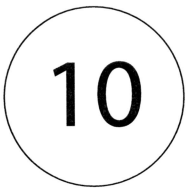

Most groups of adults do not give the reversed pairs of numbers such as 7 + 3 and 3 + 7 because, from their perspective, they are the same. Invariably, you will get the following pairs of numbers: 5,5; 6,4; 7,3; 8,2; 9,1; and 10,0. However, first and second graders never stop here, unless they have been directly told to do so. They normally go on to give the following pairs: 4,6; 3,7; 2,8; 1,9; and 0,10.

Why don't most children stop?

The reason is that addition is a *counting* activity for most young children (Fuson, 2003). So the problems 7 + 3 and 3 + 7 are extremely different for children if they are counting on. For 7 + 3, the child might say, "7 … 8, 9, 10," holding up a finger each for 8, 9, and 10. For 3 + 7, the child might say, "3 … 4, 5, 6, 7, 8, 9, 10," holding up a finger each for 4 through 10. For young children, addition is not commutative. In this example, 7 + 3 and 3 + 7 are two different problems for children because they solve them differently. They do not see beforehand that the answers will be the same. The commutative property is a concept, and children will not be able to make sense of it until they are ready.

However, as early as second grade, some children do figure out that 4 + 3 gives the same sum as 3 + 4. From an adult perspective, it is tempting to say that such children understand the commutative property of addition. We expect that they will be able to make sense of this formal statement of the property (and wonder why such a big deal is being made of it) when it is presented to them in an algebra class. However, closer examination of children's thinking about "commutativity" suggests that although they may view the equality of certain "turn-arounds" (e.g., 3 + 4, 4 + 3) as a fact, many are not certain that this would hold for any pair of numbers. For example, asked to find the sum 7 + 15, the same children who know that 3 + 4 = 4 + 3 will count on from 7 rather than reason that 7 + 15 = 15 + 7 and then count on from 15. Further, children's efforts to investigate the equality of "turn-arounds" for any pair of numbers reveal much about their developing understandings of addition. Some students check many pairs of numbers, often trying numbers larger than they usually work with. For these students, addition is a procedure applied to two numbers to get a result. Other students may use physical materials to represent the addition of two quantities. Interestingly, the use of physical materials can promote the construction of a more abstract argument because it enables students to make generalizations about how the addends and the sum are related to each other under the operation of addition. Still other students may explore whether or not the notion of "turn-arounds" holds for subtraction. This kind of experimentation can lead to ideas about negative numbers (Schifter, 1997).

The important point here is that children do develop intuitive notions about commutativity, but they do not spontaneously construct the concept in full-blown richness of detail. They need a multitude of experiences with adding numbers before they intuit the commutative property of addition, let alone name it. Their understanding can be furthered through activities that ask them to explore ideas related to commutativity and in doing so, generate hypotheses, attempt generalizations, and construct justifications. It is this type of mathematical activity that will more fully prepare them for their later study of algebra.

Multiplication

In fourth grade, most children will not give the reversed pairs for the target activity with addition. They will give the same solutions as adults. However, if the target operation were changed to multiplication many fourth graders would give reversed pairs of numbers. For example, for the target number 12, they would give 4 x 3 and 3 x 4. Eventually children figure out that 4×3 gives the same result as 3×4. Knowing that the result is the same is one thing; understanding why it is the same is quite another. Children are likely to think of 4×3 very differently than they think of 3×4. That is, they think of 4×3 as meaning 3 + 3 + 3 + 3 or four 3's and they think of 3×4 as meaning 4 + 4 + 4 or three 4's. One approach to illustrating the commutative property of multiplication is through the use of arrays. Children who have related arrays to multiplication may reason that 4×3 gives the same result as 3×4 because the same array may be viewed as four rows of 3 dots or three columns of 4 dots.

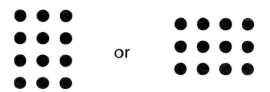

Once some children figure out that multiplication is like addition in that 4 x 3 and 3 x 4 have the same solution, they often exert peer pressure on other children and argue against the reversed pairs. The teacher may see it their way as well. Consequently, many fourth-grade classes will not give reversed pairs for multiplication but this is not an indication that every student has figured out that multiplication is commutative. More importantly, it is not an indication that children understand <u>why</u> multiplication is commutative.

Associative Property

Like the commutative property, children come to understand the associative property through multiple experiences. Sometimes, however, children's development of the associative property is discouraged by well-meaning teachers who insist that children must add from left to right and must multiply from left to right. The associative property can make problems easier and more meaningful for children and should always be encouraged. Children need problems that will support their development of the associative property. Third and fourth graders might be asked to solve the following problem mentally.

$$57 + 88 + 12$$

This problem is more difficult to add from left to right mentally, $57 + 88$, but applying the associative property it is easier to mentally add $88 + 12$ is 100 and $100 + 57$ is 157. Likewise, examples with four or more addends can be used to illustrate more general applications of the associate property.

$$99 + 78 + 1 + 22$$

To illustrate and encourage the children's development of the associative property of multiplication, problems like the following can be used.

$$17 \times 25 \times 4$$

Again note that it would be difficult to solve 17×25 mentally, but it is much easier to solve $17 \times 25 \times 4$ by applying the associative property, $17 \times (25 \times 4)$. Then, it is just a matter of multiplying 4×25, which is 100, and then, 100×17 is 1700!

As a teacher you can give children problems like these to encourage them to construct the associative property for addition and multiplication.

Distributive Property

The distributive property is very important in algebra. Unfortunately, it is typically not presented in a meaningful way to elementary children. Most upper elementary mathematics textbooks try to teach children about the distributive property by having them compute solutions in two ways as shown in the example here.

$$
\begin{aligned}
4(17 + 3) &= (4 \times 17) + (4 \times 3) \\
4 \times 20 &= 68 + 12 \\
80 &= 80
\end{aligned}
$$

In our experiences, children do not see the need to compute the solution on the right when it is easier to solve the problem without distributing the numbers. Children can develop intuitive notions about the distributive property if they are presented with the appropriate multiplication activities. Some of these are illustrated and discussed in the next section.

Identity Properties

The identity property states that if you conduct an operation on a number with its identity you will get the number you started with. For instance, in addition any number plus zero gives you the number with which you started (e.g., $5 + 0 = 5$). In addition, the identity element for any number is zero. In multiplication, the identity element of any number is 1 since 1 times any number yields that number (e.g., $5 \times 1 = 5$). Children intuitively understand these properties and think it is silly when you tell them these properties. They know that any number plus 0 is the number and any number times 1 is the number. From a child's perspective, why is something so simple given a fancy name?

Closure Property

As future teachers you will probably never teach this property to children, but it is a property that drives our creation of numbers. That is, we create new numbers so that we have closure. For example, addition of whole numbers is closed because the sum of any two whole numbers is a whole number, but subtraction of whole numbers is not closed (e.g., $2 - 5 = -3$). To make subtraction of whole numbers closed, we need negative numbers.

3.4   Problems and Exercises

<u>Solve the problems first</u> and then consider some data on how children solved the problems found in the **Children's Solutions and Discussion of Problems and Exercises** section.

1.   <u>Solve each problem mentally</u> by using the above mathematical properties (commutative, associative, and/or distributive) to make the problem easier to solve.
  a. $17 + 9 + 3 =$ ___
  b. $8 + 7 + 2 + 3 =$ ___
  c. $17 + 18 + 3 + 2 =$ ___
  d. $(16 + 87) + 13 =$ ___
  e. $4 + (96 + 17) =$ ___
  f. $1 + (45 + 99) =$ ___

2.   <u>Solve each problem mentally</u> by using the above mathematical properties to make the problem easier to solve.
  a. $28 \times 5 \times 2 =$ ___
  b. $56 \times 2 \times 5 =$ ___
  c. $17 \times 25 \times 4 =$ ___
  d. $(83 \times 25) \times 4$ ___
  e. $4 \times (25 \times 453) =$ ___
  f. $(12 \times 25) \times 8 =$ ___

3. $4 \times 0 \times 5 \times 9 =$

4. ☐ stands for a number. 7 x ☐ will always give the same answer as (TIMSS, 1995)

    a. ☐ x 7
    b. ☐ + 7
    c. ☐ - 7
    d. 7 + ☐
    e. ☐ ÷ 7

5. Which of these is equal to 370 x 998 + 370 x 2 (TIMSS, 2003)?

    a. 370 x 1000
    b. 372 x 998
    c. 740 x 998
    d. 370 x 998 x 2

3.4   Questions for Discussion

1. Why isn't addition commutative for many young children?
2. Why is the closure property important mathematically?
3. What do many children think of the identity properties?
4. Explain what it means to say, "properties are not laws, but expressions of what children already know."
5. Most adults see, 5 + 6 and 6 + 5, as the same problem, but children do not. To understand how children think, an adult has to 'unpack' or 'decompress' her thinking. Explain what it means to 'unpack' our mathematical knowledge and why this concept is important.

3.4   Children's Solutions and Discussion of Problems and Exercises

1&2. A key for helping children develop an understanding of the associative property is to provide problems which are substantially easier to solve when the associative property is applied.

Problem set 1 was given to a third grade class to solve, most students (17 out of 22) indicated they counted and did not use the associate property to make the problem easier.

Problem set 2 was given to a fifth grade class and again most students did use the associate property, this fact is also evident in the percent they were able to get correct.

    a. 52% (12/23)
    b. 52% (12/23)
    c. 35% (8/23)
    d. 39% (9/23)
    e. 9% (2/23)
    f. 35% (8/23)

Only two students indicated that they made 10 or 100 first, and they had every problem correct.

3. Only 53% of fourth graders gave the correct solution on the NAEP test (NAEP, 2003).

4. The international average of third graders responding correctly was 53% and 63% for fourth grade (TIMSS, 1995).

5.   This was a question on the eighth grade TIMSS test, 50.8% of girls and 45.7% of boys answered it correctly (TIMSS, 2003).

3.5   Algorithms

Most elementary textbooks teach "standard algorithms" in great depth. An algorithm is a series of steps or procedures that are repeated to make some task more efficient and to insure that the task yields a reliable result. The standard algorithms for addition and subtraction involve putting the addends in columns, with each column corresponding to the appropriate place value. The addition algorithm involves "carrying" a number to the top of the next column when the sum is more than 10, and the subtraction algorithm involves "borrowing" when the bottom number in a column is larger than the top number. Multiplication also involves putting the numbers in columns and multiplying by each digit and adding the products. The standard algorithm for division is called "long division." There has been a debate about whether we should spend a lot of time on long division when in real life most people will use a calculator to solve division problems with larger numbers.

Addition and Subtraction Algorithms

It took humankind thousands of years to develop these standard algorithms, and even though they are efficient, algorithms are not the only way to compute. As an illustration, consider the following subtraction algorithm that goes from left to right. Your grandparents or parents may have learned to subtract this way:

$$
\begin{array}{r}
3,458 \\
-1,769 \\
\hline
2,799 \\
1,689
\end{array}
$$

This algorithm starts on the left. First, subtract $3 - 1$ (Subtract one thousand from 3 thousand) and write down the 2 (thousand). Go to the next column where you cannot subtract 7 (hundred) from 4 (hundred) so borrow one (thousand) from the 2 (thousand), crossing it out and making it a 1 (thousand). Now you can subtract 7 (hundred) from 14 (hundred), which is 7 (hundred), so write down the 7 (hundred) and go to the next column. Here you cannot subtract 6 (tens) from 5 (tens) so borrow from the 7 (hundred), making it a 6 (hundred), and then subtract 6 (tens) from 15 (tens), which is 9 (tens). In the last column you cannot subtract 9 (ones) from 8 (ones) so borrow one (ten) and cross out the 9 (tens), making it 8 (tens). Then 18 (ones) minus 9 (ones) is 9 (ones).

This is an <u>efficient algorithm</u>, which will always work; it is just not the "standard algorithm."

Partial Sums

Partial Sums is an algorithm that is taught in some elementary textbooks for addition which is designed to encourage children to develop an understanding of the procedure.

		356
		+847
Add the 100s.	300 + 800 =	1100
Add the 10s	50 + 40 =	90
Add the 1s	6 + 7 =	13
Add the partial sums	1100 + 90 + 13 =	1203

Children are encouraged to say what they are adding in each step. For example they are encouraged to say, 'three hundred plus eight hundred is eleven hundred." Why might this method be considered more conceptually based than the standard algorithm?

Conceptual Understanding of Standard Algorithms

Even though children practice the standard algorithms, they often do not understand what they are doing. Mathematics is not meaningful; math is not a sense making activity if children simply perform an algorithm without understanding how and why it works. Consider this example which illustrates the "carrying" algorithm in addition:

$$\begin{array}{r} 1 \\ 27 \\ +28 \\ \hline 55 \end{array}$$

Now try asking children what the *1* means when they carry. Often they say that this is how you do it or that is the way that they have been taught without indicating that the *1* really represents 10.

The standard algorithms are one way to solve problems, but they are not the only way. Adults tend to think of standard algorithms as the only way to compute because this is how they were taught. However, children will invent their own ways of doing computation when not directed to follow a particular algorithm. Some research suggests that these children typically possess a greater understanding of mathematics and are more efficient in their computation than children who are directed to follow an algorithm. (Madell, 1985). On the other hand, children taught the standard algorithms for addition and subtraction before they have fully developed the concept of 10 typically experience difficulties in understanding the mathematics underlying the algorithm. The following discussion of children's own strategies illustrates why children have this difficulty.

Children's Self-Generated Algorithms

Developing a part/whole conception of numbers and an understanding of place value facilitates children's development of methods for adding and subtracting two- and three-digit numbers.

Conversely, presenting children with two- and three-digit addition problems in the appropriate contexts (e.g., with manipulatives) can help them begin to think of numbers as made up of tens and ones (or hundreds, tens, and ones). In other words, children's concept of place value and their procedures for computing with multi-digit numbers develop together.

Elementary school children invent a variety of sophisticated algorithms for addition and subtraction. For example, for the problem 37 + 24, a child might reason "37 + 10 = 47, 47 + 10 = 57" (or "37 + 20 = 57"), then "57 + 4 = 61

After children have developed their own algorithms, the standard algorithms for addition and subtraction may be much more meaningful. These are shown below as they are typically written in column format.

$$
\begin{array}{r}
\overset{1}{3}7 \\
+\ 24 \\
\hline
61
\end{array}
\qquad
\begin{array}{r}
\overset{6}{7}\cancel{2} \\
-\ \cancel{2}4 \\
\hline
48
\end{array}
$$

When children have developed a part/whole conception of ten and the ability to think of numbers as collections of tens and ones, they may be able to make sense of these standard algorithms, which rely on the notions of combining ones to make a ten and breaking a ten into ones. Still, learning these standard algorithms presents significant challenges for children. For one, the standard algorithms work from right to left, whereas children's natural tendency is to work from left to right (see examples of children's algorithms above). And if an attempt is made to teach children these algorithms before they have constructed a part/whole conception of ten and their own strategies, they are reduced to performing symbol manipulations that they don't understand. Many children in the intermediate grades and above cannot explain the meaning of the *1* above the 3 in 37 in the standard addition algorithm example above. This lack of understanding leads children to develop what are sometimes called "buggy," or error-prone algorithms. A common error for the above subtraction problem would be to subtract the 2 from the 4 in the ones column and come up with an answer of 52. Children who understand the algorithms they are using do not make these kinds of errors.

Textbooks sometimes try to explain the standard algorithms with pictures showing individual ones, sticks representing ten, and bundles of ten sticks representing one hundred. These pictures may help children who have already constructed an understanding of place value figure out what is going on in the standard algorithms, but they will be of little benefit to those children who have yet to construct such an understanding. The concept of place value cannot be apprehended from pictures. It develops from children's experiences acting on physical materials, from their own drawings representing numbers, from their mental activity of combining smaller units to make a larger unit and breaking a larger unit into smaller units, and their reflections on these activities (Cobb & Wheatley, 1988).

While a teacher may feel it necessary to guide children to use of the standard addition and subtraction algorithms, it is important to note that the role of paper-and-pencil calculation (for which these algorithms were created and are most helpful) is being reduced by the use of calculators. Furthermore, for the purposes of mental computation, the standard algorithms are rather clumsy and some children find it difficult to keep track of the numbers borrowed or carried. Children's self-constructed algorithms tend to be much better suited for performing <u>mental calculations</u> efficiently and reliably.

Despite the extensive use of calculators in the modern world, children and adults still need efficient ways to perform calculations with larger numbers.   All agree on the need for children to develop efficient and fluent mathematical calculations. One way of developing this mathematical fluency is through the teaching of standard algorithms which continues to be a major part of the elementary mathematics curriculum. Another approach to these same ends to is to encourage children use algorithms which are efficient methods and reflect their mathematical understanding about calculations with larger numbers—these would include self-generated as well as standard algorithms.

Multiplication Algorithms

The standard algorithm for multi-digit multiplication that is typically taught in elementary school is a complex procedure that alternates steps of multiplying and adding and relies on the proper alignment of place values in order to produce the correct result. Although very efficient, the compactness of this algorithm hinders efforts to give meaning to what is going on in the various steps. Children may execute the steps without understanding how the ones, tens, hundreds, etc. fit into the manipulations they are performing (National Research Council, 2001). The difficulties stemming from this lack of understanding are the same as those that arise when addition and subtraction algorithms are learned without understanding: students develop "buggy" algorithms. Children become lost if they forget a step because they have no other way to figure out the answer, and they cannot (or at least do not think to) assess the sensibleness of their answers.

Children are capable of inventing their own meaningful algorithms for multi-digit multiplication, and these algorithms become increasingly sophisticated and efficient over time. When faced with the problem of determining the number of cans of pop in 14 cartons of pop with 24 cans in each carton, children may initially use repeated addition: 24 + 24 + 24 + …. However, this strategy is soon replaced by a more efficient "doubling" strategy that makes use of adding pairs of numbers, then pairs of pairs, as illustrated below (Baek, 1998; Caliandro, 2000).

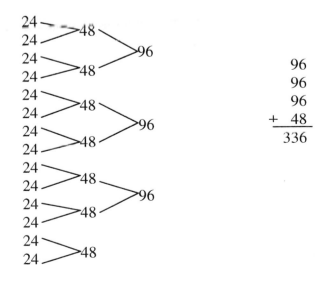

Next, students develop the strategy of partitioning one or both of the numbers in the problem, essentially breaking the problem into sub-problems that are easier and/or allow them to apply multiplication facts they already know (Baek, 1998). For example, a student comfortable with multiplying two-digit numbers by one-digit numbers might compute 24×7 and then double that result (Caliandro, 2000). We could represent this solution by writing $24 \times 14 = 24 \times (7 \times 2) = (24 \times 7) \times 2$. Another example of a partitioning strategy would be the student who reasons that ten 24's would be 240 (because $24 \times 10 = 240$) and four more 24's would be 96 (because four 25's is 100) and then adds 240 and 96 to determine the total. Note that this last strategy involves splitting one of the numbers into tens and ones. Thus, it illustrates the important role that an understanding of place value and the ability to view numbers as composed of so many hundreds, tens, and ones plays in supporting children's construction of multiplication algorithms.

A Pictorial or Area Model

For children in the fourth or fifth grade who have an understanding of the concept of area, (see chapter 10 for a discussion of the concept of area), a pictorial illustration of multiplication may be useful to teach two-digit multiplication. For children who do not have the concept of area, this model may not be appropriate. For 26 x 34, draw a box, labeling it 34 across and 26 down. Divide the numbers into tens and ones as shown, find the area of each section, and add up all the areas.

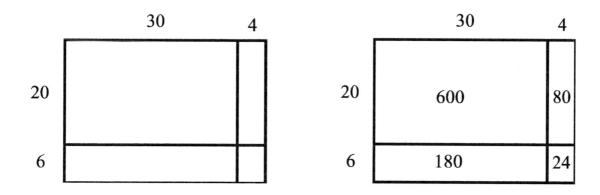

26 x 34 = 600 + 180 + 80 + 24 = 884

Division Algorithms

As children develop a part/whole conception of numbers and the ability to think multiplicatively, presenting division situations involving larger numbers will help them begin to develop efficient algorithms for division (See problems 12, 13, 14 and 15 in the **3.5 Problems and Exercises** section for more detailed examples.).

Children may find the standard division algorithm taught in schools difficult for several reasons. First, the language we typically use with this algorithm suggests the measurement model of division, but not the fair-sharing model. That is, for problems such as $38\overline{)1296}$ we begin by asking "How many times does 38 go into 129?" We are not asking "If we divide 129 into 38 groups how big is each group?"

Second, in order for the standard algorithm to work, it is necessary to find the <u>largest</u> multiple of the divisor that is less than or equal to the dividend. One cannot use the fact that 38 will go into 129 twice in the computation.

Third, these questions make it easy to lose a sense of the place value meanings of the numbers involved. For example, the 129 represents 1290 and the 3 we write above 129 really means 30 (National Research Council, 2001). Further, the question is "How many times does 38 go into 129?" but what is really being asked is "How many tens times 38 go into 1290?

Many children never become proficient at the standard algorithm for long division. And many of those who do become somewhat proficient do not necessary have a mathematical understanding of the procedure. Even if mastery of long division is not that important today with the advent of calculators, the mathematics underlying the algorithms is extremely important in everyday mathematics and in higher level mathematics, such as in dividing polynomials. Focusing on place value is the key to helping children understand.

Partial-Quotients

One method that is sometimes taught in elementary school to help children develop a mathematical meaningful algorithm for division is partial quotients. For, $600 \div 22$:

```
  22)600
    - 220      10        (10 x 22 = 220)
      380
    - 220      10        (10 x 22 = 220)
      160
    - 110       5        (5 x 22) = 110)
       50
     - 44       2        (2 x 22 = 44)
        6      27
```

The solution is 27 R 6. In this method, it is not necessarily to find the largest divisor and place value meaning is retained at each step.

3.5   Problems and Exercises

<u>Solve the problems first</u> and then consider some data on how children solved the problems found in the **Children's Solutions and Discussion of Problems and Exercises** section.

1.   Determine the total number of dots mentally.

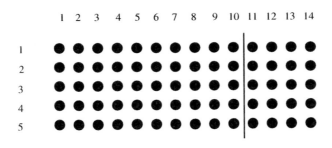

How does the positioning of the vertical and horizontal bars provide the opportunity for children to partition the dots in a way that takes advantage of place value?

2.   Solve and explain how this dot array can be used to illustrate 16 x 13?

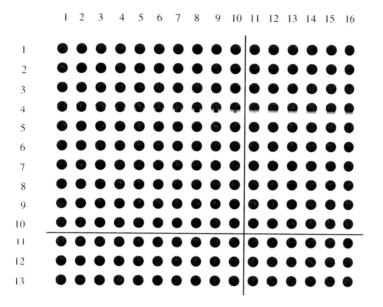

The following examples illustrate the different self-generated algorithms that children create. The next three examples are indicative of what second-grade children might use.

3.   Solve 53 – 27 using Faith's method.

There are 38 doves in a cage. Nineteen doves flew away. How many doves are in the cage now?

$$38 - 19$$

$$30 - 10 = 20$$

$$20 - 9 = 11$$

$$11 + 8 = 19$$

In this problem Faith initially dropped the 8 from the 38. She then subtracted 10 from 30. Then she subtracted 9 more. The problem for most children is what to do with the 8: should she subtract it or add it? One way to think about this question is to ask: did the eight doves leave or stay? Many children who use an algorithm similar to this have difficulty deciding whether they should add or subtract. This process can be confusing to some children, but children who do use processes like this demonstrate a fundamental understanding of mathematics. Some would argue that they are better prepared for algebra than others.

4.   Solve 48 – 16 using Pete's method.

Pete solves the problem similar to Faith but in a different way. He takes numbers apart to solve 38 – 17. :

$$38 - 10 = 28$$
$$28 - 4 = 24$$
$$24 - 3 = 21$$

Paul breaks 17 it into numbers he feels comfortable using.

5.   Solve 48 – 16 using Allen's method.

Many children solve subtraction problems by thinking of them as addition. Consider the same subtraction problem and how Allen solved it, 38– 17:

$$17 + 3 = 20$$
$$20 + 10 = 30$$
$$30 + 8 = 38$$
$$3 + 10 + 8 = 21$$

Many children add even though the problem might be an obvious subtraction problem to other children, like birds flying away. When considering this method some children may question how he knows what numbers to add.

6.   What common error might some children make in solving:

$$\begin{array}{r} 73 \\ -\,45 \\ \hline \end{array}$$

7.   Show and explain how you might use a pictorial representation or area model to demonstrate 35 x 42.

The next four solution methods; 8, 9, 10 & 11, are indicative of how third graders might initially solve multi-digit multiplication problems. In all these methods consider the important role that an understanding of place value and the ability to partition numbers in different ways play in the development of multiplicative thinking. The next four problems, give children's nonstandard solutions to the following problem:

There were 64 teams at the beginning of the NCAA basketball tournament. With 5 players starting on each team, how many starting players were in the tournament (Schifter, 1997)?

8.   Solve 43 x 6 using Jane's method.

$$5 \times 10 = 50$$
$$5 \times 10 = 50$$
$$5 \times 10 = 50$$
$$5 \times 10 = 50$$
$$5 \times 10 = 50$$
$$5 \times 10 = \underline{50}$$
$$300$$

$$4 + 4 + 4 + 4 + 4 - 20$$

$$300 + 20 = 320 \text{ (Schifter, 1997)}$$

In this example the Jane knew that 5 x 10 = 50. To solve this problem many children would count by 5 ten times. Children may likewise count the five 4's.

9.   Solve 43 x 6 using Carl's method.

$$60 \times 5 = 300$$
$$4 \times 5 = 20$$
$$320$$

Notice how this method uses the distributive property of multiplication over addition. Carl has an intuitive understanding that 64 x 5 is equivalent to (60 x 5) + (4 x 5).

10.   Solve 83 x 6 using Jason's method.

$$20 \times 5 = 100$$
$$20 \times 5 = 100$$
$$20 \times 5 = 100$$

$$4 \times 5 = 20$$

$$100 + 100 + 100 + 20 = 320$$

Jason is able to partition 64 into parts or numbers that are easier for him to multiply and then he knows to add the resulting parts together. Again his method indicates an understanding and use of the distributive property:
64 x 5 = (20 x 5) + (20 x 5) + (20 x 5) + (4 x 5)

11.   Explain the error in Jacob's method and how Dan's method illustrates an intuitive understanding of the distributive property of multiplication in this next example?

There are 17 children in a third grade class. Each child needs 12 markers for the class art project. How many markers are needed by the class?

Jacob's solution to: 17 x 12

$$10 \times 10 = 100$$
$$7 \times 2 = 14$$

$$100 + 14 = 114$$

Dan's Solution to 17 x 12:

$$17 \times 10 = 170$$
$$17 \times 2 = 34$$

$$170 + 34 = 204$$

How might partial products be useful in helping explain the error in Jacob's method to the class?

```
  17
 x12
 100      10 x 10
  70      10 x 7
  20       2 x 10
  14       2 x 7
 204
```

12.   Explain the three strategies illustrated to solve the problem. Why do you think the problem mentions a price reduction for every ten buses?

1296 fans want to visit an away soccer game of their favorite team. The treasurer of the fan club learns that one bus can carry 38 passengers and that a reduction in price will be given for every 10 buses the club books. How many buses should the club book?

```
  1296                          1296                         1296
–  380    10 buses           –  380    10 buses          – 1140    30 buses
   916                          916                          156
–  380    10 buses           –  760    20 buses          –  152    4 buses
   536                          156                            4
–  380    10 buses           –   76    2 buses
   156                           80
–   38    1 bus              –   76    2 buses
   118                            4
–   38    1 bus
    80
–   38    1 bus
    42
–   38    1 bus
     4 (Gravemeijer, 1994)
```

13.   Solve the next problem using the partial quotients method.

The captain of a stranded ship is told that there are 2000 biscuits left. The crew consists of 32 members and each man gets 1 biscuit a day. How long will this supply last?

14.   Explain the solution method used to solve this problem.

Faced with the problem of distributing 231 M&M's into 5 containers suppose a child wrote following:

```
 | 1 |      | 1 |      | 1 |      | 1 |      | 1 |
 | 5 |      | 5 |      | 5 |      | 5 |      | 5 |
 | 10|      | 10|      | 10|      | 10|      | 10|
 | 20|      | 20|      | 20|      | 20|      | 20|
 |_10|      |_10|      |_10|      |_10|      |_10|
```

$231 - 50 = 181, 181 - 100 = 81, 81 - 50 = 31, 31 - 25 = 6, 6 - 5 = 1$

$\Rightarrow$ 46 in each bin with 1 left over

15.   Explain how the following method is the partial quotients methods for solving the M&M problems.

$$
\begin{array}{r}
1 \\
5 \\
10 \\
20 \\
10 \\
\hline
5)\overline{231} \\
-50 \\
\hline
181 \\
-100 \\
\hline
81 \\
-50 \\
\hline
31 \\
-25 \\
\hline
6 \\
-5 \\
\hline
1
\end{array}
\qquad \Rightarrow \; 46
$$

3.5   Questions for Discussion

1.   What are "standard algorithms"?
2.   What does it mean to "carry a 1" when you are adding?
3.   Should elementary school students spend a lot of time learning long division? Explain your answer.
4.   If children are not taught the standard algorithm to add and subtract, what might they do?
5.   Earlier we said that children are taught standard algorithms before they are ready to understand them. What do you think?
6.   Should children be encouraged to develop their own non-standard, self-generated algorithms? What additional responsibility do allowing children to develop their own algorithms place on the teacher?
7.   Should algorithms even be taught today when both children and adults have such easy access to calculators that are quicker and more efficient than paper and pencil computations?
8.   In working with self-generated algorithms the teacher is taking on a different role in deciphering and validating individual children's constructions. Discuss this new role for teachers.

3.5   Children's Solutions and Discussion of Problems and Exercises

1.   Some students may see the 5 by 14 array as consisting of 5 tens and 5 fours. In other words, the bar helps students partition the two-digit number into tens and ones in order to make counting all the dots much easier. This solution also makes implicit use of the distributive property of multiplication: $5 \times (10 + 4) = (5 \times 10) + (5 \times 4)$.

2.   The bars provide the opportunity for partitioning the numbers into tens and ones and determining the "partial products" that correspond to this partition. By using their knowledge of place value, children can break the problem down into manageable parts. The algorithm below takes advantage of the partition suggested by the bars in the array and has been presented in some textbooks as a more accessible alternative to the standard algorithm (National Research Council, 2001).

$$
\begin{array}{r}
16 \\
\times\ 13 \\
\hline
100 \\
60 \\
30 \\
18 \\
\hline
208
\end{array}
\qquad
\begin{array}{l}
=\ 10 \times 10 \\
=\ 10 \times\ 6 \\
=\ \ 3 \times 10 \\
=\ \ 3 \times\ 6 \\
\hline
\end{array}
$$

3, 4, & 5.

If children memorize the steps to the conventional algorithm without understanding what they are doing, what have they learned? In the standard algorithms children do not have to think about place value and they do not have to decompose numbers into meaningful parts. For example, 38 is the same as 30 plus 8. If children mess up a step or go out of order in the standard algorithm then they are lost. In many cases children's use of standard algorithms is not a sense making activity. Children's self-generated algorithms help them make sense of what they are doing and in almost all cases; children's will eventually adopt standard algorithms or a slight variation thereof. However, now they understand how and why these algorithms work.

6.   Schifter (1997) and others believe that children who engage in the development of self-generated algorithms are far less likely to "subtract up" when the bottom number in the one's column is greater than the top one.

$$
\begin{array}{r}
37 \\
-19 \\
\hline
22
\end{array}
\qquad \text{because } 3 - 1 = 2 \text{ and } 9 - 7 = 2
$$

For children making this error, the subtraction algorithms is not a sense making activity.

8, 9, & 10.

Children who use methods like those described in 8, 9, & 10 have an understanding of place value and an intuitive understanding of the distributive property of multiplication over addition. By intuitive we mean they are unlikely to say that they are using the distributive property but they are applying the principles of it without naming it. Another noteworthy skill that children are employing is the ability to decompose numbers into parts and then recompose back together again e.g., $64 = 20 + 20 + 20 + 4$.

11.   As the last portion of this vignette illustrates, the transition from multiplying a two-digit number and a one-digit number to multiplying two two-digit numbers is far from trivial. Jacob attempted to adapt the process the class had used to find 64×5 by employing a strategy he was familiar with from addition, namely breaking the numbers into tens and ones, computing with the tens, computing with the ones, and then putting everything back together. However, it can be pointed out pointed out that this method missed the 7×10 that is included in 17×10 and it also missed the 10×2. Think about a 17 by 12 array like the one shown previously in problem #2.

Implicit in all the solution methods presented in the above episode is the distributive property of multiplication. For example, we could describe Carl's solution as follows:

$$64 \times 5 = (60 + 4) \times 5 = (60 \times 5) + (4 \times 5).$$

Likewise, Jacob's solution claimed that

$$17 \times 12 = (10 + 7) \times (10 + 2) = (10 \times 10) + (7 \times 2).$$

However, this solution was incomplete. Instead,

$$17 \times 12 = 17 \times (10 + 2) = (17 \times 10) + (17 \times 2)$$
$$= (10 \times 10) + (7 \times 10) + (10 \times 2) + (7 \times 2).$$

This type of understanding of how multiplication works is a critical component in children's development of efficient algorithms for multi-digit multiplication.

Children will need many more opportunities to apply their developing strategies for multiplication in order to reach Dan's level of understanding and beyond. But by providing these opportunities through engagement in the types of activities and discussions described in the account, the teacher can enable children to make sense out of multiplication by connecting it to what they already know. By undertaking discussions in which the children's' understanding of their work is the heart of the issue, the teacher is helping them construct ideas that will support their continued learning. Children's use of self-generated algorithms will have significant consequences in the later study of algebra.

Schifter (1997) argues that this type of reasoning will help children come to understand algebra. They will be far less likely to indicate that:
$(a + b)(c + d) = ac + bd$. The intent is that they will understand that
$a(b + c) = ab + ac$ like the numbers in these examples illustrate.

12.   Note that the mention of a price reduction for every ten buses is intended to encourage students to make use of multiples of 10 and thus develop an efficient repeated subtraction algorithm.

14.   The child decided to put 10 M&M's in each bin first, calculates the number remaining (i.e., 231 – 50), realized that a larger collection than 10 could still be put in each bin so allocated 20 M&M's to each bin on the second pass, calculated the number remaining (181 – 100), etc., continued in this manner until fewer than 5 M&M's remain.

15.   Notice how the alternative algorithm retains the place value meaning of all numbers involved.

- This alternative algorithm may be viewed in terms of either model of division. The fan bus problem used the measurement model, the M&M problem the fair-sharing model.

3.6   Mental Math & Estimation

Mental math and estimation are very useful in real-life applications. These skills also help children develop greater number sense. With problem solving or regular calculations, mental math and estimation are important in determining the reasonableness of the answer. However, it is important to do mental math and estimation in ways that are relevant to children. What do you think many children do with the instructions on a sheet of computation problems that read, **"Estimate your answers first and then solve the problems"**? Many will simply solve the problems and then write an estimate based on their answer. From some children's perspective, it seems silly to estimate something when you are going to get an exact answer for it anyway!

Estimation

Sowder (1992, 1989) indicated that good estimators had the following characteristics. They were confident in their mathematical ability. They had a tolerance for error. Some people are uncomfortable with estimates; they prefer exact answers and typically only estimate when they are required to do so. Finally, they believed that estimation was an important skill and saw it as something that is used in everyday experiences. Some children believe that estimation is 'just guessing' (Sowder & Wheeler, 1989).

Good estimators also had the following mathematical skills. They have a good understanding of arithmetic operations, good knowledge of basic facts and mental math, understand place value, and have the ability to work with powers of ten (Van de Walle & Watkins, 1993). Children need a strong network of concepts in order to be proficient and effective estimators.

Rounding is the predominant method of estimation suggested in elementary textbooks, but studies have shown that children prefer to compute the exact answer first and then round the answer. This preference increases with the grade level. As children become more skilled at rounding, they are less likely to deviate from this method and try others. For example, to estimate 4 x 267 most children preferred to make the problem 4 x 300 and objected to using 4 x 250 even thought it gave a better estimate (Sowder & Kelin, 1993). Children seem tied to the mechanical process of rounding and are unable to view variations of rounding as sense making activity.

Estimation involves two complex mental constructs: approximating numbers and mental computation. One theory (Case, 1985) maintains that children are unable to do both simultaneously until they are about 11years old. Accordingly, it is suggested that in the lower grades estimation not be done or done with simple problems that require minimal memorization. Appropriate tasks which should be done separately are: number size concepts and mental math (Sowder & Kelin, 1993). A number size activity might be: Which is larger 5/6 or 5/9? In one study only 10% of fourth graders indicated that 5/6 was larger (Sowder & Wheeler, 1987, cited in Sowder & Kelin, 1993)

Consider the following problem:

If I make $600 dollars per week, approximately how much will I earn in one year?

Here a likely strategy is to mentally multiply 50 x 600. Most older children would know 5 x 6 = 30. The real dilemma for most is how many zeros to put after the 30. Is the answer: 3,000 or 30,000 or even 300,000? Children's ability to mentally compute and estimate in problems like these requires them to be able to multiply and divide by powers of ten.

For estimation, the most common school activity is rounding, but in real life, people do not always round according to the rules the textbooks specify. When people are grocery shopping and have a fixed amount of money, they tend to round up (e.g., 3.19 rounds to 4.00) to make sure that they have enough money. Similarly, when people are packing food for a hiking trip, they would often rather overestimate than underestimate. In some instances, you may not round at all, such as when dividing into groups. For example, how many people will be in each group if there are 23 people and you need to divide them into 4 groups?

A real-life application involving mental math and estimation for adults but not necessarily children is figuring the tip at a restaurant. How do you figure the tip at a restaurant?

In studies of how ordinary people use mathematics in their daily lives the context of the problem plays a large part in determining the solution. When grocery shopping, what other factors besides price determine what and how much you buy? Such factors as taste, size of the object, and storage space at home play a part in influencing what people buy in the grocery store.

Mental Math

The standard algorithms are efficient methods for paper and pencil computation but they are not well suited for mental computation. When asked to add 99 + 99 + 99 mentally, many children will mentally try to write the problem in the air. They frequently make mistakes. On the other hand, a child might more efficiently solve this problem by thinking of three 100's and subtracting 3 from the total.

One key difference between people who use mental math successfully and those who do not is that they focus on the number and not the digits. For example, the child trying to use the standard algorithm to add 99 three times is looking at the digits of 99, not the whole number 99 that is almost 100. It is also important to note that the child who is thinking of three 100's is not necessarily rounding 99 to 100. A more apt description is that she is using compensation. She adds 1's to the 99's, performs a simplified calculation and then compensates for the added 1's by subtracting them. In the upper grades, another difference is that children have a more complex understanding of number concepts, especially the distributive property. For example, to multiply 12 x 25, the child may think of the problem as (2 x 25) + (10 x 25). Children in higher grades also avoided carrying, sometimes adding or subtracting left to right and keeping a running total (Sowder & Kelin, 1993).

One way to encourage the development of mental math skills is by starting with simpler problems and moving to ones where children can use thinking strategies to help them. Recall that a thinking strategy involves using a known result to figure out an unknown one. You can encourage the use of thinking strategies by sequencing problems as follows.

Third Grade	Fourth Grade
100 + 100 = ____	20 x 25 = ___
99 + 99 = ____	19 x 25 = ___
98 + 97 = ____	18 x 25 = ___

3.6   Problems and Exercises

<u>Solve the problems first</u> and then consider some data on how children solved the problems found in the **Children's Solutions and Discussion of Problems and Exercises** section.

Don't use <u>paper</u> and <u>pencil</u> or a <u>calculator</u> to solve any of the problems. Try to use estimation and/or mental math for each problem.

1. You are driving to Dallas and you have to take your 4-year-old niece and 7-year-old nephew with you. How long will the total trip take? Will you stop? How much will gas cost? What will you do to entertain your favorite relatives during the trip?

2. You are with a date that you want to impress. The bill is $37.45. How much of a tip will you leave? How did you figure it? Do you ask your date to pay for half?

3. How far do you live from the post office?

4. How often do you look at a clock in one day?

5. Think of a lake. How far is it across the lake? How did you estimate this distance?

6. How long would it take to teach a fourth grade class about Egyptian Math?

7. Solve the following problems mentally.

   40 x 50 = 2,000
   39 x 50 = ____
   40 x 49 = ____
   39 x 49 = ____

8. What two items below would provide a total of about 600 calories (NAEP, 1992).

Cheeseburger   Hot Dot   Yogurt   Cookie
393 Calories   298 Calories   214 Calories   119 Calories

9. Elena worked 57 hours in March, 62 hours in April, and 59 hours in May. Which of these is the BEST estimate of the total number of hours she worked for three months?
    a.   50 + 50 + 50
    b.   55 + 55 + 55
    c.   60 + 60 + 60
    d.   65 + 65 + 65 (TIMSS, 1995)

10. Mark's garden has 84 rows of cabbages. There are 57 cabbages in each row. Which of these gives the BEST way to estimate how many cabbages there are altogether?
    a.   100 x 50 = 5000
    b.   90 x 60 = 5400
    c.   80 x 60 = 4800
    d.   80 x 50 = 4000 (TIMSS, 2003)

11. TIMSS Eighth Grade Problems
    A.   About 7,000 copies of a magazine are sold each week. Approximately how many magazines are sold each year (TIMSS, 2003)?
         a.   8400
         b.   35000
         c.   350000
         d.   3500000

    B.   The height of a boy was reported as 140 cm. The height had been rounded to the nearest 10 cm. What are two possibilities for the boy's actual height (TIMSS, 1999)?

         Answer: _____ cm and _____ cm

12. 25 x 18 is more than 24 x 18. How much more (TIMSS, 1995)?
    a.   1
    b.   18
    c.   24
    d.   25

3.6   Questions for Discussion

1. What is a thinking strategy?
2. How do you figure the tip at a restaurant?
3. When in real life would you round a number up even though the last digit is less than 5?
4. When in real life would you round a number down even though the last digit is 5 or more?

5.   When you are grocery shopping, what other factors influence what you will buy besides estimating the price?

6.   In elementary school, when you saw the instructions, "**Estimate your answers first and then solve the problems**," what did you do? What do you think many children will do?

7.   When and where do people use mental math in their everyday lives?

3.6   Children's Solutions and Discussion of Problems and Exercises

5.   A fifth grader thought 5 miles because, "I think a pond is about 1 mile and a lake is bigger." A couple of fifth graders drew a picture of a lake and said 5 inches.

7.   A sixth grader had the following answers and explanation.

   40 x 50 = 2,000
   39 x 50 = 1,950
   40 x 49 = 19,60
   39 x 49 = 1,910

You would subtract 50 from the first one, from 2000. On the second one you would subtract 40. On the third you would subtract 90.

What error in logic did he make on the last problem?
In a different fifth grade class 57% (12 out of 21) had the correct answer for 40 x 50 but only 14% (3 out of 21) had the correct answer for 39 x 49.

8.   On the national NAEP test, 44% of fourth graders gave the correct answer (NAEP, 1992).

9.   Internationally, 33% of third graders and 52% of fourth graders gave the correct response (TIMSS, 1995).

10.   In the United States 69.6% of fourth grade children gave the correct response; however, internationally only 49.9% of children gave the correct response (TIMSS, 2003).

11.   A.   Of eighth graders in the United States, 55.4% of girls and 61.6% of boys gave the correct response.

       B.   This problem was given to eighth graders and in the United States 56% gave an answer in the proper range (TIMSS, 1999).

12.   Internationally, 30% of third graders and 45% of fourth graders had the correct response (TIMSS, 1995).

Chapter 3: References

Baek, J. (1998). Children's invented algorithms for multidigit multiplication problems. In L. J. Morrow & M. J. Kenney (Eds.), *The teaching and learning of algorithms in school mathematics* (pp. 151-160. Reston, VA: National Council of Teachers of Mathematics.

Baroody, A. J., Tiilikainen, S. H. & Tai, Y. (2006). The application and development of an addition goal sketch. *Cognition and Instruction, 24*(1), 124-170.

Caliandro, C. K. (2000). Children's inventions for multidigit multiplication and division. *Teaching Children Mathematics*, *6*, 420-424, 426.

Case, R. (1985). *Intellectual Development*. Orlando, FL: Academic Press.

Clark, F. B., & Kamii, C. (1996). Identification of multiplicative thinking in children in grades 1-5. *Journal for Research in Mathematics Education*, *27*, 41-51.

Fuson, K. (2003). Developing mathematical power in whole number operations. In J. Kilpatrick, G. Martin, & D. Schifter (Eds.), *A research companion to the principles and standards for school mathematics*. 68-113. Reston, VA: NCTM.

Gravemeijer, K. (1994). *Developing realistic mathematics education*. Utrecht: CD-β Press.

Madell, R. (1985). Children's natural processes. *Arithmetic Teacher*, *32*(7), 20-22.

National Research Council. (2001). *Adding it up: Helping children learn mathematics*. J. Kilpatrick, J. Swafford, and B. Findell (Eds.). Mathematics Learning Study Committee, Center for Education, Division of Behavioral and Social Sciences and Education. Washington DC: National Academy Press.

Piaget, J. (1987). *Possibility and necessity*. Minneapolis: University of Minnesota Press. (Original work published 1983).

Schifter, D. (1997, March). Developing operation sense as a foundation for algebra. Paper presented at the annual meeting of the American Educational Research Association, Chicago.

Sowder, J. T. (1992). Estimation and number sense. In J. Kilpatrick, G. Martin, & D. Schifter (Eds.), *A research companion to the principles and standards for school mathematics*. 371-389. Reston, VA: NCTM.

Sowder, J. T. & Kelin, J. (1993). Number sense and related topics. In D. T. Owens (Ed.) *Research Ideas for the Classroom: Middle Grades Mathematics*. 41-57. Reston, VA: NCTM.

Sowder, J. T. (1989). Affective factors and computational estimation abilities. In D. B. Mcleod & V. M. Adams (Eds.), *Affect and mathematical problem solving*. 177-191. New York: Springer-Verlag.

Steffe, L., & Killion, K. (1989). Research into practice: Children's multiplication. *Arithmetic Teacher*, *37*, 34-36.

Steffe, L. P., von Glasersfeld, E., Richards, J., & Cobb, P. (1983). *Children's counting types: Philosophy, theory and application*. New York: Praeger Scientific.

Van de Walle, J. A. & Watkins, K. B. (1993). Early development of number sense. In R. J. Jensen (Ed.) *Research Ideas for the Classroom: Early Childhood Mathematics*. 127-150. Reston, VA: NCTM.

Chapter 4: Number Theory

Number theory is widely applicable to many areas of elementary school mathematics including: finding the least common denominator when adding or subtracting fractions, finding the greatest common factor when simplifying fractions, and testing for divisibility. Studying number theory develops one's number sense or insights into the properties that numbers share and fail to share. However, number theory is not explicitly taught in the elementary schools. Number theory is important because many of its fundamental ideas are directly applicable to elementary school mathematics. While number theory is often a graduate level course, the average person can frequently understand many of the mathematical ideas of number theory. In discussing number theory, this chapter will examine how children find factors and multiples, what divisibility tests children may use in elementary school, what misconceptions preservice teachers may have about prime and composite numbers, and how children find Greatest Common Factors (GCF) and Least Common Multiples (LCM).

4.1   Factors and Multiples

The notation in number theory for divides, ' $|$ ', may be new and sometimes is confusing. Does $4 \,|\, 0$ or does $0 \,|\, 4$? Since $4 \,|\, 0$ can be interpreted as 4 x ? = 0 and $0 \,|\, 4$ as 0 x ? = 4, $4 \,|\, 0$ (four divides zero) is correct and $0 \,|\, 4$ (zero divides four) is undefined.

Determining if a number is a factor is easier for children than determining the factors of a number. For example, it is easier to determine if 3 is a factor of 48 than finding all the factors of 48. How might children determine if 3 is a factor of 48?

How would children find the factors of a number? How would they find the factors of 24? Typically, children will make a list of all the numbers that multiply together to make 24. What difficulty do you anticipate that children might have in finding all the factors of a number by making a list?

Likewise, to find multiples of numbers, children may make lists.

A mathematical point that may be confusing is that 0 is a multiple of every number. However, this is probably a mathematical idea that you will not be teaching to children.

4.1   Problems and Exercises

Solve the problems first and then consider some data on how children solved the problems found in the **Children's Solutions and Discussion of Problems and Exercises** section.

The following problem is designed to address the concept of factors. It is a good problem for elementary children, especially if they have squares as manipulatives or square dot paper.

1.   a.   What are all the ways that you can arrange 12 squares into a rectangular shape?

      b.   How can the solutions be used to represent the commutative property of multiplication?

□ □ □ □ □ □ □ □ □ □ □

2.   How might children find the factors of 40?
3.   How might children find the multiples of 7?
4.   How many numbers between 1 and 20 are multiples of 3?
5.   How many different numbers will divide 36 and 48 without a remainder?
6.   What is the fewest number of blocks that you can stack into five stacks with the same number in each stack and also stack into eight stacks with the same number in each stack?

4.1   Questions for Discussion

1.   Would you teach children that 0 is the first multiple of every number? Explain.
2.   Why do you think it is easier for children to determine if a number is a factor than to determine the factors of a number?
3.   Why is it important for children to be able to both determine if a number is a factor and determine the factors of a number?

4.1   Children's Solutions and Discussion of Problems and Exercises

1a.   In a fifth grade class, 39% (9/23) were able to draw diagrams to represent the factors of 12, (either 1 x 12, 2 x 6 or 3 x 4). Of these most only drew each factor one way and did not have for example, 3 x4 and 4 x 3.

What if a child presents the following solution for problem #1?

Would you count this solution? Does it meet the requirements of the problem? Does it alter the intended purpose of the problem, which was to teach children about factors?

1b.   Problem #1 can also be used to illustrate the commutative property of multiplication. A 3 x 4 rectangle is the same as a 4 x 3 rectangle, except that it has been rotated.

2.   In one fifth grade class, 53% (10/19) found all the factors. Most children's solutions were like the following child's explanation, "I just divided forty by all the #'s under it." Another way was described by the following child's

explanation, "First, I wondered what times what equals 40…" Some children may list factors randomly as they think of them rather than make a systematic list.

3. In a fifth grade class, 60% (12/20) confused multiple and prime and gave '1 and 7' as their solution. Of the eight who listed the multiples, **all** stopped their list, some at 35, 70 or 84. No one indicated the multiples of 7 were infinite!

4. In a fifth grade class, 50%, 10 out of 20, correctly listed them all and 20% gave partial solutions.

5. In a fifth grade class, 30%, 6 out of 20, found all the numbers, and another 30% had partially correct solutions with the most common omissions being 1 and 3.

6. Children are more likely to use actual blocks or draw pictures to solve this problem. In a fifth grade class, 60% or 12 out of 20 gave the correct solution of blocks; most drew pictures of blocks.

4.2   Divisibility Tests

Divisibility tests, shortcuts for determining whether or not one number divides another number without a remainder, are taught in the upper elementary grades, especially the tests for 2, 3, 5, 10, and sometimes 6 and 9. The tests for 4 and 8 are usually not taught in these grades. Historically, divisibility tests were very important before the advent of calculators. No one wanted to perform long division on large numbers. For example, to reduce a fraction like 34/289 one could divide 289 by the factors of 34 (e.g., 1, 2, 17, 34). With paper and pencil, this task is doable but not much fun, while with a calculator this problem is easily solved.   Today it may be just as easy to plug in numbers on a calculator as to conduct a divisibility test; however, understanding divisibility tests provide powerful insights into mathematics.

Base Ten Blocks can be used to illustrate some divisibility tests (Bennett & Nelson, 2002). For example, to test a number for divisibility by 2, represent the number with Base Ten Blocks. Since each block (1,000), flat (100) and long (10) is divisible by 2 it does not matter how many of each of these pieces one has as they will always be divisible by 2; therefore, the only pieces that need to be checked are the unit pieces (1), and if the units are divisible by 2 then the number is divisible by 2. This method is similar to asking whether the number is even or odd. One way that children may check to see if a number is even or odd is to see if they can pair all the units. If they can form pairs with the units, then the number is even, if there is 1 left over then the number is odd.

To check if 147 is divisible by 2, the one flat is divisible by 2, each of the four longs is divisible by 2, the 7 units can be put into 3 pairs with one left over, therefore the number is not divisible by 2 or the number is odd. The following picture illustrates this point.

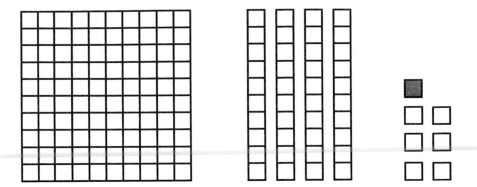

4.2   **Problems and Exercises**

<u>Solve the problems first</u> and then consider some data on how children solved the problems found in the **Children's Solutions and Discussion of Problems and Exercises** section.

    1.   Show how the divisibility test for 5 would work with Base Ten Blocks.

    2.   Why does the divisibility test for 3 work? (Base Ten Blocks may not be as helpful here.)

    3.   Find all the solutions for the last digit so that 6 divides 23,45_.
         How can you use the divisibility tests to solve this problem?

    4.   A whole number is multiplied by 5. Which of these could be the result (NAEP, 1996)?
         a. 652
         b. 562
         c. 526
         d. 265

    5.   Which of the following is both a multiple of 3 and a multiple of 7 (NAEP, 1992)?
         a. 7,007
         b. 8,192
         c. 21,567
         d. 22,287
         e. 40,040

    6.   Why does the divisibility test for 2 work? (If a number ends in 0, 2, 4, 6, or 8, it is divisible by 2.)

    7.   Why does the divisibility test for 5 work? (If a number ends in 0 or 5, it is divisible by 5.)

4.2   **Questions for Discussion**

    1.   Which divisibility tests might you teach in fifth grade?

    2.   Do you think children should still study divisibility tests? Why or why not?

4.2   Children's Solutions and Discussion of Problems and Exercises

1.   Since each block, flat, and long is divisible by 5, we only need to check the units.
2.   In some cases, the mathematical explanation is beyond most children's capabilities of understanding, yet we will still ask children to know and use the divisibility 3 test.
3.   If a number is divisible by both 2 and 3, then it must be divisible by 6.
4.   54% of fourth graders had the correct solution for this problem on the NAEP test (NAEP, 1996). They could use a calculator on this problem.
5.   77% of eighth graders correctly answered this question (NAEP, 1992). They could use a calculator on this problem.
6.   In a fifth grade class, most children simply said because the numbers are "even", One girl explained, " 2 is an even number and if you count by those numbers it always ends with an even number."
7.   One fifth grader explained, "if you count by fives every other number ends in a zero or five."

4.3   Prime and Composite Numbers

One central aspect of number theory is the study of prime and composite numbers. Prime numbers, of course, are those numbers that only have two factors – the number itself and one. Composite numbers have factors in addition to the number itself and one. The number seven is prime because its only factors are 1 and 7. The number 9 is composite because it has factors in addition to 1 and 9 (3, for instance). Elementary children do study prime and composite numbers, but these ideas will only make sense if they **understand multiplication and division**.

Consider the following misconceptions that many preservice teachers have about prime and composite numbers (Zazkis & Liljedah, 2004). Are any of the following views similar to your own?

- Prime numbers are small.
- Every large number, if composite, is divisible by a small prime number.
- Prime numbers are odd or odd numbers are prime.

If many preservice teachers have these misconceptions, then children probably have similar understandings.

Prime Number Test

Upper elementary school children may make the Sieve of Eratosthenes to determine prime and composite numbers, typically between 1 and 100. For larger numbers, the prime number test is useful. Elementary children will probably not study the prime number test, but it is based on some significant mathematical ideas.

Is 701 prime or composite? To apply the prime number test, take the square root of 701 ($\sqrt{701}$ = 26.48) and test all the primes up to 26.48 The primes up to 26.48 are: 2, 3, 5, 7, 11, 13, 17, 19, and 23. None of these numbers will divide into 701 evenly. Therefore, 701 is a prime number.

Why are only prime numbers tested? Why test only the primes up to the square root of the number? Many preservice teachers have difficulty explaining why it is only necessary to test primes up to the square root of the number (Zazkis & Liljedah, 2004).

To answer the first question, if 6 were to go into a number, the numbers 2 and 3 must also go into the number. In other words, since every composite number can be expressed as a product of prime numbers, we only need to test prime numbers. For the second question, primes larger than 23 do not need to be tested because if a larger prime went into 701 evenly, for example 29, then 29 x ? = 701, but the other factor, "?", would have to be less than $\sqrt{701}$ and all primes less than $\sqrt{701}$ have already been tested.

A Simple Question in Number Theory

An example of the accessibility of the mathematical ideas of number theory is in the movie "The Mirror Has Two Faces." The mathematician in the movie is attempting to prove that the number of twin primes, primes numbers that are 2 apart [(3,5); (5,7); (11,13); (17,19); …], is infinite. (Who plays the mathematician in this movie?) One of the beauties of number theory is that the average person can understand the question and even though we cannot answer the question, neither can mathematicians!

4.3   Problems and Exercises

Solve the problems first and then consider some data on how children solved the problems found in the **Children's Solutions and Discussion of Problems and Exercises** section.

1. Consider F = 151 x 157. Is F a prime number? Explain your decision. (Zazkis & Liljedah, 2004).
2. True or False: All prime numbers are odd.
3. Estimate the number of primes between 1 and 100. Use a sieve method to determine the number of primes between 1 and 100.
4. Are there the same number of primes between 100 and 200 as between 1 and 100? Why or Why not?

4.3   Questions for Discussion

1. What mathematical concepts should children have a good grasp of before they are taught about prime and composite numbers?
2. How many twin primes are there? How would a person even begin to prove whether or not the number of twin primes is infinite or finite?
3. How would you explain that 1 is not prime?
4. In reference to the term 'Sieve of Eratosthenes,' why is it referred to as a 'sieve'?
5. How would you respond to the statement, "One is less than prime"?

4.3   Children's Solutions and Discussion of Problems and Exercises

1. Problem #1 was given to 116 preservice teachers and 74 (64%) indicated that F was a composite number and 42 (36%) indicated F was a prime number. To

justify their solution, most that indicated that F was composite relied on the definition of a prime or composite number. Of the 42 who missed the question, over half incorrectly reasoned that the product of primes is prime (Zazkis & Liljedah, 2004).

2.   In a fifth grade class of 19, only two children explained that 2 is a prime number, the rest (10) who said it was false could not explain why.

4.   There are fewer than 25 primes between 100 and 200.

4.4   Greatest Common Factor & Least Common Multiple

A common application of number theory in elementary school mathematics involves finding greatest common factors and least common multiples. One technique to accomplish these tasks is prime factorization (factorizing a number into its constituent primes). While some elementary-school children may learn about prime factorization in fifth grade, it is more often a common middle-school activity.

Upper elementary school children may be asked to make prime-factor trees for two- and three-digit numbers with the intent of showing that the ending result is unique (Yolles, 2001). For example:

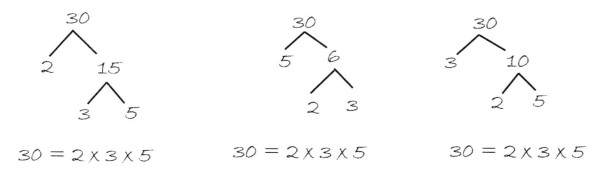

Typically, children will find the Greatest Common Factor (GCF) of two numbers by making lists of each number's factors. For 12 and 18:

        12: 1, 2, 3, 4, **6**, 12
        18: 1, 2, 3, **6**, 9, 18

In this instance 12 and 18 have several common factors (1,2,3,6), but the greatest common factor is 6.

A common activity in elementary school is to make lists of the multiples of each number to find the Least Common Multiple (LCM) for whole numbers or the Least Common Denominator (LCD) for fractions. For 7 and 8 and 1/7 and 1/8, consider:

        7, 14, 21, 35, 42, 49, **56**, 63, 70, ...
        8, 16, 24, 32, 40, 48, **56**, 64, 72, 80

While this method works well for smaller numbers it becomes very cumbersome for pairs of larger numbers like 210 and 144. Here, the prime factorization method is more efficient.

Children may get confused with the notion of "greatest" and "least'. The **greatest** common factor of 12 and 18 is 6 but 6 is smaller, not greater, than 12 and 18. Likewise the **least** common multiple of 7 and 8 is 56 but 56 is greater, not less, than 7 and 8. For children, the solutions for GCF and LCM may seem to be asking for just the opposite of the meaning of the words.

Children's study of the greatest common factor and least common multiple foreshadows their future study of algebra. Traditionally, a significant amount of time is devoted to factoring in first year algebra courses. In algebra students must also find common multiples to expressions such as $1/(x+1)$ and $1/(x^2-1)$.

4.4   Problems and Exercises

Solve the problems first and then consider some the data on how children solved the problems found in the **Children's Solutions and Discussion of Problems and Exercises** section.

1.   How may children find the LCM of 9 and 12?
2.   How may children find the GCF of 24 and 36?
3.   How are the concepts of prime, composite, factor, multiple, and divisibility related?
4.   Two trains both begin their runs at 6:00 AM from the same station. Train A takes 60 minutes to complete its loop and Train B takes 72 minutes to complete its loop. When will both trains arrive simultaneously at the station provided that the trains are on time?
5.   There are 1,000 lockers in a school numbered 1 to 1,000 and 1,000 students. The first student goes through and opens every locker. The second student goes through and shuts every other locker (i.e., the lockers numbered 2,4,6, …). The third student goes through the school and changes the state of every third locker (that is, if the locker is open she shuts it and if the locker is shut she opens it), the fourth student either opens or shuts every fourth locker, and so on. Which lockers will be open when all the students are finished?
6.   Randolph Street is 50 blocks long. The bus stops every 6 blocks and the subway stops every 4 blocks. At which streets can a passenger switch from the bus to the subway?
7.   The windows on the subway train are washed every 5 days and the windows on the bus are washed every 6 days. All the windows were washed today. When is the next time all the windows will be washed?
8.   Six students bought exactly enough pens to share equally among themselves. Which of the following could be the number of pens they bought?
    a. 46
    b. 48
    c. 50
    d. 52 (NAEP, 2003)
9.   Two whole numbers, each greater than 2, are multiplied together. The product is 126. What could the two numbers be (NAEP, 2003)?

10.   The least common multiple of 8, 12, and a third number is 120. Which of the following could be the third number?
   a. 15
   b. 16
   c. 24
   d. 32
   e. 48

11.   Find the mystery number using these hints: When you count by 4's, you say the number. When you count by 3's you say the number. The number is less than 25.

12.   The numbers in the sequence 7, 11, 15, 19, 23, ... increase by four. The numbers in the sequence 1, 10, 19, 28, 37, ... increase by nine. The number 19 is in both sequences. If the two sequences are continued, what is the next number that is in BOTH the first and second sequence (TIMSS, 2003)?

4.4   Questions for Discussion

1.   Will you be teaching prime factorization to children? Explain your answer.
2.   How does problem #4 relate to number theory?
3.   In a fifth-grade class a child wrote the following in trying to find the factors of 18:

$$\frac{18}{}$$
1 x 18
2 x 9
3 x 6

The teacher thought the child had given all the factors, but when asked to list the factors of 18 the child wrote: 1,2,3. Can you explain how this child was thinking?

4.4   Children's Solutions and Discussion of Problems and Exercises

1.   In one sixth grade class, the children overwhelmingly found the greatest common factor, and had 3 as their solution rather than the least common multiple. They also overwhelmingly correctly found the GCF of 24 and 36 for problem #2. In both cases they interpreted the problem to mean, 'find the GCF'.

2.   In one fifth grade class of 21 students:
   * 8 children said 12.
   * 10 children said 6
   * 3 children said 4

All the children that had the correct solution listed the factors, as did some of those with incorrect solutions, but many with incorrect solutions simply tried dividing both numbers by the factor.

6.   In one fourth grade class, 29% (5/17) were able to give at least one solution. No one gave all the solutions!

8.   54% of fourth graders got this problem correct on the NAEP test (NAEP, 2003).

9.   Only 15% of the fourth graders obtained a correct solution on the NAEP test (NAEP, 2003). Some erroneous solutions included: 2 and 63, also 63 and 63.

10.   Only 18% of eighth graders could correctly answer this question (NAEP, 1990).

12. In the United States, 46.1% of eighth grade girls gave the correct response and 43.7% of eighth grade boys gave the correct response. Internationally, the average was only 31% (TIMSS, 2003).

Chapter 4: References

Bennett, A. B. & Nelson, L. T. (2002). Divisibility tests: So right for discoveries. *Mathematics Teaching in the Middle School, 7, 460-464.*

Yolles, A. (2001). Making connections with prime numbers. *Mathematics Teaching in the Middle School, 7,* 84-86.

Zazkis, R. & Liljedahl, P. (2004). Understanding primes: the role of representation. *Journal of Research in Mathematics Education, 35,* (3) 164-186.

Chapter 5: Integers

In elementary school, the integers are typically only briefly covered in different grade levels. In grades two through four children may explore what a negative number is, and in grades five and six they perform some basic calculations with integers. Some children are able to use and even invent negative numbers in their self-generated subtraction algorithms. In its discussion of integers, this chapter explores children's understandings of negative numbers, the different ways that children might learn addition and subtraction of integers, some possible explanations for multiplying negative and positive numbers, and children's thinking about negative numbers in the context of problems.

Where in everyday life might people use or need negative numbers? List some situations where negative numbers are used.

_____
_____
_____
_____
_____
_____

5.1   Children's Understanding of Negative Numbers

Young children have informal understandings of negative numbers which are often action based. For example, in games they lose points and this can lead to scores below zero or "in the hole" (National Research Council, 2001). Temperatures dropping below zero is another example of action based negative numbers.

Two possible representations of negative numbers are: a location on a number line or a quantity representing a deficit, such as a debt of two dollars. Are these two different representations different for children? Consider the following two activities which are adapted from tasks that Goldin & Shteingold (2001) presented to various elementary school children. How do you think children will solve the problems?

Number Line Representation

Children are given several blank spaces which are connected. Next children are asked to fill in the spaces on the path using numeral cards, 0-6.

We might expect children to fill in the spaces as follows:

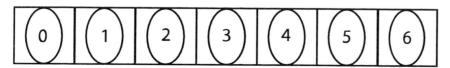

To test children's understanding of negative numbers, a blank space is added to the left of the 0. Children are told they cannot change the numbers in the other spaces, they cannot reorder the numbers. What number do you think children will put in the blank space?

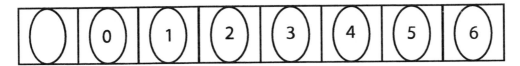

Number as a Quantity Representation

In this activity children are shown a spinner where they either add a point to their score or take a point away.

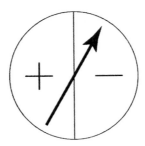

After some practice with the game, children are asked to tell what would happen if a person had no points and the spinner landed on the side where a point was taken away.

These two activities are designed to illustrate children's different understandings of negative numbers – as a location on a number line or as a quantity. Goldin & Shteingold (2001) concluded that children can develop informal internal representations of negative numbers, often not relating one context to the other. In a sample of 34 second-grade children, Goldin & Shteingold (2001) found that 19 had a partial understanding of negative numbers in one context or the other. For the spinner question, one little boy said, "Probably negative one … or zero. You could see it either way. I would say zero." While this child has the vocabulary for expressing negative numbers, he is not very confident in his thinking on negatives and really does not understand them in this context.

Children's Use of Negative Numbers in Algorithms

Children in third grade have been known to "invent" negative numbers in the process of solving subtraction problems such as 83 – 27. These children typically reason as follows: "80 – 20 is 60. Then 3 – 7 goes 4 below 0 because 3 – 3 is 0 and 7 is 3 + 4 so there are still 4 more to take away. Then I do 60 – 4 and get my answer, 56." As this example illustrates, some children invent negative numbers on their own, without being formally introduced to them.

Children's Understanding of Negative Numbers in a Different Context

What number do you think most fourth-grade children will put in the blanks for this "Find the Pattern" activity? (Patterns either increase or decrease by the same number each time, and the children have had prior experiences working with this type of activity.)

___, 11, ___, 7, 5, ___, 1, ___

When presented with this sequence, many fourth graders will put "0" in the last blank on the right instead of "-1".

In this context, the possibility of a negative number does not yet occur to them. However, in different contexts, children may discuss temperatures below freezing or a loss of yardage on a football play meaningfully. As a teacher, it is important to help children understand the meaning of negative numbers as they arise in various contexts of instruction to help prevent children's development of misconceptions.

5.1   Problems and Exercises

<u>Solve the problems first</u> and then consider some data on how children solved the problems found in the **Children's Solutions and Discussion of Problems and Exercises** section.

    1.   Fill in the missing numbers in the pattern and give the rule.

        ___, _11_, _8_, ___, _2_, ___
        Rule _____

        Why do you think many children put "0" in the space on the right?

For problems 2 through 5, fill in the blank with <, >, or =.
2. -3 ___ -7
3. -6 ___ 4
4. 3 ___ -3
5. -0.12 ___ -0.11

How do you think children will explain their solutions to problems 2 through 5?

6. The following is a fourth Grade TIMSS Problem (2003):

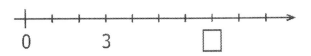

On the number line above, what number goes in the box?

Number in ☐ = _____

7.   A second grader solved the following problem using negative numbers. How might she have done it?

> Ethan had 72 pieces of candy. He and his brothers ate 33 pieces of candies. How many candies does Ethan have left (Behrend & Mohs, 2005/2006)?

5.1   Questions for Discussion

1.   In what contexts do you think children have an understanding of negative numbers? Why?
2.   What does the expression "go into the red" mean? How does it relate to integers?
3.   How would you explain to a second grader why -7 is smaller than -2?

5.1   Children's Solutions and Discussion of Problems and Exercises

1.   In one fourth grade class, 39% (9/23) put -1 in the last slot; however in a fifth grade class only 8% (2/26) had -1. The most common incorrect answer was 0.
2.   In a fifth grade class, 54% (14/26) filled in the blank correctly.
3.   In a fifth grade class, 50% (13/26) filled in the blank correctly.
4.   In a fifth grade class, 46% (12/26) filled in the blank correctly, (8 had =).
5.   In a fifth grade class, 23% (6/26) filled in the blank correctly.
6.   In the United States, 65.6% of fourth graders put the correct number in the box. This problem used only positive integers, what do you think children would do with negative integers?
7.   She broke 72 into 70 and 2, 33 into 30 and 3. Then she reasoned that 70-30 = 40 and 2 – 3 = -1. Finally she concluded that 40 + -1 is 39.

5.2   Addition and Subtraction of Integers

Some children make recurrent errors with negative numbers that center on the rules for performing calculations with them, specifically; subtracting negative numbers, multiplying or dividing positive numbers by negative numbers, and multiplying or dividing two negative numbers.

How could you explain 4 − (−2) to children? A double negative in the English language provides a nice example of why a double negative is a positive. **If I am not, not going to the store then I am going to the store!**

Parentheses

Why do we use parentheses to separate two signs next to each other?

If we write 4− −2, some may see one big minus sign and interpret this as 4—2 instead of 4 − (−2) as intended. Similarly, for 5 + −3, an extended horizontal dash on the plus sign might lead some children to interpret it as 5 + 3.

Thus, we use parentheses for neatness and to avoid confusion.

Number Line

A number line is a tool frequently used to illustrate addition and subtraction of integers with children. While it works fairly well for adding and subtracting positive integers and even for adding negative integers, it frequently causes children some difficulty when used to subtract a negative integer. For 4 − (−3), a child could go to the 4 on the number line, but in what direction should he go for − (−3)? To the left twice? Mathematically we can explain subtraction as addition of the additive inverse, but for children this explanation may be confusing.

Black and Red Chip Model

The black and red chip model uses colored chips to represent positives and negatives. Sometimes the notion of credits and debits are used so that one black chip represents a $1 credit and one red chip represents a $1 debit. In this model, children must not only learn the conventions of operating with the chips, but they also must figure out how the model maps onto, or corresponds to, rules for operating with positive and negative numbers. In order to use the chip model to calculate −8 − (1), students must represent −8 as 9 red (negative) chips and 1 black (positive) chip (or 10 reds and 2 blacks, 11 reds and 3 blacks, etc.). Then one black chip may be taken away, leaving a set of chips that represents −9. However, we have found some students who, although able to conceive of −8 as −9 + 1, or 9 red chips and one black chip, seem unable to operate with this representation. For them, the red chip and the "extra" black chip are either "imaginary" or "don't really exist" or else they see these two chips as locked together in such a way that they cannot be uncoupled.

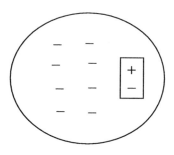

Here, −8 is represented as 9 negatives and one positive with an "imaginary" or "bonded" plus/minus pair. For these children, the conventions of the model seem to get in the way of their efforts to learn the rule for subtracting a positive number from a negative number. Even in middle school, different models for adding and subtracting positive and negative numbers are sometimes confusing (Petrella, 2001).

Absolute Value

In later mathematics, the absolute value of a positive or negative number is its distance from the origin on a number line. For example, −6 is $|{-6}| = 6$ units from the origin.
A possible source of confusion involving negative numbers arises when absolute value symbols are used in an expression like, $-|{-7}|$. A child may erroneously argue that two negatives make a positive, so the answer is 7. How might you explain to a child why this answer is incorrect?

Absolute value symbols act like parentheses in regards to the order of operations, in that we perform any operations inside of the symbols first, then we take the absolute value of the result. So, $-|{-7}|$ can be thought of as $-(|{-7}|)$ or $|7-4|$ is the same thing as $|(7-4)| = |3| = 3$.

Absolute value is important in algebra. High school students need a good grasp of integers and absolute value to solve problems such as: $|8| = -a$?

5.2   Problems and Exercises

Solve the problems first and then consider some data on how children solved the problems found in the **Children's Solutions and Discussion of Problems and Exercises** section.

1. $7 + \underline{\quad} = -9$
2. $13 + \underline{\quad} = 6$
3. $4 - (-2) = \underline{\quad}$

4. $\begin{aligned} 23 \\ \underline{-35} \end{aligned}$

In the bat and ball game of 500, a player hits the ball and the other players try to catch it. If a player catches the ball, he or she score points as indicated. If he or she misses the ball, the player loses that many points. The first player to reach 500 points is the next batter.

Catch	Points
Fly	100
One Bounce	75
Two Bounces	50
Grounder	25

Determine the score of each player.

5.   Mary caught one fly ball, but missed two on the first bounce.
6.   Jack caught a grounder, dropped a fly ball, and missed another ball on the second bounce.
7.   Susan dropped a grounder, but caught two fly balls.
8.   Who is ahead and who is farthest behind? How far ahead is the leader?
9.   When Tracy left for school the temperature was minus 3 degrees.

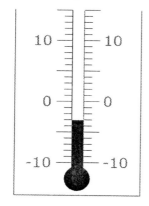

At recess, the temperature was 5 degrees.

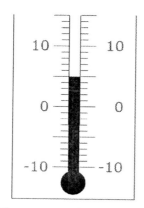

How many degrees did the temperature rise (TIMSS, 2003)?
a. 2 degrees
b. 3 degrees
c. 5 degrees
d. 8 degrees

10.   What temperature would be 15° F more than the temperature shown on the thermometer (NAEP, 2005)?

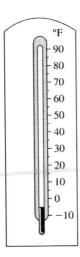

5.2   Questions for Discussion

1.   How would you introduce addition and subtraction of negative numbers to children?

2.   When children are first learning subtraction, they learn, "You cannot take a larger number from a smaller number." If you were teaching second grade, is there anything you would do to qualify this statement knowing that in later mathematics, "You can take a larger number from a smaller number."

5.2   Children's Solutions and Discussion of Problems and Exercises

1,2,&3. In a sixth grade class, 94% (17 out of 18) correctly answered problem #1, 67% problem #2, and 89% problem #3. Most children explained their solutions by citing the rules, e.g., a negative times a negative is a positive. A few children used a number line.

4.   In one fifth grade class, 20% (4/20) had the correct solution, 6 children had 12, and the rest had various other incorrect solutions.

9.   In the United States, 45.1% of the fourth grade girls and 58.8% of the fourth grade boys answered the problem correctly. In Norway, 65.1% of the fourth graders answered the problem correctly.

10.   70% of eighth graders answered this question correctly on the 2005 NAEP test.

5.3   Multiplication and Division of Integers

It is important to explain the rules for the multiplication and division of integers even though these rules are very basic. Children need to know why mathematics works or at least see an explanation of why it works. If children are familiar with thinking of multiplication as repeated addition and are able to represent 2×3 as 2 groups of 3 (i.e., 3 + 3), then multiplication of a whole number times a negative number can likewise be explained as repeated addition.

$$3 \times (-4) = -4 + (-4) + (-4)$$

However, a negative number times a whole number (e.g., −2 x 4) may be more difficult to explain as repeated addition. What does −2 x 4 mean? −2 groups of 4? Since multiplication is commutative, the numbers can be switched and repeated addition can again be used to explain the process.

Those teaching arithmetical operations with positive and negative numbers are faced with a difficult choice: just present the rules as "the way it is" and something to be memorized, knowing that some children will forget or apply the rules incorrectly, or use a representational model such as the chip model in order to provide a context for the rules, knowing that some students will struggle with the conventions of the model. For example, try to figure out how the black and red chip (credit and debit) model can be used to illustrate $8 \div (-2) = -4$.

An alternative to either of these choices that is sometimes recommended involves using patterns to suggest the appropriate rules and encouraging students to draw on their previous knowledge of operations with whole numbers (e.g., the relationship between multiplication and division and/or the commutativity of multiplication) in order to extend the rules. For example:

$2 \times 4 = 8$		$4 \times -2 = -8$
$2 \times 3 = 6$		$3 \times -2 = -6$
$2 \times 2 = 4$		$2 \times -2 = -4$
$2 \times 1 = 2$		$1 \times -2 = -2$
$2 \times 0 = 0$	$\Rightarrow$	$0 \times -2 = 0$
$2 \times -1 = \underline{\quad}$ (−2)		$-1 \times -2 = \underline{\quad}$ (2)
$2 \times -2 = \underline{\quad}$ (−4)		$-2 \times -2 = \underline{\quad}$ (4)
$2 \times -3 = \underline{\quad}$ (−6)		$-3 \times -2 = \underline{\quad}$ (6)
$2 \times -4 = \underline{\quad}$ (−8)		$-4 \times -2 = \underline{\quad}$ (8)

The first column extends the pattern of a positive times a positive to a positive times a negative. The second column extends the pattern of a positive times a negative to a negative times a negative.

Division of positive and negative numbers can be illustrated by changing division problems to multiplication. For the problem $8 \div (-2) = \underline{\quad}$, one might reason as follows:

> Knowing that division is the opposite of multiplication, we can represent,
> $8 \div (-2) = \underline{\quad}$, $-2 \times \underline{\quad} = 8$, and since $-2 \times (-4) = 8$, then $8 \div (-2) = -4$.

However, not all children will "see" the patterns in these examples. This approach may only help some children understand the rules for multiplying and dividing negative numbers. As a future teacher, it is important for you to understand the different approaches that you may use with children.

How Children Solve some Integer Word Problems

Oftentimes, we give children problems that are intended to illustrate multiplication and division of negative numbers, but children do not think of the problems in these ways.

If I lost 4 pounds a week for 3 weeks, how many pounds did I lose?

Mathematically, we might represent the problem as $3 \times (-4) = -12$, but how do you think children and most adults really solve the problem? Probably, they think $3 \times 4 = 12$ but indicate the solution is 'a 12 pound loss'.

If a school lost 10 students a year, how many more students did the school have 2 years ago?

Mathematically this problem may be represented as $-2 \times -10 = 20$, but especially here children will just multiply and think of it as $2 \times 10 = 20$.

The way children think about problems involving negative numbers may be very different than the intended formal approach to mathematical thinking.

5.3   Problems and Exercises

Solve the problems first and then consider some data on how children solved the problems found in the **Children's Solutions and Discussion of Problems and Exercises** section. As you solve these problems, you may also want to consider how children might solve or think about the following problems.

1.   Jim's football team lost 5 yards on 2 consecutive plays. How many yards did the team lose?

2.   A video is made of a train traveling 20 feet per second. If the video is played in reverse, describe the location of the train after 4 seconds.

3.   A video is made of a train going in reverse at 15 feet per second. If the video is played in reverse describe the location of the train after 5 seconds.

4.   How would you explain this pattern to children?

$$2(-5) = -10$$
$$1(-5) = -5$$
$$0(-5) = 0$$
$$-1(-5) = \underline{}$$
$$-2(-5) = \underline{}$$

5.   Solve: $(-5)(-7)$

6.   If x = –3, what is the value of –3x? (TIMSS, 2003)
      a. –9
      b. –6
      c. –1
      d. 1
      e. 9

7.   If n is a negative integer, which of these is the largest number (TIMSS, 2003)?
      a. 3 + n
      b. 3 x n
      c. 3 – n
      d. 3 ÷ n

8.   What is the value of 1 – 5 x (–2) (TIMSS, 2003)?
      a. 11
      b. 8
      c. –8
      d. –9

5.3   Questions for Discussion

1.   Should teachers ever teach the rules for integer operations without explaining them? Explain your answer.

2.   As a teacher, do you think all children will understand the explanations for integer operations? If not, why give the explanations?

3.   For problems 1 through 3 and the examples given, is it acceptable for children to represent and solve these types of problems using whole numbers when the problems are intended to be represented with integers? Explain your response.

5.3   Children's Solutions and Discussion of Problems and Exercises

1.   In a third grade class, only 26% (5/19) had the correct solution, and in fifth grade, 83% (19/23) had the correct solution. However, no child with the correct answer used negative numbers; they either multiplied, (2 x 5 = 10), or added, (5 + 5 = 10).

2.   In a fifth grade class, 57% (13/23) had a correct solution. Again, no child used negative numbers. The incorrect solutions, (10/23), were all between 20 and 60 feet.

3.   In one fifth grade class, 81%, (13/16), indicated the correct solution, but only 3 children clearly explained that the train had moved that many feet forward.

4.   In a fifth grade class, 56% (10/18) could correctly extend the pattern, but many of them were still unsure why a negative times a negative equals a positive.

5.   Only 50% of eighth graders could correctly solve this problem (NAEP, 1996).

6.   In the United States, 65.5% of eighth graders and internationally 48.4% gave the correct response (TIMSS, 2003).

7.   In the United States, 48.2% of eighth graders and internationally 39.9% gave the correct response (TIMSS, 2003).

8.   In the United States, 38% of eighth graders and internationally 35.9% gave the correct response (TIMSS, 2003).

Chapter 5: References

Behrand, J. L., & Mohs, L. C. (2005/2006). From simple questions to powerful connections: A two-year conversation about negative numbers. *Teaching Children Mathematics*, 260-264.

Goldin, G. & Shteingold, N. (2001). Systems of representation and the development of mathematical concepts. In A. Cuoco & F. Curcio (Eds.) *NCTM 2001 Yearbook: The role of representation in school mathematics.* 1-23. Reston, VA: NCTM.

National Research Council. (2001). *Adding it up: Helping children learn mathematics.* J. Kilpatrick, J. Swafford, and B. Findell (Eds.). Mathematics Learning Study Committee, Center for Education, Division of Behavioral and Social Sciences and Education. Washington DC: National Academy Press.

Petrella, G. (2001). Subtracting integers: An affective lesson. *Mathematics Teaching in the Middle School, 7,* 150-151.

Chapter 6: Rational Numbers – Fractions

The overarching intent of this supplement is to describe how children understand and learn mathematics. For the most part, describing how children come to know fractions depends on how fractions are taught or presented to children. Children possess some informal knowledge of sharing or partitioning by halves, thirds, and fourths, but most do not have everyday experiences with fractions. Other than sharing something equally, children are unlikely to encounter anything other than the most basic fractions such as 1/2, 1/4, and 1/3. Although some children may encounter fractions in recipes, their understanding is usually very contextualized; they do not usually transfer this knowledge to other fraction contexts. Children simply do not come across fractions in their everyday experiences the way they do whole numbers and geometry. Consequently, their understanding or misunderstanding of fractions is most often dependent upon their experiences with fractions in the school setting. This section will describe children's intuitive notions of fractions, the typical representation of fractions to elementary school children, other conceptions of fractions which are essential in children's understanding of later mathematics, and many of the common misconceptions or errors that children make with fractions.

6.1   Fractions

One approach to developing a concept of fraction is to use children's sense of fairness in sharing parts of a whole equally, which is also referred to as equal-sharing. Piaget et. al. (1960) was able to show how children are developmentally able to make partitions. Working with 4 and 5 year olds, he found that children could first make the 2–partition (they could make equal shares for two people), then the 4-partition, and with substantial struggle the 3-partition and multiples, and finally the 5-partion and others (Smith, 2002). Initially, many children are more concerned that each person gets an equal number of things than with the size of each thing. But early on in elementary school they become more aware of the size of the parts and can partition quantities into equal shares corresponding to halves, fourths, and eighths (National Research Council, 2001).

A part/whole concept of natural numbers (see Chapter 3) is invaluable in helping children construct fraction concepts. Children begin to understand that a whole is made up of parts and sometimes these parts are the same size and sometimes they are not. Once they are able to think of natural numbers as units composed of smaller units, children's informal notions of partitioning and sharing may play an important role in the development of their concept of fractions. Central to understanding fraction is the idea that fractions name the relationship between the parts and the whole and not the size of the whole or the size of the parts (Smith, 2002). For example, a child might be asked, "What is 1/4 in this picture?"

Research indicates that children have sound informal knowledge of 1/2 and powerful strategies for halving (Empson, 2002). Studies also suggest that children in first and second grades are capable of formulating the concept of fraction, provided they are encouraged to use manipulatives, and fractions are described orally by fraction words (Payne, Towsley, & Huinker, 1990). It is important that children have oral names for the equal-sized pieces before they are exposed to written symbols. **Numerical symbols should not be introduced at this early stage of fraction concepts.**

Children typically develop an understanding of 1/2, 1/4, and 1/3 in that order, but their understanding of other fractions drops off rapidly, especially when numbers other than 1 are used in the numerator.

Fraction as a Part–whole Relationship

Fraction as part of a whole has two forms: a fraction of a **whole** (continuous) or a fraction of a **set** (discrete). These are by far the most prevalent conceptions of fraction presented to children in K-5 elementary mathematics textbooks. Elementary school textbooks tend to emphasize the part-whole conceptualization of fractions and fraction symbols while only giving a cursory look at other fractional representations (Empson, 2002). A popular model has always been a pizza or a pie. What models do you remember using in learning about fractions?

Fraction of a Whole (continuous)

The most common representation of a fraction is that of a fraction of a **whole** or of a **continuous region**. The following picture is a representation of this concept:

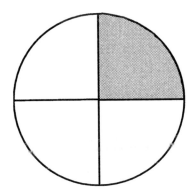

Fraction of a Group (discrete)

The following picture is a representation of this concept:

What is the difference between the two previous pictorial representations of fractions?

Most children have more experiences with fractions of a whole (continuous), but they also need experiences with fractions of a group (discrete)! One conception is not more difficult than the other. It is just that in most cases children do not get as much experience with fractions of groups.

Research also indicates that children will develop a deeper conceptual understanding of fractions by using multiple modes of representation—pictorial, manipulative, verbal, real-world, and symbolic. Emphasis should also be placed on the use of multiple physical models and the connection between them. For example, children may be given a fraction model with 2/3 of a circle shaded and then asked to show that same fraction with a set of chips (Cramer, Post, & delMas, 2002).

Manipulatives that are sometimes used to illustrate the part-whole relationship of fractions include: Fraction Bars, Cuisenaire Rods, Fraction Sticks, Fraction Circles, and Pattern Blocks. Cuisenaire Rods are not marked off in length so children have to solve the problem of determining the relationship among them. However, working with manipulatives does not guarantee that children will develop the intended mathematical knowledge (Ball, 1992). The mathematical ideas are not in the manipulative. Manipulatives are tools intended to help children construct the mathematical ideas.

Fraction as a Quotient

Another conceptualization of fractions is as division. One interpretation of the fraction 1/2 is as division, $1 \div 2$. This understanding is useful later on in mathematics, but it probably does not make sense to children when they are first learning about fractions. Understanding the connection between fractions and division seems to be especially difficult for children. That is, they do not understand the connection between 3/4 as a number (one entity), and $3 \div 4$ (two entities and an operation). How are these two perspectives of the same fraction connected?

Fraction as a Location on a Number Line or as a Measure

Your college textbook may discuss fractions as locations on a number line. While at times a useful representation, it is not how children initially make sense of fractions. A fraction as a measure might be 3/4 of an inch on a ruler or, more generally 3/4 of the way from the beginning of the unit to the end of the unit.

Fraction as a Ratio

Fractions may also be viewed as a ratio. For example, 3 cats for every 4 dogs. A 'fraction of a group' is a ratio. However, the concept of ratio also includes part-to-part comparisons. The ratio interpretation can also present significant difficulties. For example, in the whole group of cats and dogs for which there are 3 cats for every 4 dogs, the fraction of cats relative to the whole is 3/7 and the fraction of dogs relative to the whole is 4/7. In this case, 3/4 is actually comparing two parts and does not represent a part and the whole.

Fraction as an Operator

A fraction may be applied as an operator that enlarges or reduces something. For example, 3/4 of 8 is 6 (National Research Council, 2001). In other words, this example illustrates the process of 'three-fourthing' a number. This conceptualization of fraction is more useful to middle and high school students.

Equivalent Fractions

While finding and making equivalent fractions is a common elementary school experience (children are almost always required to put their fraction solution in **simplest form**), equivalent fractions are a very important mathematical concept.

Consider how to show that 1/2 is equivalent to 4/8. Start with a diagram of 1/2.

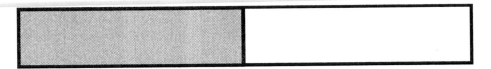

One way to show that these fractions are equivalent is to divide each half into four sections. The picture of 1/2 is the same size as 4/8.

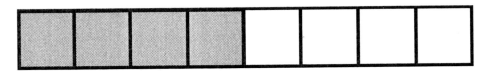

Another way to demonstrate this concept is to divide the figure horizontally into four sections; again illustrating that 1/2 is the same size as 4/8

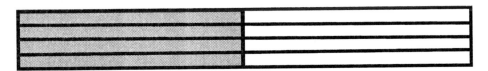

One means of examining children's understanding of equivalent fractions is to ask them to make a diagram (Smith, 2002). How would you show that 4/8 and 6/12 are equivalent with a picture?

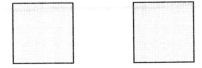

When answering such questions, it is important to remember that there are an <u>infinite</u> number of equivalent fractions!

At the <u>symbolic level</u>, children will need a good understanding of multiplicative relationships when working with equivalent fractions. For example, 2/3 = 8/12 because "8 is 4 times 2" and "12 is 4 times 3" or "2 is one-fourth of 8" and "3 is one-fourth of 12."

Improper Fractions

For many, the word fraction means less than 1; however, fractions can be equal or greater than 1. These latter fractions are given the name "improper fractions." This name is not a good one for this type of fraction because there is nothing improper or wrong with an improper fraction. A common elementary school activity is for children to change improper fractions to mixed numbers and vice versa.

Pictorial representations of improper fractions may be confusing to children. How would you make a drawing, using circles, to represent the improper fraction 5/2 to a fifth grade class?

One solution is to draw 3 circles and shade in 5 half-circles.

Some children might interpret this picture as showing 5/6 because 5 out of 6 parts are shaded. A confusing aspect of fractions is keeping track of the referent or whole that the fraction refers to. For the above drawing to represent 5/2, the referent is <u>one circle</u> as it was in the previous representation of proper fractions. Children are correct to say 5/6 if the whole is taken to be the <u>3 circles</u> combined. Clearly defining the whole can be a very confusing aspect of fractions!

Another representation may be 5 full circles cut in half with half of each shaded.

Still another representation might be just 5 half-circles.

Common Misconceptions with Fractions

The National Assessment of Educational Progress, NAEP (Carpenter, et. al., 1981), documents a low level of performance on fraction computation tasks and a lack of understanding of fractions among nine, thirteen, and seventeen year olds.

Estimate $\frac{12}{13} + \frac{7}{8}$

    a.   1
    b.   2
    c.   19
    d.   21

On the NAEP test, 55% of thirteen-year-olds chose either 19 or 21.

These answers stem from a common error children make when adding fractions: adding numerators (i.e., the top number in a fraction) and denominators (i.e., the bottom number in a fraction), (e.g., 1/3 + 2/5 = 3/8). This mistake may result from thinking that operations on

fractions are just like operations with natural numbers. In fact, many properties of fractions and rules for performing operations on fractions conflict with well-established ideas about natural numbers. For example, children may believe that
1/3 > 1/2 because 3 > 2, or they may think that 4/5 and 5/6 are the same because, in each case, the numerator is one less than the denominator. In other words, children sometimes use properties learned from working with natural numbers even though those properties do not apply to fractions (National Research Council, 2001).

In a videotaped interview, a ninth-grade general math student estimated 3/4 + 3/4 was less than 1. His notion of fraction was that all fractions were less than 1.

Another source of difficulties in developing sound fraction concepts stems from the depiction of fractions using pre-partitioned shapes. Children are frequently asked to identify various fractions or show them by shading (again using pre-partitioned shapes), but research shows children complete these exercises without focusing on the geometrical properties of the whole or the parts. These exercises do not provide opportunities for children to use physical models or to draw their own diagrams to solve problems. Thus they do not engage children in activities where they must do the partitioning. Activities with pre-partitioned shapes may contribute to the misconception that the pieces of the whole do not have to be the same size.

For example, some children will say that one-third of the following figure is shaded.

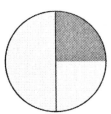

This type of response suggests that when children only encounter figures that are already partitioned into equal-sized pieces, they can obtain correct answers without constructing the fundamental notion that a fraction such as 1/3 refers to one out of three equal-sized pieces, not just one out of three pieces. When using pre-partitioned shapes, children tend to focus on "filling-in the blanks" rather than focusing on the meaning of the numbers (e.g. one shaded piece becomes a "1" as the top number of the fraction and three pieces altogether becomes a "3" in the bottom number of the fraction).

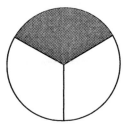

Children frequently are expected to abstract fraction concepts before they fully understand them. For example, children are told that one of two equal-sized parts is called "one-half" and written "1/2." The problem is that this symbol is confusing for children who have previously dealt with only natural numbers because it requires them to recognize that the numbers 1 and 2 represent how many of how many equal-sized parts, but at the same time, these numbers represent another number, which is the number 1/2 (Bezuk, 1988). The same fraction can be viewed as either a number, or as a relationship among two numbers, or as both. A key idea is that a fraction is a number, not two numbers, and that number can be added, subtracted, multiplied, divided, etc.

Further, children must learn that the two numbers that make up a fraction (numerator and denominator) are related through <u>multiplication</u> and <u>division</u>, not addition. Further the names of the numbers, (numerator and denominator), are not as important as the meaning of the location of the number (e.g., the number on top is the number of equal pieces in relationship to the number on the bottom which is the total number of pieces or the whole).

Because fractions involve complex part/whole relationships and some situations involve not only multiple parts, but also multiple wholes, children sometimes "<u>lose track of</u>" the whole. For example, when asked to share two whole pizzas among 4 people, a child may cut each pizza in half, distribute the four halves to the four people, and conclude that each person gets 1/4. In other words, the child sees each person as receiving one out of four equal parts, but loses sight of the fact that each part is 1/2 of a pizza (Charles & Nason, 2000). Additionally, when presented with the problem of sharing 3 pizzas among 4 people, children often give the following answers for the amount of pizza each person gets:

 1/4 of a pizza   1/4 of each pizza   3/4 of three pizzas   1/4 of all the pizzas

For the problem of sharing 4 cookies among 3 people, they often give the answer of "1 1/3 of two cookies." Which of these answers would you consider incorrect? Which, if any, would you consider incomplete, but not necessarily incorrect? All of these responses indicate that children have difficulty understanding the unit (or whole) to which a fraction is referring.

6.1   Problems and Exercises

Problem Set A

The problems in Set A are activities. The first is a set of interview questions that can be done with a child. The second is a hands-on activity that can be done as a class activity or individually.

Fraction Interview

What do children understand about fractions and how will you find out what they know? One means might be to interview a child asking varied questions about fractions.

Your assignment is to conduct an interview with a child and then write a description summarizing your assessment of that child's understanding of fractions. Try to choose a child who has some understanding of fractions, but not one with an advanced understanding. Most students in grades 4-9 would fall into this category. A high school student without a thorough understanding of fractions would also be fine. Try to figure out what they know about fractions. Use specific examples to justify your conjectures about his/her understanding.

Suggested Questions:

1. What fractions do you know or use?

2. What does 5/8 mean?

3. What does 5/3 mean?

4. Which is larger, 1/8 or 1/3? How do you know?

5. Which is larger, 2/3 or 3/4? How do you know?

6. What is the largest fraction you know? What is the smallest fraction you know?

7. Draw a picture representing 3/4.

8. Draw a picture representing 5/2.

9. Does this picture represent 4/5? Why or why not?

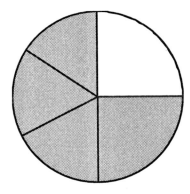

10. What is 1/2 + 1/3?

Fraction Bars

A hands-on activity to help children develop a conceptual understanding of fractions is to use Fraction Bars.

Cut up strips of equal length, approximately 8 per person. (The paper slicer works nicely. Try to make each strip approximately 1 inch wide.)

I.   Label the first strip 1.

1

II.   Fold the next strip in half and label each section 1/2. Suggestion: put a line or dotted line through the fold to highlight it. If a strip is folded incorrectly, start over with another strip. The folds are very important.

1/2	1/2

III.   Fold the next strip into thirds. This can be done by folding the strip like a letter to be put in an envelope or by making <u>1 and 1/2</u> loops with the strip and folding it at the ends. Label each section 1/3.

1/3	1/3	1/3

IV.   Next fold a strip into fourths. Fold the strip in half once and then repeat the procedure. Label each section 1/4.

1/4	1/4	1/4	1/4

V.   Fifths may be the most difficult to make, but fifths are essential for the subsequent problems. You can make fifths by making a circle with <u>2 and 1/2</u> loops. Crease or fold the strip wherever the ends of the strip fall. This is the most challenging strip!

1/5	1/5	1/5	1/5	1/5

VI.   Next make sixths. This can be done by first making thirds and then folding the thirds in half. Another way is to make <u>3</u> loops and fold the strip at the ends.

1/6	1/6	1/6	1/6	1/6	1/6

VII.   Sevenths are *optional*. They can be made by making <u>3 and 1/2</u> loops and creasing the circle at the ends of the strip.

VIII.   The last fraction bar is eighths. Fold the strip in half three times.

1/8	1/8	1/8	1/8	1/8	1/8	1/8	1/8

Notice that sixteenths are not too difficult to make but other fraction bars may prove tricky.

1.   **Individually or with a partner, <u>using your fraction bars,</u> find as many different ways as possible to make 1 or a whole**. Pretend that you do not know how to add fractions by finding a common denominator!

As an example, 1/2 and 2/4 (or children may think of 2/4 as two 1/4s) can be put together to make a whole. Record your solutions. For the previous solution, write:

$$1/2 + 2/4 = 1$$
$$\text{or}$$
$$1/2 + 1/4 + 1/4 = 1$$

As you are working make sure that you use three fraction bars to make a whole and also that you use the fifths fraction bar.

2.   Using your fraction bars, make inequalities. Do not use any 1's in the numerator. For example: 2/3 < 3/4.

Problem Set B

<u>Solve the problems first</u> and then consider some data on how children solved the problems found in the **Children's Solutions and Discussion of Problems and Exercises** section. In addition, the mathematical purposes or instructional intent is given in italics for many of the following problems.

Problems 1-9 are intended to help conceptualize fractions as quantities. Problems posed in the context of money can help children view fractions as quantities. Children can focus their attention on the value of a bill or coin that is part of a larger bill or coin that represents the whole.

1.   A nickel is what part of a quarter?
2.   A nickel is what part of a dollar?
3.   A dime is what part of a dollar?
4.   A dime is what part of two dollars?
5.   A dime is what part of five dollars?
6.   This nickel is one tenth of what I have under here [indicating some money covered under a cloth]. What amount of money is under the cloth?
7.   These two nickels are two twentieths of what I have under here [indicating some money covered under a cloth]. What amount of money is under the cloth?
8.   Which is bigger, one-tenth or one-twentieth of 1000 dollars?
9.   Which is bigger, five-tenths or one-half of 1000 dollars? (Sáenz-Ludlow, 1994).

Problems 10a and 10b are intended to help children focus on the importance of the unit (whole) in relation to the parts using fraction circles.

10a.   If in the first circle the cost of one piece is 1 dollar, what is the cost of one piece in the second circle?

10b.   If the cost of one piece in the second circle is 1 dollar, what is the cost of one piece in the third circle?

In problem 11 children are encouraged to produce different partitions of the same shape, questions like that below aid in their development of logical part/part and part/whole relationships:

cookie A   cookie B

11.   If one child gets one piece of cookie A and another child gets one piece of cookie B, will they get the same amount? Who will get more? Why? (Pothier & Sawada, 1990).

Problem 12 is designed to help children construct equivalent fractions, as it requires the comparison of two fractional units of the same whole.

12.   If Grandpa gave one-fifth of his money to Sam and one-tenth of his money to Sue, what part of his money did he give to the two children?

Problems 13a -13d focus on the simultaneity of different partitions of the same whole (fifths and tenths) and foster the need to correlate them. This type of activity may also lead to the generation of equivalent fractions.

```
┌─────────────────────────┐
│           A             │
│      ┌─────────┐        │
│      │    B     │       │
│      │   ┌───┐  │       │
│      │   │ C │  │       │
│      │   │   │  │       │
│      │          │       │
│      └──────────┘       │
│           D             │
└─────────────────────────┘
```

13a.   D is what part of the large square?
13b.   B is what part of the large square?
13c.   C is what part of the large square?
13d.   A is what part of the large square?

14.   Draw a picture representing 12/5.

15.   Without finding a common denominator, which is larger 5/7 or 7/9?

16.   Slime man eats 5 food pellets in 7 days and snake woman eats 3 food pellets in 4 days. Who is getting more food (Lamon, 2001)?

17.   Why might a child think that 7/8 = 11/12?

18.   How might a child use the fraction 1/2 as a referent to determine if 3/7 or 5/8 is larger?

19.   How would you show that 5/3 = 1 2/3?

20.   Consider these next three problems from either NAEP or TIMSS. How are they different? What makes the problems more difficult for children?

I.   Which shows 3/4 of the picture shaded (NAEP, 2003)?

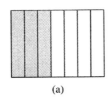

(a)

(b)

(c)

(d)

II.   In this diagram, 2 out of every 3 squares are shaded.

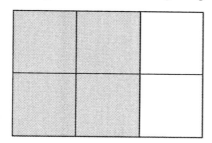

Which diagram has 3 out of 4 squares shaded (TIMSS, 2003)?

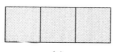

(a)

(b)

(c)

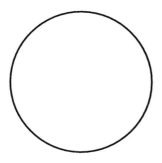

(d)

III. Sam said that 1/3 of a pie is less than 1/4 of the same pie.

Is Sam correct? _____

Use the circles below to show why this is so.

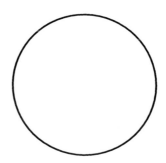

Shade in 1/3 of this circle.   Shade in 1/4 of this circle.

21.   How many fourths make a whole (NAEP, 1996)?

22.   Each figure represents a fraction. Which two figures represent the same fraction (TIMSS, 1995)?

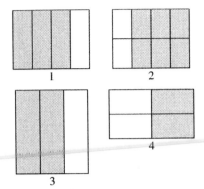

            a.   1 and 2
            b.   1 and 4
            c.   2 and 3
            d.   3 and 4

23.   Luis had two apples and he cut each apple into fifths. How many pieces of apple did he have (NAEP, 2003).
            a. 2/5
            b. 2
            c. 5
            d. 10

24.   Each figure represents a fraction. Do they represent the same fraction?

6.1   Questions for Discussion

1.   Why do you think a five year-old can more easily figure a way to share 3 cakes among 4 people rather than share 2 cakes among 3 people?

2.   Why would you have children make fraction bars before you had them use manufactured fraction bars?

3.   As you read this section, what misconceptions about your own understanding of fractions did you discover?

4.   Why are fractions difficult for children to grasp?

6.1   Children's Solutions and Discussion of Problems and Exercises

Problem Set A

1.   Common responses are 1/2, 1/4, etc.
2.   Children most often use a picture either of a whole or sets to describe 5/8. One fourth grader explained, "five eights [sic] means there are eight wholes and five of them are shaded."
3.   In one fourth grade class, 58% (14/24) were able to describe 5/3. Many drew two circles each divided into thirds and shaded in 5 parts.
4.   A question that children frequently ask is, "Do you mean the size of the pieces or the number of pieces (Bezuk & Bieck, 1993)?"
5.   Many fourth and fifth graders drew pictures to successfully answer this question. However, some used incorrect reasoning to reach the correct conclusion e.g., "3/4 is larger because three is larger than two and four is larger than three."
6.   Some fourth graders responses were;
      Largest fraction: 1/2, 1/1, 12/12, 99/100, 100/100, 999,999,999/999,999,999
      Smallest fraction: 1/2, 1/1, 0/0, 3/4
      Some children said the smallest fraction was 1/1 and the largest was 100/100. Another said that 1/2 was the largest and 3/4 was the smallest.
7.   Many second graders could do this activity, but their pieces were usually not equal.
8.   Some fourth graders believe that 5/2 should be written as a mixed number.
9.   In a fourth grade class, 56% said the picture did not represent 4/5. One child indicated, "The coloring (shading) is correct, but the pieces are not divided equally."
10.   In a fourth grade class, 91% (21/23) gave the incorrect solution 2/5! Only two children knew to find the common denominator.

Problem Set B

3.   In a third grade class of 16 children, 5 gave 1/10 as their solution, 5 gave 10/100 as their solution, and 6 children had incorrect solutions (e.g., 1/2, 10, .90, 10/10 and 1/4).
8.   Problem 8 is intended to allow children to use natural number comparisons to generate fractional comparisons. For example, by determining that one-tenth of 1,000 dollars is 100 dollars and one-twentieth of 1,000 dollars is 50 dollars, a child may reason that one-tenth is larger than one-twentieth. In this way, such questions enable children to take advantage of their natural number knowledge to learn about fractions while at the same time avoiding the overgeneralization of natural number properties that, in the absence of any meaningful context, often leads children to say one-twentieth is larger than one-tenth because twenty is larger than ten.
10a. In a fifth grade class, 55% (12/22) indicated the correct cost.
11.   The more pieces a figure is divided the smaller the pieces.
12.   In a fifth grade class, only 26% (5/19) were able to find the correct solution.

13. By sequencing the questions appropriately, children are required to generate new partitions "on top of" previous ones. This activity leads to the construction of a nested system of partitions that allows children to find equivalent fractions (Sáenz-Ludlow, 1994).

14. Answers will vary, the key is the referent!

15. If one tries to answer this question by drawing the fractions, it may be too close to tell. However, if children look at the unshaded pieces and there are two of each, they may see that sevenths are larger than the ninths because the whole is divided into fewer pieces; therefore the sevenths are missing more, so 5/7 must be smaller than 7/9 or 5/7 < 7/9.

16. Children may reason with ratios rather than find a common denominator. For example, one child reasoned, "3/5 = 21/35 and 7/11 = 21/33, they are both getting the same number of pieces but the first one has smaller pieces so it is less" (Lamon, 2001).

17. Some children reason, 8 – 7 = 1 and 12 – 11 = 1; they are the same!

18. A child may reason 1/2 is larger than 3/7 and 1/2 is smaller than 5/8; therefore, 3/7 is less than 5/8.

19. This illustration can be done with division, but if children are not comfortable with division another way might be to show 5 one-thirds and then combine 3 of the one-thirds into a whole.

20. I.   83% of fourth grades were able to correctly identify the correct figure (NAEP, 2003).

    II. In the United States 63.3% of fourth graders were able to correctly identify the correct figure (TIMSS, 2003).

    III. Internationally only 26% of fourth graders and 13% of third graders could correctly shade in both circles (TIMSS, 1995).

21. 50% of fourth graders had a correct solution to this problem (NAEP, 1996).

22. Internationally 54% of fourth graders and 46% of third graders gave the correct pair (TIMSS, 1995).

23. In the United States, 53% of fourth graders indicated that he had the correct number of pieces of apple (NAEP, 2003).

24. Children may say that since the shaded pieces in the second figure are not together the figures do not represent the same fraction.

6.2   Addition and Subtraction of Fractions

Traditional instruction on fraction computation tends to be rule based, focusing on symbol manipulation, and does not emphasize understanding (National Research Council, 2001). The problem with this approach is that it is very dependent upon memory, and it is easily forgotten. Children without an understanding of fractional computation often solve one problem correctly, and then apply the wrong rule to the next problem. Their answers are hit or miss! Exasperating the problem further is the fact that even children who have correct solutions frequently do not understand what they are doing (National Research Council, 2001). They have become proficient in rote procedures which they do not understand and consequently cannot monitor their work or judge the reasonableness of their solutions.

Models for Adding and Subtracting Fractions

The addition or subtraction of fractions with common denominators (e.g., 2/8 + 3/8 = 5/8) can be demonstrated with pictures and diagrams. It is somewhat more challenging to demonstrate the addition or subtraction of fractions <u>without</u> common denominators (e.g., 1/3 + 1/2 = 5/6).

It is important to provide a model for adding fractions with unlike denominators to help children develop an understanding of the process. Fraction bars offer one means of doing so.

Consider how fraction bars might be used to show 1/3 + 1/2. To add 1/3 + 1/2, take the fraction bar divided into thirds and fold it so you have a strip 1/3 long. Do the same with the bar divided into halves to make 1/2. Put the two strips together. Holding them together, compare them to the other fraction bars until the 1/3 + 1/2 strip lines up exactly on a fold. If you hold up eighths, the end falls in between folds, but if you compare it to sixths, it falls at the last fold, which is 5/6.

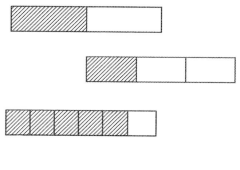

1/2 + 1/3 = 5/6

You can illustrate subtraction in the same way. For 1/2 − 1/3, hold up the 1/2 strip and put the 1/3 strip over it. Now you are trying to find the difference of the two strips, which should match up with 1/6.

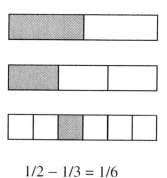

1/2 − 1/3 = 1/6

Pick examples carefully—if you try 1/2 − 1/5, there are no fraction bars (tenths) created in **Problem Set A** that will work.

Fraction addition and subtraction can also be illustrated pictorially. Textbooks may have different ways or variations of the same way. Consider 1/2 + 1/3. When we look at pictorial representations the pieces are different sizes. **We must have the same size pieces to add or subtract fractions.** This is an important idea in fraction addition and subtraction that children may come to understand through working with various representations (manipulatives, pictures, etc.)!

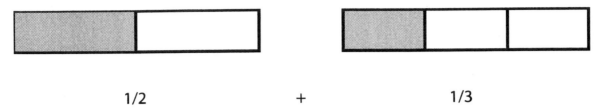

1/2   +   1/3

Take the original representations and divide each piece by what the other piece was divided, that is divide each half piece into thirds and divide each third into halves.

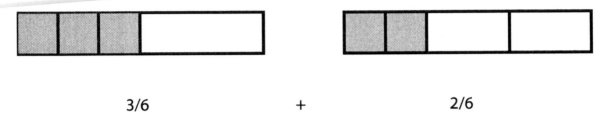

3/6   +   2/6

Now we have the same size pieces, sixths, and the 3 sixths can be combined with the 2 sixths to make 5 sixths.

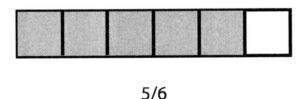

5/6

Common Misconceptions Adding and Subtracting Fractions

Why are operations with fractions so difficult for children? Research shows that an expert or experienced person in mathematics might look at the problem 2/3 + 4/5 as one operation on two numbers. An inexperienced child might view this as 4 numbers with 3 operations. (Operations may not necessarily mean interpreting the fraction bar as the division operation, but as something that must be done.) Most children in elementary school are not ready to work with 4 numbers and 3 operations.

Another common difficulty with fractions is illustrated by the following problem: **What is 1/2 of a large pizza plus 1/2 of a small pizza?** Is the solution 1 medium pizza? These fractions cannot be added because they do not refer to the same whole. Such a problem illustrates yet again how operations on fractions can be very confusing. Here's another problem where the fractions do not have the same referent:

What do you get when you add 1/2 of an apple and 1/2 of an orange?

It is important to remember that the algorithm for adding fractions is not the only procedure for operating on fractions that children do not understand. Significant portions of children do not understand most of the computational procedures they use with fractions. For example, children may know the rule for converting a mixed number to an improper fraction e.g., $3\frac{1}{4} = \frac{(3\times4)+1}{4} = \frac{13}{4}$ but they often do not understand why they do this. Likewise, children do not understand why they "invert and multiply" to divide fractions. As a result of this lack of understanding, children's algorithms develop "bugs," such as inverting the dividend instead of the divisor before multiplying or multiplying fractions by "cross multiplying." **These errors typically result when children try to memorize the steps of an algorithm that do not make sense to them**.

Part of the reason for the aforementioned difficulties is that the use of manipulatives in developing the concept of fraction is abandoned too quickly and an insufficient amount of time is spent on the concept of fraction and on ordering and equivalence of fractions before operations on fractions are introduced. As a result, children's experiences with fractions become a meaningless application of rote procedures that prohibit them from assessing the reasonableness of their results when applying those procedures (Bezuk, 1988). Furthermore, for a conventional arithmetical algorithm to become meaningful to a child, it must represent the coordination of the child's thinking and conventional notation. Introducing conventional notations too soon may also impede children's learning by having them use symbols that are foreign to them to represent their thinking (Sáenz-Ludlow, 1995).

When adding fractions, it is useful to ask children to estimate the size of the sum before solving the problem with manipulatives or diagrams. This estimate not only engages their understanding of the meaning of the fractions involved, but it will also help them judge the reasonableness of the answer they obtain. For instance, in the problem above, a child may reason that the sum should be greater than 1/2 because 1/4 + 1/4 = 1/2 and 1/3 is larger than 1/4. Thus, an answer of 2/7, obtained by adding numerators and denominators is not reasonable here.

6.2   Problems and Exercises

<u>Solve the problems first</u> and then consider some data on how children solved the problems found in the **Children's Solutions and Discussion of Problems and Exercises** section.

1. Why might a child say that 3/5 + 2/3 = 5/8? How would you explain this problem to a child?
2. What two fractions can you add from the following set, {1/2, 1/3, 1/4 and 1/6} to make 2/3? How is this problem better in encouraging mathematical understanding than just having children add two fractions?
3. Estimate your answer for this problem.
    Tyra ate 1/4 of a small cake and Michael ate 1/3 of the cake. What part of the cake did the two of them eat?
4. Now solve problem 3 using manipulatives, such as fraction circles or fraction bars or make diagrams.
5. Show how you could use fraction bars to demonstrate how to add or subtract the following fractions with unlike denominators:
    a.   1/3 + 1/6
    b.   1/2 - 1/6
    c.   3/8 + ½

6. $4/6 - 1/6 =$ (NAEP, 2003)
     a. 3
     b. 3/6
     c. 3/0
     d. 5/6

7.   Janis, Maija, and their mother were eating cake. Janis ate 1/2 of the cake. Maija ate 1/4 of the cake. Their mother ate 1/4 of the cake. How much of the cake is left (TIMSS, 2003)?
     a. ¾
     b. ½
     c. ¼
     d. none

8.   What is the value of $4/5 - 1/3 - 1/15$ (TIMSS, 1999)?
     a. 1/5
     b. 2/5
     c. 3/4
     d. 4/5

6.2   Questions for Discussion

1.   How might a child explain why you can't add 1/2 of a large pizza and 1/2 of a small pizza?
2.   Explain how a child might see $1/2 + 3/4$ as three operations with four numbers.
3.   Why is it helpful to use manipulatives in demonstrating addition and subtraction of fractions?
4.   Why is it especially important for children to estimate their answers before adding or subtracting fractions?

6.2   Children's Solutions and Discussion of Problems and Exercises

2.   The intent is to encourage children to not just automatically do the calculation without thinking about the size of the fractions (Smith, 2002).
3.   In a fourth grade class, 19% (4/21) gave a reasonable estimate typically 1/2, and two children actually added the fractions to get 7/12.
6.   53% of fourth graders answered this problem correctly (NAEP, 2003).
7.   In the United States, 64.7% of fourth graders answered this problem correctly (TIMSS, 2003).
8.   In the United States, 55% of eighth graders answered this problem correctly (TIMSS, 1999).

6.3   Multiplication and Division of Fractions

It is important to try to explain multiplication of fractions to children. Multiplication of a whole number times a fraction can be explained as repeated addition.

$$4 \times 1/2 = 1/2 + 1/2 + 1/2 + 1/2$$

Since all the properties are retained (see Integers 5.3), multiplication of a fraction times a whole number can be reversed because of the commutative property.

However, it is much more difficult to explain a fraction times a fraction. The repeated addition representation does not work very effectively when we look at 2/3 x 4/5. How do you show 2/3 of 4/5? If we think of 3 x 4 as meaning 3, 4 times, then 2/3 x 4/5 is 2/3, 4/5 times. Or we can interpret 3 x 4 to mean 3 groups of 4, then 2/3 x 4/5 is 2/3 groups of 4/5. Would these explanations make sense to a child?

Models for Multiplying and Dividing Fractions

One way to demonstrate multiplication of fractions between 0 and 1 is with the following diagram. This diagram is also a good model for multiplication of decimals when the decimals are in tenths.

To solve 2/3 x 4/5 or 2/3 of 4/5 using a diagram, begin by drawing a rectangle, partitioning it vertically into fifths, and shading in four-fifths.

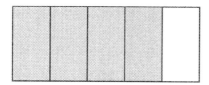

Now partition the rectangle horizontally into thirds.

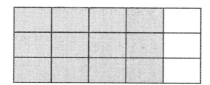

This partitions the 4/5 (the shaded region) into thirds so we can now shade in 2/3 of the 4/5.

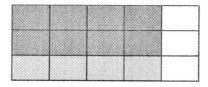

Thus, we see that 2/3 of 4/5 is 8/15.

Note that we began with 5 vertical strips. We divided each of the 5 vertical strips into 3 parts, giving us 5 x 3 (the product of the denominators) = 15 total pieces. Then, to find 2/3 of 4/5, we only wanted to count 2 of the pieces in each of the 4 shaded vertical strips. This gave us 4 x 2 (the product of the numerators) = 8 double-shaded pieces.

Division is much more difficult to explain.

If we have common denominators, then, for example, 3/4 ÷ 1/4 can be thought of as "how many 1/4's are in 3/4?". A picture may be useful to illustrate.

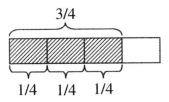

3/4

1/4   1/4   1/4

There are three 1/4's in 3/4 so 3/4 ÷ 1/4 = 3.

However, when the fractions do not have common denominators, it is more difficult to explain unless the fractions are changed to the common denominators.

One way to explain why we invert and multiply is to change division of fractions to a complex fraction.

$$4/5 \div 2/3 =$$

$$\frac{4/5}{2/3} = \frac{4/5 \times 3/2}{2/3 \times 3/2} = \frac{4/5 \times 3/2}{1} = 4/5 \times 3/2$$

There is also a way to illustrate division of fractions with paper folding. For 1/2 ÷ 1/4, fold a paper in half and then fold the half in half again. Upon unfolding, one may see that there are two 1/4's in 1/2. However, this model only works well if the answer is a whole number.

Common Misconceptions Multiplying and Dividing Fractions

What else is different about fractions?

In third and fourth grade children learn intuitively that multiplication makes numbers bigger. Teachers often say this to their children, and even if they do not, most children intuit the idea. This idea is true for whole numbers.

6 x 2 = 12, and 12 is larger than 6.

But this same idea does not hold for fractions. 6 x 1/2 = 3, but 3 is smaller than 6.

Likewise, children learn intuitively that division makes numbers smaller.

12 ÷ 2 = 6, and 6 is smaller than 12.

But again, this idea does not hold for fractions. 12 ÷ 1/2 = 24, but 24 is larger than 12.

Even when children are proficient with the multiplication and division of fractions, they have difficulty with word problems that require the multiplication and division of fractions. Many teachers have observed that children can solve what the teacher would call multiplication and division fraction word problems, but the children don't see the problems as involving multiplication or division (i.e., they don't write multiplication or division number sentences for the problems). This difficulty may be related to their natural number notions of multiplication and division, namely that multiplication makes numbers bigger and division makes smaller numbers smaller. In the case of division, such confusion may also stem from thinking only in terms of the sharing model of division. For example, children may believe that you can't divide 3 by 4 because the dividend must be greater than the divisor, or they may believe that the number sentence 4 ÷ 1/4 does not make sense because the divisor must be a whole number (how can you share 4 things among 1/4 people?), or they may believe that 1 ÷ 1/2 = 2 is impossible because "division makes smaller," that is, the quotient must be less than the dividend. In spite of such beliefs, children are able to construct viable strategies for solving problems like the following:

> You are giving a party for your birthday. From Ben and Jerry's Ice Cream Factory, you order 6 pints of each variety of ice cream that they make. If you serve 3/4 of a pint of ice cream to each guest, how many guests can be served from each variety?

A typical solution produced by sixth graders was to draw a picture to represent six pints of ice cream, separate each pint into four equal sections, and distribute three of those sections at a time to guests. From this they concluded that eight guests could be served from each variety.

1	1		2	3		3	4		5	5		6	7		7	8
1	2		2	3		4	4		5	6		6	7		8	8

Although, on the surface, the children' solution strategies did not appear to vary greatly, the number sentences they wrote for this problem did:

24 ÷ 3 = 8 (because there are 24 pieces, 3 pieces to a serving, so 8 people can be served.)
8 × 3/4 = 6 (because 8 servings of 3/4 of a pint gives you 6 whole pints)

3/4 + 3/4 + 3/4 + 3/4 + 3/4 + 3/4 + 3/4 + 3/4 = 6 (because 3/4 each gives you 6 whole pints)

6 - 3/4 - 3/4 - 3/4 - 3/4 - 3/4 - 3/4 - 3/4 - 3/4 = 0 (because you take away 3/4 of a pint for each serving and you can do this 8 times)

A teacher who was expecting children to write the number sentence 6 ÷ 3/4 = 8 for this problem may feel that the children's number sentences do not match what is going on in the problem. However, the children's number sentences do match what was going on in the problem <u>for them</u>. By writing number sentences involving division of whole numbers, multiplication of a fraction by a whole number, and repeated addition and subtraction of fractions, the children were expressing the variety in their levels of understanding and ways of thinking about multiplication, division, and fractions. This multiplicity of ideas provided the teacher with an opportunity to help children see how these ways of thinking about the problem are related to each other and to division of fractions (Schifter, 1997). (Think about how multiplication, subtraction, and addition are all involved in the standard algorithm for dividing <u>whole</u> numbers.) If the children are familiar with the measurement concept of division, a teacher in the above situation might, after encouraging children to compare the different number sentences, say, "Here's another number sentence we could write for this problem: 6 ÷ 3/4 = 8 because there are 8 3/4's in 6." This example illustrates why it is important for children to have experiences with both the sharing concept of division and the measurement concept of division. If children have only thought in terms of the sharing concept, the teacher's justification of why the number sentence 6 ÷ 3/4 = 8 is appropriate for this problem is not likely to make sense to them.

6.3 Problems and Exercises

Solve the problems first and then consider some data on how children solved the problems found in the **Children's Solutions and Discussion of Problems and Exercises** section.

1. You have 3/4 of a whole cake. You and your friends eat 1/2 of that amount. What part of the whole cake did you and your friends eat?
2. Use a diagram to solve 3/4 x 5/6.
3. a. Why is 5/0 undefined?
   b. Why is 0/0 undefined?
   c. How is the explanation of 3a different from 3b?
4. Create "real-life" problems that could be represented by each number sentence:
   a. 1/2 + 1/3
   b. 1/2 x 1/3
   c. 1/2 ÷ 1/3

We have discussed two interpretations of division: sharing and measurement. An example of a sharing division word problem is
Mother divided 6 candies evenly among her 3 children. How many candies did each child receive?

An example of a measurement division word problem is:
Six candies were divided among some children. Each child got two candies. How many children received candies?

5a. Write sharing and measurement division word problems, using fractions instead of natural numbers, and discuss the problems you faced when doing so.
5b. What constraints do each of these models impose?

Solve the following word problems. Try to give possible difficulties you think children may have when solving these problems and describe the possible sources of the difficulties.

6a. An 8-meter-long stick was divided into 13 equal pieces. What was the length of each piece?
6b. Six kilograms of cheese were packed in boxes, each box containing 3/4 of a kilogram. How many boxes were needed to pack all the cheese?

7.   Jim has 3/4 yards of string which he wishes to divide into pieces 1/8 of a yard long. How many pieces will he have (NAEP, 2003)?
    a. 3
    b. 4
    c. 6
    d. 8

8.   If 1 1/3 cups of flour are needed for a batch of cookies, how many cups of flour will be needed for 3 batches of cookies (NAEP, 1992)?
    a. 4 1/3
    b. 4
    c. 3
    d. 2 2/3

9.   There are 600 balls in a box, and 1/3 of the balls are red. How many red balls are in the box (TIMSS, 2003)?

    Answer _____ red balls

10.   Eighth Grade TIMSS questions
    I.   3/5 + (3/10 x 4/15) =
        a. 3/51
        b. 1/6
        c. 6/25
        d. 11/25
        e. 17/25 (2003)
    II.   6/55 ÷ 3/25 =
        Answer: _____ (1999)
    III.   Robin and Jim took cherries from a basket. Robin took 1/3 of the cherries and Jim took 1/6 of the cherries. What fraction of the cherries remained in the basket?
        a. 1/2
        b. 1/3
        c. 1/6
        d. 1/18 (1999)
    IV.   Laura had $240. She spent 5/8 of it. How much money did she have left?
        Answer _____ (1999)

6.3   Questions for Discussion

1. Is it okay to teach third grade children that multiplication makes numbers bigger and division makes numbers smaller? Why or why not?
2. Why do we need to get a common denominator when adding or subtracting fractions?
3. Why do we "invert and multiply" when dividing fractions?
4. Why do we multiply numerator times numerator and denominator times denominator when multiplying fractions?
5. When converting a mixed number to an improper fraction, why do we multiply the whole number times the denominator of the fractional part, add this product to the numerator of the fractional part, and write the result over the denominator of the fractional part?
6. Why does the strategy for comparing two fractions by cross-multiplying work?

6.3   Children's Solutions and Discussion of Problems and Exercises

1.   Three children's solutions to this problem follow:

"Three-fourths is the same as $\frac{1}{4} + \frac{1}{4} + \frac{1}{4}$. So I took half of $\frac{1}{4}$, which is $\frac{1}{8}$, and three times that is $\frac{3}{8}$."

"Three-fourths is $\frac{1}{2} + \frac{1}{4}$. So I took half of $\frac{1}{2}$, which is $\frac{1}{4}$, and half of $\frac{1}{4}$, which is $\frac{1}{8}$. Since $\frac{1}{4}$ is the same as $\frac{2}{8}$, I added $\frac{2}{8}$ and $\frac{1}{8}$ and got $\frac{3}{8}$."

"I changed $\frac{3}{4}$ to $\frac{6}{8}$ and took half of $\frac{6}{8}$, which is $\frac{3}{8}$."
(Warrington & Kamii, 1998).

The second pictorial solution here involves the coordination of multiple partitions of the same whole, that is, the previously discussed idea of (mentally) placing one partition on top of another one. In this way the child was able to generate an equivalent fraction for $\frac{1}{4}$ that provided a common denominator and made it possible to add the two parts.

In one fourth grade class, only 41% (7 out of 17) had the correct solution to this problem.

3.   A fraction like 5/0 is undefined because there is no solution but 0/0 is undefined because there are an infinite number of solutions.

7.   Only 27% of fourth graders successfully answered this question on the NAEP test (NAEP, 2003).

8.   Only 21% of fourth graders successfully answered this question on the NAEP test (NAEP, 1992).

9.   In the United States, 31.9 % of fourth grade girls and 44.8% of fourth grade boys gave the correct response. Internationally 49.4% of fourth graders gave the correct response.

10.   I.   In the United States, 36.2% of eighth graders gave the correct response (TIMSS, 2003).

II.   In the United States 37% of eighth graders gave the correct response (TIMSS, 1999).

III.   In the United States, 52% of eighth graders gave the correct response (TIMSS, 1999).

IV.   In the United States, 25% of eighth graders gave the correct response (TIMSS, 1999).

6.4   Properties of Rational Numbers

Can you list the natural numbers in order from least to greatest? Whole numbers? Integers?

Try to list the rational numbers in order from least to greatest. For example, we might start as follows:

1/2, 1/3, 1/4, 1/5, 1/6, 1/7, 1/8, 1/9, …

But between 1/7 and 1/8 there is another fraction, in fact more than one fraction. We can show this fact by finding a common denominator, 1/7 = 8/56 and 1/8 = 7/56, and then multiplying by 2/2 to get 14/102 and 16/102. Now we see that 15/102 lies between 1/8 and 1/7. Or put another way, 15/102 is the average of 1/7 and 1/8. Another way to show this fact is to begin by multiplying by 2/2, which gives 2/14 and 2/16. This means that 2/15 must lie between 1/8 and 1/7. We can keep finding fractions forever (i.e., now we could find a fraction between 2/14 and 2/15). Therefore, between any two fractions, there is always another fraction. This property is called the Denseness Property of Rational Numbers. Or put another way, between any two fractions there are an <u>infinite</u> number of fractions. This property is important in mathematics.

How is the denseness property addressed in elementary mathematics textbooks? Common problems include asking children to find a fraction between two other fractions. In elementary school, we typically do not talk about the denseness of fractions.

Correspondence of Rational Numbers and Points on the Number Line

For each rational number, there is a point on the number line. However, for each point on the number line is there is not a corresponding rational number. If we were somehow able to magnify the number line and see each point that makes up the line, we would see many points that do not correspond to rational numbers. The ratio of the circumference of a circle to its diameter is not a rational number. It is π! We do not have rational numbers for the points π, $\sqrt{2}$, $\sqrt{3}$, etc. We need more than integers to obtain a one-to-one correspondence with the points on the number line and numbers. We need real numbers. Real numbers will be discussed in chapter 7.

6.4   Problems and Exercises

<u>Solve the problems first</u> and then consider some data on how children solved the problems found in the **Children's Solutions and Discussion of Problems and Exercises** section.
1.   Find a fraction between 1/6 and 1/7.
2.   On the portion of the number line below, a dot shows where 1/2 is. Use another dot to show where 3/4 is (NAEP, 2003).

3.   Students in Mrs. Johnson's class were asked to tell why 4/5 is greater than 2/3. Whose reason is best (NAEP, 1990)?
        a. Kelly said, "Because 4 is greater than 2."
        b. Keri said "Because 5 is larger than 3."
        c. Kim said, "Because 4/5 is closer than 2/3 to 1".
        d. Kevin said, "Because 4 + 5 is more than 2 + 3."

4.   Write a fraction that is larger than 2/7 (TIMSS, 1995).

      Answer _____

5.   Write a fraction that is less than 4/9 (TIMSS, 2003)

      Answer _____

6.4   Questions for Discussion

1.   Why can't we list all the rational numbers in order from least to greatest?
2.   In what context will you be teaching the essence of the denseness property to children?
3.   In Chapter 2 we discussed children's one-to-one correspondence while counting. Explain the concept of one-to-one correspondence from a child's perspective and from a mathematical perspective as it relates to fractions.

6.4   Children's Solutions and Discussion of Problems and Exercises

2.   Only 37% of fourth graders were able to correctly locate 3/4 on the number line (NAEP, 2003).
3.   35% percent of children in fourth grade identified the correct explanation (NAEP, 1990).
4.   Internationally 57% of fourth graders and 41% of third graders gave a correct response (TIMSS, 1995).
5.   In the United States, 65.5% of eighth grade girls and 73.7% of eighth grade boys gave a correct response (TIMSS, 2003).

Chapter 6 References

Ball, D. (1992). Magical hopes: Manipulatives and the reform of math education. *American Educator*, 16 (14-18), 46-47.

Bezuk, N. S. (1988). Fractions in the early childhood mathematics curriculum. *Arithmetic Teacher*, 35 (6), 56-60.

Bezuk, N. S. & Bieck, M. (1993). Current research on rational numbers and common fractions: Summary and implications for teachers. In D. T. Owens (Ed.) Research ideas for the classroom: Middle grades mathematics. 118-136. Reston, VA: NCTM.

Carpenter, T. P., Corbitt, M. K., Kepner, H. S., Jr., Lindquist, M. M., & Reys, R. E. (1981). *Results form the second mathematics assessment of the National Assessment of Educational Progress. Reston*, VA: NCTM.

Cramer, K., Post, T., & delMas, R. (2002). Initial fraction learning by fourth- and fifth-grade students: A comparison of the effects of using commercial curricula with the effects of using the Rational Number Project Curriculum. *Journal for Research in Mathematics Education, 33*, (2), 111-144.

Empson, S. B. (2002). Organizing diversity in early fraction thinking. In B. Litwiller & G. Bright (Eds.) NCTM *2002 Yearbook: Making sense of fractions, ratios, and proportions.* 29-40. Reston, VA: NCTM.

Lamon, S. J., (2002). Part-whole comparisons with unitizing. In B. Litwiller & G. Bright (Eds.) NCTM *2002 Yearbook: Making sense of fractions, ratios, and proportions.* 79-86. Reston, VA: NCTM.

Lamon, S. J. (2001). Presenting and representing: From fractions to rational numbers. In A. Cuoco & F. Curcio (Eds.) *NCTM 2001 Yearbook: The role of representation in school mathematics.* 146-165. Reston, VA: NCTM.

National Research Council. (2001). Adding *it up: Helping children learn mathematics.* J. Kilpatrick, J. Swafford, and B. Findell (Eds.). Mathematics Learning Study Committee, Center for Education, Division of Behavioral and Social Sciences and Education. Washington DC: National Academy Press.

Payne, J.N., Towsley, A.E., Huinker, D.M. (1990). Fractions and decimals. In J.N. Payne (Ed.) Mathematics *for the young child.* 175-200. Reston, VA: National Council of Teachers of Mathematics.

Piaget, J. G. (1960). *The child's conception of geometry.* New York: W. W. Norton.

Pothier, Y., & Sawada, D. (1990). Partitioning: An approach to fractions. *Arithmetic Teacher,* 38(4), 12-16.

Sáenz-Ludlow, A. (1994). Michael's fraction schemes. *Journal for Research in Mathematics Education, 25,* 50-85.

Sáenz-Ludlow, A. (1995). Ann's fraction schemes. *Educational Studies in Mathematics, 28,* 101-132.

Schifter, D. (1997, March). *Developing operation sense as a foundation for algebra.* Paper presented at the annual meeting of the American Educational Research Association, Chicago.

Smith, J. P. (2002). The development of students' knowledge of fractions and ratios. In B. Litwiller & G. Bright (Eds.) NCTM *2002 Yearbook: Making sense of fractions, ratios, and proportions.* 3-17. Reston, VA: NCTM.

Tirosh, D. (2000). Enhancing prospective teachers' knowledge of children's conceptions: The case of division of fractions. *Journal for Research in Mathematics Education, 31,* 5-25.

Warrington, M., & Kamii, C. (1998). Multiplication with fractions: A Piagetian, constructivist approach. *Mathematics Teaching in the Middle School, 3,* 339-343.

Chapter 7: Decimals, Percents, and Real Numbers

Chapter seven covers a variety of topics including place value, decimals, decimal computation, ratio and proportion, percents, and real numbers. These topics are related in that they are topics children study in the upper elementary grades 4, 5 and 6, and several of them are mathematically related, especially place value less than one, decimals, and percents. These topics are also related in that they require children to do higher level thinking such as proportional reasoning. The topics in this chapter are interconnected and studying one concept may involve using or knowing another concept in this chapter. For example, using decimal numbers and performing decimal computations are frequently required in solving proportions

7.1 Place Value

Understanding place value requires more than just memorizing that the location of a particular digit in a number represents a certain value (i.e., the 6 in 463 represents 6 tens). Typically, many elementary school children spend a great deal of time learning about the place value chart without understanding place value. Many children do not understand place value and just memorize the locations and places. The concept of ten is the key to understanding place value (see chapter 3). Children with a concept of ten can think of 10 as 10 individual units or as one unit or chunk. In addition, they can go back and forth between these two conceptions. For example, to add 28 + 43, they might: add 20 and 40 to get 60, (note they decompose the numbers into tens), then take 2 from 3 and add it to the 8 to make a 10, then add the 10 to the 60 to get 70, and finally, put the 7 tens together with the 1 one to make 71.

Returning to the first example of 463, if 72 is added to 463, then a child might take 4 tens or 40 from 70 and add 60 and 40 to make 100, add the hundred to the 4 hundreds to make 500, add the ones, and then combine the hundreds, tens, and ones to get 535. This process may seem complicated from our perspective of knowing algorithms, but children need these kinds of understandings in order to truly comprehend place value. An illustration of an understanding of place value is when children understand that 463 can be thought of as containing 46 tens and not just that the 6 represents 6 tens!

If children understand ones and tens, then an understanding of hundreds, thousands, etc. can be developed based upon the concept of ten. These understandings can serve as building blocks for an understanding of decimal numbers as well.

7.1   Problems and Exercises

<u>Solve the problems first</u> and then consider some data on how children solved the problems found in the **Children's Solutions and Discussion of Problems and Exercises** section.

1. How many pennies are in $2.63?
2. How many dimes are in $32.46?
3. How many tens are in the number 234?
4. Which number is equal to eight tens plus nine tens (TIMSS, 2003)?
    a. 17
    b. 170
    c. 1700
    d. 17000
5. For the school fund fair the principal needs to buy one balloon for each of the 524 students in the school. If balloons come in packages of 10, how many packages of balloons does the principal need to buy?
6. For the upcoming election, the mayor wants to buy a campaign button for each voter in her city. If there are 23,893 voters in her city and campaign buttons come in packages of 100, how many packages of buttons should she buy?
7. Write the number that is 1,000 more than 56,821 (TIMSS, 1995).
    Answer: _____
8. The Target number is 5, the Target operation is subtraction, and the first number is 1,000,000. What is the second number?
9. What problems do you anticipate fourth and fifth grade children might have in solving Problem #8?
10. What is the smallest whole number that you can make with the digits 4, 3, 9, and 1? Use each digit once (TIMSS, 1995).
    Answer: _____
11. By how much would 217 be increased if the digit 1 were replaced by a digit 5 (NAEP, 1992)?
    a. 4
    b. 40
    c. 44
    d. 400
12. Which of the following is 78.2437 rounded to the nearest hundredths (TIMSS, 2003)?
    a. 100
    b. 80
    c. 78.2
    d. 78.24
    e. 78.244
13. In which list are the numbers ordered form greatest to least (TIMSS, 2003)?
    a. 0.233, 0.3, 0.32, 0.332
    b. 0.3, 0.32, 0.332, 0.233
    c. 0.32, 0.233, 0.332, 0.3
    d. 0.332, 0.32, 0.3, 0.233

14.   What is 4 hundredths written in decimal notation (NAEP, 2005)?
a. 0.004
b. 0.04
c. 0.400
d. 4.00
e. 400.0

15.   What number is represented by point A on the number line (NAEP, 2005)?
a. 0.0010
b. 0.0054
c. 0.0055
d. 0.006
e. 0.055

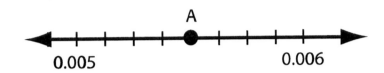

16.   Decimal Puzzle: I am a decimal number. My tens' digit is the first prime odd number; my thousandths' digit is twice my tens digit; my hundredths' digit is a dozen less 4. My hundreds' digit is one-fourth of my hundredths' digit; my thousands' digit is one-half of my hundreds digit. My ones' digit is the only number you cannot divide by, and my tenths' digit is 9 times my ones' digit. What number am I?

7.1   Questions for Discussion

1.   Suppose the mathematics elementary textbook you are using emphasizes the learning of the names for the locations on a place value chart. How could you help children develop a conceptual understanding of place value versus just memorizing the place values and their names?

2.   How can a conceptual understanding of the concept of ten help children construct an understanding of place values such as hundreds and thousands?

3.   How can a conceptual understanding of the concept of tens and hundreds help children construct an understanding of decimals?

7.1   Children's Solutions and Discussion of Problems and Exercises

1.   In a third grade class, 94% (17 out of 18) had the correct solution for this problem. One child's explanation was, "I figured out how many pennies were in two dollars and then I added 63¢ on to it."

2.   In one third grade class, only 25% (4 out of 16) had the correct solution to this problem. Some of their answers were: 86, 88, 205, 300, 310, 370 and 3,256. In a sixth grade class, 42.9 % (9 out of 21) had the correct number of dimes.

3.   In a fourth grade class, 71.4% (15 out of 21) said the answer was 3. Most explained that they "just looked in the tens place." 19% (4 out of 21) indicated that there were 23 tens in 234. Two children had incorrect solutions, 34 and 9. The child who had 9, added the digits 2 + 3 + 4.

4.   In the United States, 64.7% of fourth graders answered this question correctly (TIMSS, 2003).

5.   In one third grade class, only 31% (5 out of 16) were able to derive the correct solution.

6.   A fifth grade class that had not focused on division struggled with this problem as only 1 out of 20 children solved it correctly. No one looked at place value; about half the children tried to divide, seven multiplied the numbers, and four subtracted the numbers.

7.   Internationally, 30% of third graders and 48% of fourth graders gave the correct solution (TIMSS, 1995).

8 &9.   Some erroneous solutions given by fourth and fifth grade children were: 9,999,995; 1,000,005; 995,000. What does a solution of 100,995 indicate about the child's understanding of place value?

10.   Internationally, 29% of third graders and 43% of fourth graders gave a correct response (TIMSS, 1995).

11.   Only 36% of fourth grade children gave the correct solution to this problem (NAEP, 1992).

12.   In the United States, 65.6% of eighth graders correctly rounded the number correctly.

13.   In the United States, 47.9% of eighth graders gave the correct response.

14.   67% of eighth graders successfully gave the correct decimal notation (NAEP, 2005).

15.   Only 42% of eighth graders gave the correct response (NAEP, 2005).

7.2   Decimals

Many children have difficulty developing a conceptual understanding of decimals (Hiebert, Wearne & Taber, 1991). One of the problems children have with decimals is that they try to understand them by relying on their prior understanding of whole numbers. Relying on understandings of whole numbers creates misconceptions about decimals which children have difficulty abandoning (Carpenter, Fennema, & Romberg, 1993). For example, when asked what is 1/8 as a decimal, a child might respond 0.8 (Moss, 2000). Why do you think the child would give this response?

Children need to develop an understanding of decimals beyond just a word or a location on a place value chart. Such an understanding should enable children to answer:
- What is a decimal number?
- What does 0.26 mean?

A Foundation for Decimal Understanding

One way that children develop an understanding of decimals is to build upon their prior conceptual understanding of place value with whole numbers. The following example is taken from an article in the *Arithmetic Teacher,* January 1994, by Diana Wearne and James Hiebert. Consider the explanations given by two girls for a word problem given to them in second grade and then a word problem given to them in fourth grade.

The school cafeteria has 347 ice-cream bars in one box and 48 in another box. How many ice-cream bars does the cafeteria have in two boxes?

Both girls used the standard algorithm to solve the problem and their written work looked similar:

$$
\begin{array}{r}
347 \\
+\ 48 \\
\hline
395
\end{array}
$$

Marcy explained her work as follows: "Right is right. You always line up the numbers on the right and then you add the numbers starting from the right" When questioned about her explanation she explained, "That is the way my teacher said to do them. Right is right."

A second child, Angela explained her work in this way: "7 and 8 is 15, so I had enough ones to make another 10; 4 and 4 is 8 tens, and one more ten makes 9 tens; I have nothing to add to the hundreds so it is 3 hundreds." When she was questioned about why she aligned the digits the way she did, she explained that she knew the two 4's were both tens and the 7 and 8 were both ones. "… it's easier when they are together."

Both girls have the correct solution, but Angela appears to have a conceptual or relational understanding of what she is doing. On the other hand, Marcy appears to have a procedural or instrumental understanding of what she is doing. Two years later, in fourth grade, the girls are asked to solve a problem which involves adding decimals.

Jeremy had 3.5 pounds of oranges in one bag and 0.62 pounds of oranges in another bag. How many pounds of oranges does Jeremy have?

Below is what Marcy's written work looked like:

Marcy
$$
\begin{array}{r}
3.5 \\
+.6\,2 \\
\hline
.9\,7
\end{array}
$$

Marcy's explanation indicated her lack of understanding of decimals: "First you line up the numbers and then you add: 5 plus 2 is 7 and 3 plus 6 is 9. Then you bring down the decimal point." She indicated that she brought down the decimal point in the .62 and not the decimal point in 3.5

Angela on the other hand had a much more conceptual explanation. She knew the 2 represented hundredths and the 5 and 6 represented tenths. Here is her written work:

Angela
$$
\begin{array}{r}
3.5 \\
+\ .62 \\
\hline
4.12
\end{array}
$$

Helping children build a strong conceptual understanding of mathematics will help them throughout their lives in mathematics! As this example illustrates, if children have a conceptual understanding of place value for whole numbers then it can be carried over to a decimal understanding of place value. What is even more apparent is the fact that if a child does not have a conceptual understanding of basic mathematical ideas then he or she will find it difficult to develop a conceptual understanding of higher level mathematics.

Models for Decimal Numbers

Four of the most common models used with children working with decimals are: decimal squares, Base Ten Blocks, money, and a number line.

Decimal Squares

One common pictorial model used in elementary school textbooks to help children develop the concept of decimals is a decimal square. Decimal squares can be used as a pictorial model to represent the decimal. For example 0.23 can be represented by the picture that follows:

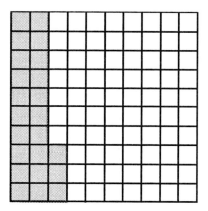

Decimal squares can also be used to compare decimal numbers as in the case of which is greater, 0.23 or 0.32?

         0.23   0.32

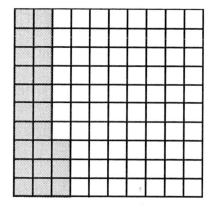
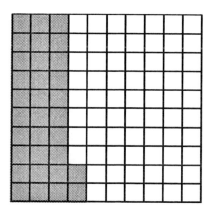

Decimal squares can also be used to illustrate addition or subtraction of decimals as well as multiplication and division. The following example can be used to illustrate addition: 0.24 + 0.36 = 0.60.

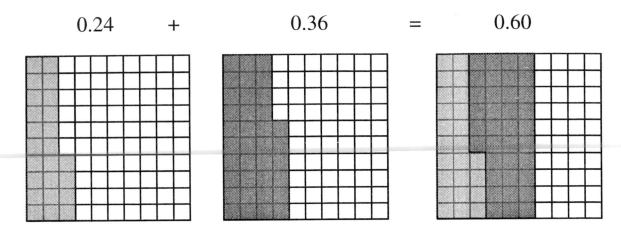

Base Ten Blocks

Another common model used to teach children about decimals is Base Ten Blocks (See Chapter 3 for a discussion of the advantages and disadvantages of Base Ten Blocks.). It is important to note that in the decimal model, the values of the manipulatives are changed from their original values to these values:

> A flat is one, (1).
> A long is a tenth, (.1).
> A cube is a hundredth, (.01).

The change in the values of the Base Ten Blocks may be confusing for children because the flat that they learned was 100 now becomes 1. However, Base Ten Blocks are a common manipulative found in most schools, and may be one of the few available for decimals. Another problem is that most schools only have one or two sets of Base Ten Blocks and not enough for the entire class. The Base Ten Blocks representation as decimals corresponds well with the decimal square.

Money

A third model to use when teaching children about decimals is money. Children might be asked to count money and write the solution using the dollar sign and decimals: $0.46. Working with money is also a life skill that children will need and use.

Note that all the approaches and models mentioned are only useful **for tenths and hundredths**. There is not a good hands-on manipulative for thousandths or smaller decimal numbers.

Number Line

A fourth model for teaching decimals is a number line. Number lines may help children in ordering decimals. Common textbook exercises are to locate a given decimal on a number line or given a mark on a number line and give the decimal number it represents. For example, what numbers are represented by the points labeled A, B and C?

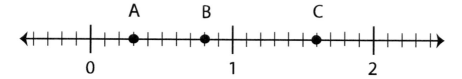

Rounding Decimal Numbers

Another common exercise dealing with decimals is to round decimal numbers to the nearest tenths, ten, etc. The intent behind this exercise is not so much to teach children about rounding, but it is to teach children the name of the location of the digits in the number. Rounding activities with decimals often focus on an instrumental understanding of decimal place value.

Children's Understanding of Decimals

Children's understanding of decimals is analogous to their understanding of negative numbers. In both instances, different children have different understandings of these concepts in different contexts. Children may appear to understand decimals using some models, but they are unable to carry over this understanding to other contexts or models. As an example, 46 sixth graders were asked to illustrate **six tenths and six hundredths** in four ways. In the parentheses are the number out of 46 who had the representation correct and the corresponding percentage.

      1. On a number line   (11 – 26%)
      2. On two 10 x 10 decimal squares   (28 – 65%)
      3. Using money   (28 – 65%)
      4. Using place value   (25 – 58%)

Only six students or 14% were able to get all four situations correct. 14 or 33% were able to get three. 12 or 28% were able to get two. 7 or 16% were able to get one, and 4 or 9% did not get any correct. While most students demonstrated some understanding of decimals, very few were able to demonstrate a conceptual understanding in all areas. Why do you think these children responded the way they did? Marintee & Bay-Williams (2003) suggest "To make sense of decimals, students need multiple experiences and contexts in which to explore them." Others suggest that what children need to explore is not the study of the different representations but rather the essential sameness of the representations. What is the essential sameness of these four representations of decimals? Earlier we said the important idea was that 10 units make one ten and now we see that 10 tenths make 1 unit and that 10 hundredths make 1 tenths. In general if a digit is moved one place to the left, it represents 10 times the value (and if it is moved the right, it represents one-tenth).

A significant point to consider is that most adults already have an understanding of decimals and therefore see how the mathematics of decimals works or fits with each model or representation. This knowledge often helps adults understand how the physical model should work. Children, on the other hand, do not yet have an understanding of decimals, so they do not necessarily see the decimal representation in the models. At times, they are figuring out both the mathematics and the model. The key question becomes which models or representations will help children develop a mathematical understanding of decimals.

Scientific Notation

An understanding of both decimals and place value is necessary for understanding scientific notation (e.g., 23,000 is 2.3×10^4 in scientific notation). However, in grades K-5, children typically do not encounter scientific notation even though children may multiply large numbers on a calculator, in which case the calculator will display the number in scientific notation. Elementary teachers should be able to explain the meaning of these displays. Scientific notation is useful when working with very small numbers and very large numbers such as the speed of light.

7.2   Problems and Exercises

Solve the problems first and then consider some data on how children solved the problems found in the **Children's Solutions and Discussion of Problems and Exercises** section.

1. Illustrate 0.63 using a decimal square.
2. Use a model to illustrate to a child which is larger: 0.3 or 0.03.
3. Show how you could illustrate addition using decimal squares for 0.32 + 0.49.
4. Show how you could illustrate addition using Base Ten Blocks for 0.32 + 0.49.
5. Round 34.4561 to the nearest tenth.
6. Round 34.4561 to the nearest ten.
7. Which is closer to 0.5?   0.46   or   0.53   Why?
8. Find three decimals between: 0.4 and 0.5 _____ _____ _____
9. Which of these numbers is between 0.07 and 0.08 (TIMSS, 1999)?
    a. 0.00075
    b. 0.0075
    c. 0.075
    d. 0.75
10. The mean distance from Venus to the Sun is 1.08×10^8 kilometers. Which of the following quantities is equal to this distance (NAEP, 2005)?
    a. 10,800,000 kilometers
    b. 108,000,000 kilometers
    c. 1,080,000,000 kilometers
    d. 10,800,000,000 kilometers
    e. 108,000,000,000 kilometers

11.   Carol wanted to estimate the distance from *A* to *D* along the path shown on the map. She correctly rounded each of the given distances to the nearest mile and then added them. Which of the following sums could be hers (NAEP, 1992)?

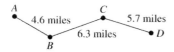

   a.   4 + 6 + 5 = 15
   b.   5 + 6 + 5 = 16
   c.   5 + 6 + 6 = 17
   d.   5 + 7 + 6 = 18

12.   Which number represents the shaded part of the figure (TIMSS, 1995)?
   a. 2.8
   b. 0.5
   c. 0.2
   d. 0.02

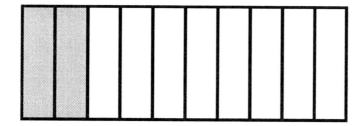

13.   0.4 is the same as
   a. four
   b. four tenths
   c. four hundredths
   d. one-fourth

14.   Which of these means 7/10 (TIMSS, 2003)?
   a. 70
   b. 7
   c. 0.7
   d. 0.07

7.2   Questions for Discussion

1.   What if Marcy was told to align the decimal points? Would she understand what she is doing?
2.   What do you hope children might learn about decimals by using a decimal square?
3.   What do you hope children might learn about decimals by using Base Ten Blocks?
4.   What do you hope children might learn about decimals by using money?
5.   What do you hope children might learn about decimals by using a number line?
6.   In what ways may your understanding of decimals differ from children's understanding?

7.2   Children's Solutions and Discussion of Problems and Exercises

1.   In a fourth and fifth grade split class, 82% (14 out of 17) were able to draw a representation of 0.63 on a decimal square.

5.   In a fourth and fifth grade split class, 60% (9 out of 15) rounded correctly; they wrote their answer as: 34.5000.

7.   In a fourth grade class, 60% (15 out of 25) indicated that 0.53 was closer to 0.5 and 0.46. All the children that had the correct solution changed 0.5 to 0.50!

8.   In the same fourth grade class, 54% (14 out of 26) gave three decimal numbers between 0.4 and 0.5. Some incorrect solutions were: 0.4 1/4, 0.4 2/4, 0.4 3/4 and 4.1, 4.2, 4.3.

9.   In the United States, 70% of eighth graders gave the correct response (TIMSS, 1999).

10.   Only 41% of eighth graders marked the correct response (NAEP, 2005).

11.   25% of fourth graders and 75% of eighth graders successfully answered this question (NAEP, 1992).

12.   Internationally, 33% of third graders and 40% of fourth graders answered correctly (TIMSS, 1995).

13.   Internationally, 21% of third graders and 39% of fourth graders answered correctly (TIMSS, 1995).

14.   In the United States, 61.8% of fourth graders answered this problem correctly.

7.3   Decimal Computation

The standard algorithms for adding, subtracting, multiplying and dividing decimal numbers are similar to the standard algorithms for whole numbers with a few key procedures added. We believe teachers **should be able to explain each of the key procedures for decimal computation**. These procedures include:

1.   Lining up the decimal points when adding or subtracting decimals;

2.   Counting the number of decimal places in the factors to find the number of decimal places in the product when multiplying decimal numbers; and

3.   Moving the decimal point in the dividend and the divisor when dividing using long division.

If mathematics is going to be presented as a sense-making activity, teachers must be able to explain why these procedures work. Consider how you would illustrate or explain these rules to a fifth-grade class.

Lining Up the Decimal Points

Solve 1.45 + 3.624 + 23.9 + 0.473 + 12 without a calculator.

What do you do with the "12" since it has no decimal point?

```
  1.45
  3.624
 23.9
  0.473
+12.____
```

Why do we line up the decimal points? We line up the decimal points because when the numbers are put in columns each column is the same place value, i.e., we are adding tens to tens, ones to ones, tenths to tenths, hundredths to hundredths and so on.

Counting the Number of Decimal Places in the Factors when Multiplying Decimals

Solve 2.4 x 0.68 without a calculator.

```
    2.4
 x 0.68
    192
    144
  1.632
```

Why do we count the number of decimal places in the factors? One explanation that might be presented to children is to change the decimals numbers to fractions.

24/10 x 68/100 = (24 x 68)/ (10 x 100) =1632/1000

When we multiplied the numerators we did exactly the same thing as in the problem by ignoring the decimal points and multiplying the numbers 24 x 68. In addition, 1632/1000 is 1.632. Dividing by 1,000 is the same as moving the decimal point three places to the left or in our case counting the decimal places in the original two numbers.

To fully understand this explanation, children need an understanding of place value and fluency with fractions.

Moving the Decimal Point in the Dividend and the Divisor when Dividing

Solve 4.8 ÷ 1.25 without a calculator and use long division.

```
1.25)‾4.8‾
```

Why do we move the number of decimal places in the divisor to make a whole number and move the decimal point in the dividend the same number of places?

We move the decimal point in this fashion because $4.8 \div 1.25 = 4.8 / 1.25$. To change 1.25 to a whole number one must multiply by 100 which is the same as moving the decimal point two places to the right. It is easier to divide by a whole number than a decimal. In our fraction, 4.8/1.25, if we multiply the denominator times 100 then we must multiply the numerator by 100, which is the same thing as moving the decimal point in the dividend two places to the right. Thus, $4.8 \times 100 / 1.25 \times 100 = 480/125$ or $48 \div 125$.

Why is it important that teachers be able to explain these rules? One reason is some students and children believe that mathematics is "magic". However, mathematics is not "magic;" there is a logical mathematical reason for rules and procedures. Mathematics should be a sense making activity (see section 1.3).

Do you expect that all fifth and sixth grade children will understand these explanations? To reiterate, we believe teachers should understand and be able to demonstrate these explanations to a typical fifth-grade class or higher. Further, we believe that even though some or many will not understand these explanations such explanations are a valuable educational experience.

More on Decimal Computation

Add $1.04 + 3.893 + 26$.

Some textbooks might suggest that we add zeros if we were to put these numbers in columns and perform the standard algorithm.

$$
\begin{array}{r}
1.040 \\
3.893 \\
+ \ 26.000 \\
\end{array}
$$

However, in measurement we talk about **accuracy**. If these were measurements, then writing 26 as 26.000 implies that this measurement is accurate to three decimal places. Some elementary mathematics textbooks, such as the series *Everyday Mathematics*, suggest that decimal computation problems not be written with extra zeros. In the example above, adding zeroes implies that the answer 30.933 is accurate to three decimal places; however the number 26 is only accurate to a whole a number. A more appropriate answer in measurement would be 31. As a future teacher you may decide to use or not to use this procedure; however, as a professional educator you should be able to justify your decision.

Partial Sums of Decimals

Another method to add decimals is the partial sums method.
We can use the previous example of: 1.04 + 3.893 + 26 to illustrate. In the partial sums method, the numbers are put in columns, added from left to right, and finally the partial sums are added.

```
      1.04
      3.893
   + 26.
     20.
     10.
      .8
      .13
      .003
   30.933
```

This is a viable method for decimal computation and may be found either in the elementary textbook you will be using or may be developed by one of your children. Consequently, as a teacher, you may need to understand this method and perhaps even explain it. In Chapter 3, partial sums, partial products, and partial quotients are used to illustrate a method other than standard algorithms to compute with whole numbers. These same methods can be used for decimals computation as well.

7.3   Problems and Exercises

Solve the problems first and then consider some data on how children solved the problems found in the **Children's Solutions and Discussion of Problems and Exercises** section.

1.   Find the missing numbers in the pattern and give the rule.

____ ____ 0.16 ____ 0.22 ____ 0.28 ____

          Rule: _____

2.   When you add, 16.4 + 1.25 + 40.63, why do you line up the decimal points?
3.   Explain mathematically why you count the number of decimal places in the factors of a decimal multiplication problem to find the number of decimal places in the product. Use 2.16 x 1.4 as an example.
4.   Explain mathematically why you move the decimal point in the dividend the same number of places you move it in the divisor of a decimal division problem. Use 37.68 ÷ 1.2 as an example.
5.   Mrs. Jones bought 6 pints of berries. Each pint cost 87¢. Mrs. Jones used her calculator to find the cost of the berries and the display showed 522. What was the cost of the berries (NAEP, 2003)?
      a. $522
      b. $52.20
      c. $5.22
      d. $0.52

6.   The Breakfast Barn bought 135 dozen eggs at $0.89 per dozen. What was the total cost of the eggs (NAEP, 2003)?

7.   George buys two calculators that cost $3.29 each. If there is no tax, how much change will he receive from a $10 bill (NAEP, 1992)?

8.   a.   Arthur priced two skateboards. The Super X cost $49.67, and the Triple Y cost $63.04. How much more expensive is the Triple Y than the Super X?

     b.   One third-grader's solution was 11,271. How did he or she get this answer?

9.   What type of subtraction problem is Problem 8? Can you use the same numbers in #6 and make a **take-way** problem?

10.   Sam can purchase his lunch at a school. Each day he wants to have juice that costs 50¢, a sandwich that costs 90¢, and fruit that costs 35¢. His mother has only $1.00 bills. What is the least number of $1.00 bills that his mother should give him so he will have enough money to buy lunch for 5 days (NAEP, 1996)?

11.   Melissa bought 0.46 of a pound of wheat flour for which she paid $0.83. How many pounds of wheat flour could she buy for one dollar (Post et. al., 1991)? Explain how you solved the problem.

12.   What is the sum of 2.5 and 3.8 (TIMSS, 2003)?

      a. 5.3
      b. 6.3
      c. 6.4
      d. 9.5

13.   Subtract:

$$\begin{array}{r} 4.03 \\ -1.15 \\ \hline \end{array}$$

      a. 5.18
      b. 4.45
      c. 3.12
      d. 2.98
      e. 2.88 (TIMSS, 2003)

14.   Julie put a box on a shelf that is 96.4 centimeters long. The box is 33.2 centimeters long. What is the longest box she could put on the rest of the shelf (TIMSS, 1995)?

      Answer _____

15.   Divide 0.003 $0.003\overline{)15.45}$

      a. 0.515
      b. 5.15
      c. 51.5
      d. 515
      e. 5150 (TIMSS, 1999)

7.3   Questions for Discussion

1.   Why is it important for teachers to understand the whys behind the rules used in decimal computations?

2.   How much of the explanations for decimal computations do you think fifth grade students will understand?

7.3   Children's Solutions and Discussion of Problems and Exercises

2.   The following are some of the reasons given by fourth graders on why the decimal points are lined up when adding: "To separate the wholes from the other parts;" "I do it because the teacher tells us to;" "Because you'll get confused if you don't," and "Because you will get the wrong answer."

5.   70% of fourth graders successfully answered this question on the 2003 NAEP test (NAEP, 2003).

6.   59% of fourth graders successfully answered this question (NAEP, 2003).

7.   Only 21% of fourth graders gave the correct solution to this problem (NAEP, 1992).

8.   a.   This problem was given to 53 third graders; 42% or 22 out of 53 solved the problem correctly.

b.   He added the numbers and did not bring down the decimal point in his solution.

10.   Only 17% of fourth graders had the problems completely correct. Another 20% gave a partially correct solution (NAEP, 1996).

11.   55% of <u>teachers</u> answered this problem incorrectly, and only 10% of those who gave a correct solution could give a reasonable explanation of their solution.

12.   In the United States, 72% of fourth graders gave the correct response (TIMSS, 2003).

13.   In the United States, 72.3% of fourth graders gave the correct response (TIMSS, 2003).

14.   Internationally, only 12% of third graders and 26% of fourth graders answered this problem correctly (TIMSS, 1995).

15.   In the United States, 39% of eighth graders gave the correct response (TIMSS, 1999).

7.4   Ratio and Proportion

Problems: If 4 oranges cost $5.00, how much do 24 oranges cost?
            If 4 apples cost $2.00, how much do 15 apples cost?
How might children solve these problems?

There are many variations as to how children might solve these problems, and educators have given similar methods different names. What follows are examples of a few of the most common methods. These are not all the methods, and children may use variations of these methods. The context, the situation, and the numbers will also influence children's strategies.

Unit or Unit Rate Method

In this method, children find a unit rate and multiply by the total. In the first problem, 1 orange costs $1.25 and then 24 x 1.25 = $30.00. Note that in some problems they might find the unit rate per dollar. In this case such an approach is not as meaningful because it leads one to the conclusion that one can get 0.8 of an orange for $1.00 which does not work well in reality. What store would let someone buy 0.8 of an orange? However, in the context of the apple problem, children might reason 2 apples for $1.00. Notice the propensity for error here, since children must first perform long division and then multiply, especially if whole numbers are not obtained in the process (Lamon, 2002). In real life settings, such as estimating in the grocery store, this may not be a practical method as most cannot do long division mentally.

Scale Factor or Composite Unit Rate

Because there are 6 times as many oranges, the cost will be 6 times as much. 6 x $5.00 = $30.00. This method does not work as well when the composite unit rate is not a whole number. For example, in the apple problem 15 is how many times 4?

Building-Up

This common strategy of children is an <u>additive</u> strategy. They may draw a picture or make a table similar to the following when using this method:

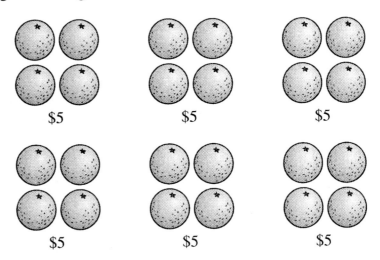

$5 $5 $5

$5 $5 $5

Oranges	Dollars
4	5
8	10
12	15
16	20
20	25
24	30

Cross Multiplication

To cross multiply, a proportion could be set up: 4/5 = 24/x. Then one cross multiplies (4x = 120) divides both sides of the equation by the coefficient of x, (4x/4 = 120/4; x = 30).   At first, children have difficulty with this method, yet it is the preferred method of secondary and college students. Even after children have been taught this method, many sixth and seventh graders still do not use it (Lamon 1993; Kaput, & West, 1994). Why? First, it does not match the building-up method which many children use, and secondly, consider the cross product, 4x = 120; the 120 has no meaning (Smith, 2002). A 120 what? Children typically do not develop cross multiplication on their own either.

Proportional reasoning is immensely important in mathematics. However, being able to solve problems by cross multiplication is not necessarily an indication that children understand proportional reasoning. This method is efficient and children will eventually need to know how to use it, but the underlying concept of proportionality is fundamental in many areas of higher level mathematics. "Understanding ratio and proportion depends on one's ability to view a relationship as a single quantity and then to operate with it" (Lamon, 1994). For example, this type of reasoning is necessary to <u>understand</u> fractions.

The following are some questions to consider as you are solving ratio and proportion problems:

- Is there only one way to solve the problems?
- Must you use a proportion each time or are there other ways?
- Do all the ways make sense to you?
- What is the best way for each problem?

Rate, Ratio and Scale Factor

What is the difference between **ratio** and **rate**? Some elementary mathematics textbooks do not distinguish between rate and ratio, others do. Typically, **rate** refers two different units such as miles per hour. **Ratio** refers to a comparison between numbers or measures with the same units. For example, the ratio the weight of a man on earth to the man on the moon is about 6:1. A 240 pound man would weigh 40 pounds on the moon. On earth or on the moon the unit is pounds, therefore the comparison is a **ratio**.

One way to think of a **scale factor** or scaling is as enlarging or shrinking on a copy machine. A picture enlarged by 200% has a **scale factor** of 2. Finding the **scale factor** is actually the same as finding the composite unit rate. Preschool children have an intuitive understanding of scale (Smith, 2002). For example, many realize that an enlarged picture will have all the parts proportionately enlarged. Note that scale refers to linear measurement and not to area or volume.

Proportional Reasoning

The NCTM Standards (2000) place a heavy emphasis on proportional reasoning in elementary school mathematics. The previous discussion describes how children solve proportional reasoning problems, but proportional reasoning is a process that is applicable to more than just problems labeled as ratio and proportion. In real life problems are not labeled "Ratio and Proportions." Children should have extensive experience with proportional reasoning. These experiences may not always be in the form of ratio and proportion problems but in basic reasoning skills. For example, a child may reason: if 2 x 17 is 34, then 4 x 17 must be 68 because 34 + 34 = 68. How is this an example of proportional reasoning? Notice how this reasoning is similar to the building-up process or applying a scale factor of 2 to the ratio 17:34. Proportional reasoning is an important concept that entails some of the most sophisticated thinking required of children.

7.4 Problems and Exercises

<u>Solve the problems first</u> and then consider some data on how children solved the problems found in the **Children's Solutions and Discussion of Problems and Exercises** section.

1.   The children who visit a booth at the science fair are going to build models of butterflies. For each model, they will need the following:

   4 wings   1 body   2 antennae

   When the model is put together it looks like this:

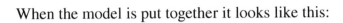

   If there is a supply of 29 wings, 8 bodies, and 13 antennae, how many complete butterfly models can be made?

   Answer: _____

   Use drawings, words, or numbers to explain how you got your answer (NAEP, 1996).

2.   A fourth-grade class needs 5 leaves each day to feed its 2 caterpillars. How many leaves would they need each day for 12 caterpillars?

3.

   Answer: _____

   Use drawings, words, or numbers to explain how you got your answer (NAEP, 1996).

4.   On a certain map, the scale indicates that 5 centimeters represents the actual distance of 9 miles. Suppose the distance between two cities on this map measures 2 centimeters. Explain how you would find the actual distance between the two cities (Weinberg, 2002).

5.   Ellen, Jim, and Steve bought 3 helium filled balloons and paid $2.00 for all three. They decided to go back to the store and get enough balloons for everyone in their class. How much did they have to pay for 24 balloons (Lamon, 1994)? How do you think 24 sixth grade children who have neither had formal instruction in ratio and proportion nor been taught cross multiplication might solve this problem?

6.   If 7 girls must share 3 pizzas and 3 boys must share 1 pizza, who gets more pizza, the girls or the boys (Lamon, 1994)?

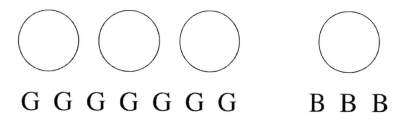

G G G G G G G   B B B

7.   The following 9 problems, a-i, were given to 115 sixth-grade children who had not had formal instruction on ratio and proportion (Kaput & West, 1994). Solve each one and then put them in rank order of difficulty from easiest to most difficult for these sixth graders.

a) A large restaurant sets tables by putting 7 pieces of silverware with 4 pieces of china on each placement. If it used 392 pieces of silverware in its settings last night, how many pieces of china did it use?

b) A car of the future will travel 8 miles in 2 minutes. How far will it travel in 5 minutes?

c) Joan used exactly 15 cans of paint to paint 18 chairs. How many chairs can she paint with 25 cans?

d) The Park committee found that 15 maple trees can shade 21 picnic tables. If they make the park bigger and buy 50 maple trees, how many picnic tables can be shaded in the bigger park?

e) The two sides of figure A are 9 cm high and 15 cm long. Figure B is the same shape but bigger. If one side of Figure B is 24 cm high, how long is the other side?

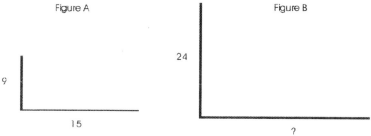

f) Simon worked 3 hours and earned $12. How long does it take him to earn $36?

g) To make Italian dressing, you need 4 parts vinegar to 9 parts oil. How much oil do you need for 828 ounces of vinegar?

h) To make donuts, Jerome needs exactly 8 cups of flour to make 14 donuts. How many donuts can he make with 12 cups of flour?

i) In a certain school, there are 3 boys to every 7 girls in every class. How many girls are there in a class with 9 boys (Kaput & West, 1994)?

7.   A man who weighs 175 pounds on earth would weigh 28 pounds on the moon. How much would his 50 pound dog weigh on the moon?

8.   At Boston Elementary School, the ratio of girls to boys is 5:3. If there are 400 students at this school, how many boy and girl students are there?

9.   A teacher marks 10 of her pupils' tests every half hour. It takes her one and one-half hours to mark all her pupils' tests. How many pupils are in her class (TIMSS, 1995)?

10.   For every soft drink bottle that Fred collected, Maria collected 3. Fred collected a total of 9 soft drink bottles. How many did Maria collect (TIMSS, 2003)?
a. 3
b. 12
c. 13
d. 27

7.4   Questions for Discussion

1. What is the difference between rate, ratio, and scale factor? What if the elementary mathematics textbook you are using does not make a distinction?
2. Give an example and describe how proportional reasoning is more than just solving word problems using proportions.
3. What difficulties, if any, did you encounter in solving the problems in 7.4? What difficulties would you expect children to face?

7.4   Children's Solutions and Discussion of Problems and Exercises

1.   This was a challenging problem for fourth grade children as only 3% gave a correct response with a complete explanation. Another 30% gave a correct response with no explanation or a partial explanation (NAEP, 1996).

2.   For the caterpillar and leaves problems, only 6% gave a correct solution and a complete explanation while 7% gave a correct answer with a partial or no explanation. In a separate study (Kenney, Lindquist, & Heffernan, 2002) of 172 students with similar results, the most common incorrect solutions were: 60 and 19 leaves. How do you think children arrived at these solutions?
What do these results tell you about children's skills at explaining their solutions in writing?
Some selected two numbers from the problem and multiplied 5 x 12 = 60; others added all the numbers given in the problem: 5 + 2 + 12 = 19.

3.   The map problem was given to 387 middle school children in sixth, seventh, and eighth grade. Out of all 387 children, only 23% (90) correctly answered this problem, and only 39 of these children provided a complete explanation. The majority of children with incorrect answers gave no explanation! 43 of the 90 correct used the unit rate, (1 mile is equivalent to 1.8 centimeters). 27 of the 90 used cross multiplication while 20 of the 90 used various other methods (Weinberg, 2002).

4. For the balloon problem, the 24 children used the following methods:
    - 10 multiplied by the **scale factor** of 8
    - 2 used the building-up process
    - 3 used the unit rate
    - 1 used another method
    - 8 had an incorrect solution (Lamon, 1994)
5. Children do not always solve problems in the ways that have been described. The context of the problem often influences children's solution methods. 18 of the 24 children used an unexpected solution strategy. Their solution method was:

3 boys must share 1 pizza,
then if you do the same for the girls,
the first 3 girls would share 1 pizza,
the next 3 girls would share 1 pizza,
and the last girl would be left with a whole pizza,
so the other girls could "go over to that one to get some more."
The girls would have more than the boys (Lamon, p.109, 1994).

6. One study found that the order for the easiest to the most difficult for these 9 problems are:
    f, b, i, a, d, h, c, g, e (Kaput & West, 1994).
    Why do you think this was so?
7. In a sixth grade class, only 1 child out of 17 had the correct solution, and she found a unit rate.
8. In a sixth grade class, only 4 out of 14 were able to determine the correct solution.
9. Internationally, 30% of third graders and 46% of fourth graders indicated the correct number of pupils (TIMSS, 1995).
10. In the United States, 54.8% of fourth graders gave the correct response (TIMSS, 2003).

7.5   Percents

What is percent? The word percent is derived from the Latin phrase 'per centum' meaning "for each 100." Many of the same <u>activities</u>, <u>models</u>, and <u>approaches</u> used with decimals can be used with percents.

Children's Knowledge of Percents

A survey of one fourth grade class indicated that they encountered percents everyday in: school marks, sales at stores, and in taxes on restaurant bills (Moss, 2002). These same children understood that 100% meant "everything," 99% meant "almost everything," 50 % meant "exactly half," and 1% meant "almost nothing" (Moss, 2002).

A pervasive activity in elementary school mathematics texts is to give a number in one of the forms: **fraction, percent, or decimal and then have children convert the number to the other two forms**.

A better problem might be to add: 1/8 + 0.25 + 35%. Children's choice of form will provide an indication as to which form they know the best or feel most comfortable using.

The decimal squares described in section 7.2 are models that can be used for percents. For example, the decimal square used to represent 0.23 can also be used to represent 23% as well as the fraction 23/100.

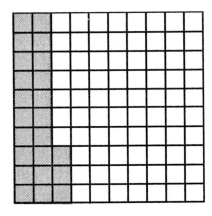

One could convert 0.23 to 23%, showing how the above representation works for both or one could refer back to the definition of percent to show that 23 parts out of 100 are shaded.

Mental Computation with Percents

Consider how a child might find 75% of 60. He or she may first find 50% of 60 which many can do mentally (50 % of 60 is 30.). Next he or she could apply a halving strategy and take half of 50% which is 25% and half of 30 which is 15 (therefore 25% of 60 is 15). Finally, he or she could add the two percentages 50% + 25% which is 75%, so 30 + 15 is 45; therefore, 75% of 60 is 45.

A survey of children who had no formal training with percents indicated that they were able to invent strategies like the one above and that they were more successful on percent tasks than older students with formal training (Lembke & Reys, 1994). Children have intuitive understandings of percents and operations on percents prior to formal instruction. Percents are typically introduced after children have had instruction on decimals and fraction in the sixth grade or beyond, yet they still have a great deal of difficulty with percents (Parker & Leinhardt, 1995). Formal instruction on percents is not always based on children's intuitive knowledge of percents or how they think about percents!

More and more textbooks are presenting percents in the upper elementary grades. At the introductory stage, the goal should be to help children develop a conceptual understanding of percents. In addition, people compute mentally with percents almost daily, and it is significant to show **how people use percents mentally in real life**. Benchmarks such as 50%, 200%, and 10% are commonly used in mental calculations of percents. For example, 50% is considered a **benchmark** because children can easily compute 50% of most numbers by dividing by 2. Benchmarks are essential for working with percents mentally!

7.5   Problems and Exercises

Solve the problems first and then consider some data on how children solved the problems found in the **Children's Solutions and Discussion of Problems and Exercises** section.

1.   Find 65% of 160 as the child did in the example. (Hint you may have to subtract 10 %.)
2.   Is 40% of 50 the same as 50% of 40? Why or why not?
3.   The boss at a local factory discovered that 40% of all sick days are taken on Mondays and Fridays. What would you tell this boss?
4.   I have $60.00. I spent 40% of my money on a new CD. How much was the CD?
5.   There were 90 employees in a company last year. This year the number of employees increased by 10 percent. How many employees are in the company this year (NAEP, 2005)?
     a. 9
     b. 81
     c. 91
     d. 99
     e. 100
6.   Ms. Thierry and 3 friends ate dinner at a restaurant. The bill was $67. In addition they left a $13 tip. Approximatcly what percent of the total bill did the leave as a tip (NAEP, 2005)?
     a. 10%
     b. 13%
     c. 15%
     d. 20%
     e. 25%
7.   A shop increased its prices by 20%. What is the new price of an item which previously sold for 800 zcds (TIMSS, 2003)?
     a. 640 zeds
     b. 900 zeds
     c. 960 zeds
     d. 1,000 zeds
8.   At a play 3/25 of the people in the audience were children. What percent of the audience was this (TIMSS, 2003)?
     a. 12%
     b. 3%
     c. 0.3%
     d. 0.12%

9.   What percent of each figure is shaded?

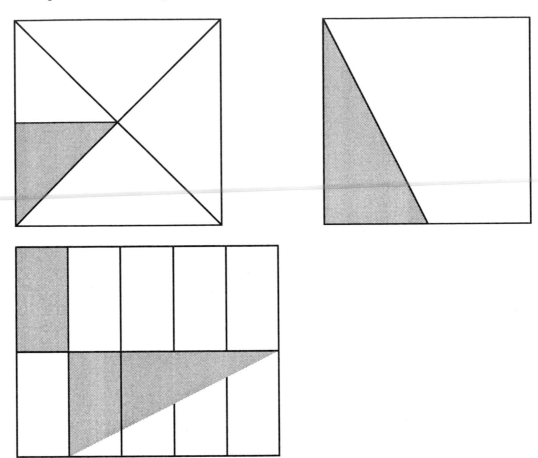

7.5   Questions for Discussion

1.   Where in everyday life do people encounter and use percents?
2.   What do you think children intuitively understand about percents?
3.   What strategies did you use to solve the problems in 7.5? In what ways are the strategies you used similar or different from the strategies children might use? Explain your answer.

7.5   Children's Solutions and Discussion of Problems and Exercises

4.   When this problem was given to a fifth grade class and sixth grade class, no one had the correct solution. No one even set the problem up correctly: 60.00 x 0.40.
5.   Only 37% of eighth graders gave the correct response (NAEP, 2005).
6.   Only 30% of eighth graders correctly figured the percent of tip (NAEP, 2005).
7.   In the United States, 57% of eighth graders solved the problem correctly (TIMSS, 2003).
8.   In the United States, 70.5% of all eighth graders had a correct solution (66.6% of the girls and 74.9% of the boys) (TIMSS, 2003).

7.6   Rational, Irrational, and Real Numbers

Realistically, about the only irrational number that children in grades K-5 will encounter is π. They will use π in the calculation of the circumference and area of circles. However, irrational and real numbers are essential to the development of later mathematics that children will eventually study.

Earlier chapters attempted to illustrate that the numbers that we use arose out of need. The ancient Greeks, as well as other cultures, encountered a dilemma when they constructed a 1 by 1 square and tried to calculate the diagonal of the square exactly. Likewise, they encountered a dilemma when they tried to calculate the ratio of the circumference of a circle divided by its diameter, which we know is π. For centuries, mathematicians all over the world tried to develop an exact rational number for π: 22/7, 25/8, 223/71, 355/113, 3927/1250, etc., but none worked exactly. Since these numbers were needed and used in many calculations, and they were not Rational Numbers, a new set of numbers, Irrational Numbers, was developed.

Section 7.6 does not have a Problems and Exercises section because children are very unlikely to be studying problems with real numbers, aside from π and a perchance mention of square roots.

7.6   Questions for Discussion

1.   In fifth grade, children will likely use π. How would you explain to children how π is different from the other numbers they have studied?
2.   Is π really different from other numbers from a child's perspective?
3.   How are real numbers important in the later study of mathematics?

Chapter 7: References

Carpenter, T., Fennema, E., & Romberg, T. (1993). *Rational numbers: An integration of research.* Hillsdale, NJ: Lawrence Erlbaum Associates.

Hiebert, J; Wearne, D; & Taber, S. (1991). Fourth Graders gradual construction of decimal fractions during instruction using different physical representations. *Elementary School Journal*, 91, 321-41.

Kaput, J. & West, M. (1994). Missing-value proportional reasoning problems: Factors affecting informal reasoning patterns. In G. Harel & J. Confrey (Eds.) *The development of multiplicative reasoning in the learning of mathematics.* 235-287. Albany, NY: State University of New York Press.

Kenney, P.A., Lindquist, M., & Heffernan, C. L. (2002). Butterflies and caterpillars: Multiplicative and proportional reasoning. In B. Litwiller & G. Bright (Eds.) *NCTM 2002 Yearbook: Making sense of fractions, ratios, and proportions.* 87-99. Reston, VA: NCTM.

Kouba, V., Zawojewski, J. S., & Strutchens, M. E. (1997). What do students know about numbers and operations? In P. Kenney & E. Silver (Eds.) *Results form the sixth mathematics assessment of the national assessment of educational progress.* 87-140. Reston, VA: NCTM.

Lamon, S. J. (1993). Ratio and proportion: Children's cognitive and metacognitive processes. In T. Carpenter, E. Fennema, & T. Romberg (Eds.) *Rational numbers: An integration of research*. 131-156. Hillsdale, NJ: Lawrence Erlbaum Associates.

Lamon, S. J., (1994). Ratio and proportion: Cognitive foundations in unitizing and norming. In G. Harel & J. Confrey (Eds.) *The development of multiplicative reasoning in the learning of mathematics*. 89-120. Albany, NY: State University of New York Press.

Lamon, S. J., (2002). Part-whole comparisons with unitizing. In B. Litwiller & G. Bright (Eds.) NCTM *2002 Yearbook: Making sense of fractions, ratios, and proportions*. 79-86. Reston, VA: NCTM.

Lembke, L. & Reys, B. (1994). The development of, and interaction between, intuitive and school-taught ideas about percent. *Journal for Research in Mathematics Education, 25,* 237-59.

Lesh, R., Post, T. R., & Behr, M. (1988). Proportional reasoning In J. Hiebert & M Behr (Eds.), Number concepts and operations in the middle grades. 93-118. Reston, VA: NCTM.

Marintee, & Bay-Williams, (2003, January). Investigating students' conceptual understandings of decimal fractions using multiple representations. *Teaching Mathematics in the Middle School, 8,* (5) 244-247.

Moss, J. (2002). Percents and proportion at the center: Altering the teaching sequence for rational number. In B. Litwiller & G. Bright (Eds.) NCTM *2002 Yearbook: Making sense of fractions, ratios, and proportions*. 109-120. Reston, VA: NCTM.

Parker, M. & Leinhardt, G. (1995). Percent a privileged proportion, *Review of Educational Research, 65 (4).* 421-81.

Post, T. R., Harel, G., Behr, M., & Lesh, R. (1991). Intermediate teachers' knowledge of rational number concepts. IN E. Fennema, T.P. Carpenter, & S. J. Lamon (Eds.) *Integrating research on teaching and learning mathematics*. 177-198. Ithaca, NY: SUNY Press.

Smith, J. P. (2002). The development of students' knowledge of fractions and ratios. In B. Litwiller & G. Bright (Eds.) NCTM *2002 Yearbook: Making sense of fractions, ratios, and proportions*. 3-17. Reston, VA: NCTM.

Tall, D. O. (2004). Three Worlds of Mathematics and the Role of Language. In D. O. Tall *Mathematical Growth: from Child to Mathematician* (in preparation; see the Academic link Draft for Mathematical Growth at http://www.davidtall.com/).

Thompson, P. W., & Altamaha, L.A. (2003). Fractions and Multiplicative Reasoning. In J. Kilpatrick, G. Martin, & D. Schifter (Eds.), *A research companion to the principles and standards for school mathematics*. 95-113. Reston, VA: NCTM.

Wearne, D. & Hiebert, J., (1994, January). Place value and addition and subtraction. *Arithmetic Teacher,* 272-274.

Weinberg, S. L. (2002). Proportional reasoning: One problem, many solutions! In B. Litwiller & G. Bright (Eds.) *NCTM 2002 Yearbook: Making sense of fractions, ratios, and proportions*. 138-144. Reston, VA: NCTM.

Chapter 8: Geometry

More so than many of the other chapters, this chapter will focus on <u>how</u> children learn geometry in addition to describing their geometrical thinking. Simply stated, children learn geometric concepts through repeated manipulation and motor actions on objects (this includes drawing), and their internal reflection upon these actions and ideas (Piaget & Inhelder, 1967). To elaborate, children learn through their active manipulation of objects and things around them and their reflection upon these actions (Clements, 2003). Children need to *build, tear down, manipulate, draw and <u>reflect</u>* upon their physical activity! Children need to interact with shapes extensively in order to understand them. Pictures are useful in teaching geometry to children. However, manipulatives or children manipulating objects are always superior to just seeing pictures. For the most part, children cannot act on or manipulate pictures! Activities such as making shapes with their bodies or making shapes with toothpicks and marshmallows are invaluable in helping children develop rich understandings of geometry. Children's work in computer environments, where they have to draw pictures, may also serve as an interactive tool similar to working with manipulatives!

A key factor that influences children's learning of geometry is mental imagery (Wheatley, 1994). In order to understand and do geometry, children must create mental images. At the most basic level, they must have a mental image of a rectangle to determine if a given shape is a rectangle. As they get older, they may have to mentally double the length and the width of a rectangle to determine its effect on the area. Imagery plays a vital role in children's construction of geometric ideas.

8.1 Basic Geometric Concepts

<u>Geometry in Elementary School</u>

What geometric concepts are typically taught in elementary school? More specifically:

K-1 _____

2-3_____

4-5_____

Every elementary school's series of textbooks varies somewhat, but typically anywhere from 10-20% of each grade level's book is devoted to geometry while another 10-15% is devoted to measurement. Traditionally, elementary school geometry instruction has been little more than recognizing and naming shapes and figures (Clements, 2003). In contrast, geometry in the elementary school could and should also focus on the development of children's spatial abilities, the characteristics and relationships of two and three dimensional shapes, and mathematical justification.

This supplement is focused on how children think about mathematics; however, this next math joke also illustrates how children think in general.

What did the acorn say when he grew up?

When the answer was told to a fourth-grade child, he responded with "Spell it". The teacher answered, G, E, ..., and he said, "No spell **IT**." While this example may not be mathematically rich, it does give a sense of how children think! The answer backward is: yrtemoeg

Concept Image

One way both children and adults make sense of shapes is that they form a concept image of a shape. A concept image of a shape is ones' conglomeration of all mental pictures of the shape (Vinner & Hershkowitz, 1980). This collection of mental images does not take into consideration the definition of a particular shape, but rather is a generalized image. Once children and adults develop concept images they can have difficulty changing them (Burger & Shaughnessy, 1986; Fuys, Geddes, & Tischler, 1988; Vinner & Hershkowitz, 1980). In the formal world of geometry with definitions and properties, a child's concept images may be in conflict with a formal approach to geometry. For example, if children experience rectangles as quadrilaterals with 4 right angles of which two sides are always longer and two sides are shorter, they may have difficulty conceptualizing that a square is a rectangle. A square may not fit their concept image of a rectangle! With concept images, children may not be focused on the properties of the rectangle, but rather on their collection of mental images. However, concept images are powerful mental models that young children are encouraged to construct. Concept images allow children to differentiate between shapes such as a square and a triangle. Young children can make sense of new concepts by building on what they already understand. A concept image allows children, especially young children, to know what things are without knowing the definition or properties. The notion of concept images also illustrates that our formal community view of mathematics does not exactly fit how children and some adults make sense of the world.

Children learn geometric concepts by looking at both examples and non-examples. These non-examples are sometimes significant in helping children develop viable concept images of difficult concepts (Fuys & Liebov, 1993). On another note, some cultures have different spatial understandings. For example, some African and Polynesian cultures have a different understanding of rectangles than ours (Geddes & Fortunato, 1993). Spatial visualization skills are learned and dependent upon our experiences.

van Hiele Levels

The van Hiele levels are descriptions of learners' development of geometric thinking. Their five levels include: 1) visual, 2) descriptive/analytical, 3) abstract/relational, 4) formal deduction, and 5) rigor. In simpler terms: level 1 refers to seeing, level 2 refers to describing, level 3 refers to using the properties to define the objects, level 4 refers to relating the properties of one kind of object to another, and level 5 refers to the ability to construct formal proofs. For example, a child functioning at level 1 can distinguish between a circle and a square; a child function at level 2 can describe a square as having 4 corners; a child functioning at level 3 can define a square as, "a quadrilateral with 4 right angles and 4 'equal' sides." Children functioning at the Visual Level can recognize shapes, but they do not think about the attributes or the properties of a shape. For instance, for these children a figure is a rectangle because "it looks like a door" (Clements, 2003). A child functioning at the descriptive/analytical level (level 2) can recognize and characterize shapes by their properties. However, children functioning at level 2 have difficulty seeing relationships between shapes. For these children, the statement that, "a square is a rectangle," is confusing. In contrast, a child functioning at the abstract/relational level (level 3) understands why a square is a rectangle. Many high school students are unable to function at the fourth level of formal deduction in the construction of formal proofs. Traditionally, elementary school geometry has only focused on the van Hiele's first two levels.

Contrary to the way the van Hiele levels are typically presented, **they were not meant to categorize learners or describe the ordered development of geometric thinking.** These levels were designed to describe thinking at a particular time in a child's life (Mason & Johnston-Wilder, 2004). A child is said to be **functioning** at a level, not <u>at</u> a level. Also, a child's thinking about a geometric shape may be at one level when focusing on one aspect and at another level on another aspect. For example, when considering triangles, an older child may be able to reason abstractly (level 3) about congruence but only visually (level 1) about similarity.

Points, Lines, and Planes

Your college mathematics textbook probably indicates that **points, lines**, and **planes** are undefined terms. Your book may go on to elaborate as to why these terms are undefined and discuss non-Euclidean geometries. **However, in most children's world, these terms are defined!** Children will point to a dot, '.', and indicate that it is a point. They know what is and is not a line. Point, line, and plane are also defined in most elementary mathematics textbooks. Distinctions that are made in higher level mathematics are not always relevant to children's thinking.

Congruence

In geometry, there is a need to distinguish between the concept of congruence and the equality. You may understand this distinction more fully by considering the following two line segments. How are they similar and how are they different?

The two line segments have the same measure, but one is vertical and one is horizontal. In geometry we often need a way to distinguish between equal measures and orientations. If we said they were equal, it would not quite be true, since the lines are not exactly the same. Hence, we introduce the concept of congruence.

What does it mean to a child to say that two shapes are congruent? Many times congruence is explained to children as: If you can take one shape cut it out and put it exactly on top of the other, then the two shapes are congruent. Another way to explain congruence is to imagine that we copy the shape with a copy machine and then place the copy on top of the original. The shapes should line up exactly if they are congruent because congruent shapes have all the same sides and angles. However, initially, children may not notice that both the angles and the lengths of the sides stay the same.

Parallel and Perpendicular Lines

Parallel lines are defined differently in children's textbooks than in the typical college textbook. Typically in your college textbook, parallel lines are defined as two lines in a plane that do not intersect. For children, parallel lines are defined as: Lines that never meet and are everywhere the same distance apart (Bell et. al., 2002). Children are likely to focus on the aspect that parallel lines stay the same distance apart, are equidistant, yet the formal definition does not include any mention of equidistant. These understandings of the definition of parallel lines can lead to some misconceptions. For example, some eighth grade students still believe that curved lines might be parallel (Mansfield & Happs, 1992).

Another misconception that children have is that perpendicular lines must be horizontal and vertical (Mitchelmore, 1992). For these children, the following two intersecting lines are not perpendicular. We could say that these lines do not fit their *concept image* of perpendicular.

8.1   Problems and Exercises

Solve the problems first and then consider some data on how children solved the problems found in the **Children's Solutions and Discussion of Problems and Exercises** section.

1.   Are the following two angles equal or congruent? Explain.

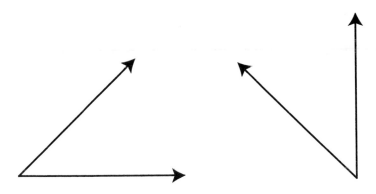

2.   Circle the sets of parallel lines. Explain your answer.

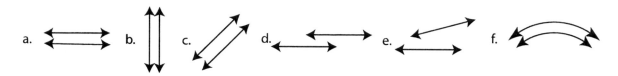

3.   Circle the sets of perpendicular lines. Explain your answer.

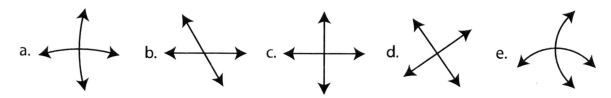

4.   From a child's point of view:
        a.   What is a point?
        b.   What is a line?
        c.   What is a plane?
5.   If I cut a pizza by making 6 different cuts through the center and each cut is a diameter, how many pieces of pizza will I get?
6.   What does it mean to say that two shapes are congruent?
7.   According to the map in the figure that follows, which streets appear to be parallel to each other (NAEP, 1990)?

        a. Park and Main   b. Tyler and Maple
        c. Park and Tyler   d. Main and Tyler

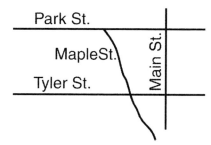

8.   Which letter has two parallel lines [line segments] (NAEP, 1992)?

9.   Which of the following figures contains line segments that are perpendicular (NAEP, 1990)?

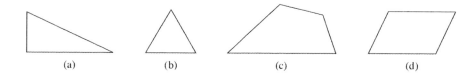

10. A sheet of paper is folded once and a piece is cut out as shown. Which of the following looks like the unfolded paper (NAEP, 1992)?

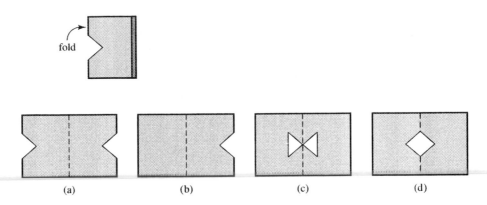

(a)   (b)   (c)   (d)

11. In the picture there are a number of geometric shapes, like circles, squares, rectangles, and triangles. For example, the sun looks like a circle.

Draw lines to three other different objects in the picture and write what shapes they look like (TIMSS, 2003).

8.1   Questions for Discussion

1.   What geometry do you remember learning in elementary school?
2.   If point, line, and plane are undefined in geometry, how can they be the basic building blocks for all of geometry?
3.   How might you involve children in learning geometric concepts, where they actively manipulate objects?
4.   How do you use mental imagery in geometry?
5.   Where do you use mental imagery in real life?

8.1   Children's Solutions and Discussion of Problems and Exercises

1.   Many children misunderstand the question and responded that the angles were either were "equal" or "congruent". They did not make a distinction between "equal" and "congruent!"
2.   This question was given to a class of 26 fourth graders. Their responses for which sets of lines are parallel were:
   a-26   b-25   c-24   d-2   e-0   f-6
   Most of these children did not believe that the lines in d. were parallel because they were not lined up! We might say the lines did not fit their **concept image** of parallel. When asked to give their definition of parallel, the most common response was: "The lines go the same way without going into each other." A few children, 6, indicated in f. that curved lines were parallel.
3.   This question was given to the same fourth grade class, and their responses to which lines are perpendicular were:
   a-1   b-4   c-26   d-23   e-1
   Two explanations given were: "The lines cross evenly." "The lines are straight and connect in the middle."
6.   In a third grade class, 58% (11 out of 19) could give satisfactory written explanations of what congruent meant. Most correct responses were similar to the following response, "They are the same size and the same shape."
7.   44% of fourth graders gave the correct answer c. on the 1990 NAEP test.
8.   Only 27% of fourth graders gave the correct answer d. on the 1992 NAEP test.
9.   This problem was given to eighth graders and only 20% gave the correct answer a. (NAEP, 1990).
10.   65% of fourth graders gave the correct response d. as compared to 87% of eighth graders (NAEP, 1992).
11.   In the United States, 72.9% of girls and 66.1% of boys in fourth grade correctly identified three shapes. Internationally, the average was 58.6% (TIMSS, 2003).

8.2   Basic Shapes

Shapes

In early childhood, children learn to name and recognize basic shapes. In a study of the shape recognition abilities of 5 year olds, 85% could name a circle, 78% a square, 80% a triangle, and 40% a rectangle (Klein, Starkey, & Wakeley, 1999).

One common type of problem given to children to help them problem solve with shapes is to ask them how many squares, (rectangles, triangles, etc.,) are in a given shape. Chapter 1, Section 1.1, Problem Set A, problem #8 is one example of this type of problem.

Convex

Why study the concept of convex? The concept of convex is typically not directly taught in elementary schools. Consider the typical shapes that elementary-school children study: square, rectangle, triangle, rhombus, pentagon, etc. One characteristic that many of these shapes have in common is that they are all convex. So even though you may not teach this concept explicitly to children, they may have an intuitive sense or a 'concept image' of convex.

One fifth grade series defines convex as: "a polygon in which all the sides are pushed outward" (Everyday Mathematics, *Student Reference Book*, 2002). How does this definition differ from the one given in your college textbook? Which is easier to understand? Which is not as precise? Remember, in formal geometry precision matters.

Shapes, Interior, and Exterior

It is sometimes helpful to think of or define a "simple closed figure" as a figure that divides a plane into three sections: the interior, the shape itself, and the exterior.

If a kindergarten teacher points to the center of a square on the board and asks her class what she is pointing to, she would hope that they would say a square. However, from a formal geometry perspective, she is not pointing at a square but at the interior region of the square. This is a technical point and not one that you would emphasize with kindergarten children. Most teachers would be happy if children at this age could recognize shapes such as squares, triangles, rectangles, and circles. However, in the upper elementary grades a distinction is made between the interior, the shape itself, and the exterior.

It is important to constantly consider how the formal geometry you are learning relates and does not relate to children. In addition, consider that these formal ideas of geometry will eventually be introduced to children, and this more formal approach may create misconceptions. Children may have difficulty making sense of new ideas at that time in their learning. It is important to remember that constructing an understanding of geometric concepts is a process.

Triangle

The following first grade child's description of triangle is unique and not typical. This example is taken from, *Logo and Geometry, NCTM Monograph #10.*

Interviewer: Pretend you are talking on the telephone to someone who has never seen a triangle. What would you tell that person to help them make a triangle?

Andrew: I'd ask, "Have you ever seen a diamond?"

Interviewer: Let's say that they said, "Yes."...

Andrew: They have never seen a triangle. Well, cut it off in the middle. Fold it in the middle, on the top of the other half, then tape it down, and you have a triangle. Then hang it on the wall so you'll know what a triangle is!

Notice how the child in his explanation mentally visualized and manipulated shapes. This child demonstrates a powerful use of mental imagery! He also displays the ability to reason mathematically and think about shapes beyond just naming and recognizing them.

Rectangle

In the early elementary grades a rectangle is often defined as a four sided figure with four right angles (corners), and, whether explicitly stated or implied, with two longer sides and two shorter sides. However, in fifth and perhaps fourth grade elementary textbooks, the definition of a rectangle is given as a quadrilateral with four right angles. Consequently, every square is a rectangle. As a future teacher, you should be aware of this definition and realize the difficulty it may cause fifth graders, and in all likelihood, many of your classmates in this course.

Parallelogram

Many children refer to a parallelogram as a slanted rectangle. They also have difficulty remembering the name of this shape. What would you do as the teacher if a first-grade child referred to a parallelogram as a slanted rectangle? What would you do if a fifth-grade child did the same?

Invariance of Shape

In the early elementary grades (K-2), children are taught to name (recognize) shapes and some basic properties of shapes. Almost every elementary school textbook defines a square as a quadrilateral with four right angles and four congruent sides. If the shape is held parallel to the floor, ☐, children and prospective elementary teachers refer to the shape as a square. However, if the same shape is rotated 45 degrees, ◇, prospective elementary teachers refer to it as a rhombus because it fits the definition in the textbook. Children invariably refer to the shape as a diamond. For young children the two shapes are not the same (Lehrer et al., 1998). For adults and older students, the second shape is both a rhombus and a rotated square. This is an example of the <u>concept</u> of "invariance of shape." Shapes and their properties do not change when the shape moves. Young children see these as two different shapes and do not always see the relationship between the figures.

Further, invariance of shape is a concept, and a concept cannot be taught directly to children. One might erroneously believe that you could simply tell a child that they are in essence the same shape, but such a statement will not make sense to a child until the child is ready. Children learn concepts, like "invariance of shape," through continued sensory-motor activity with manipulatives such as tangrams, pentominoes, pattern blocks, and attribute blocks AND through reflection upon these activities.

An important connection teachers can make at this level is to help children mentally visualize and manipulate shapes. This ability is valuable in geometry and calculus. If students can learn to rotate and mentally manipulate shapes, such as squares, then they will be better prepared to visualize and solve calculus tasks such as finding the surface area of a three-dimensional donut cut in half. The ability to mentally visualize and manipulate shapes, spatial visualization, is a valuable skill that will be especially useful to children in middle and high school.

Computer Tools

There are several computer tools which are considered dynamic computer environments used to help children learn geometric concepts. They are different from drill programs that allow children to create and manipulate figures on the computer screen. They may be stand-alone applets readily available on the Web or interactive software such as Geometer's Sketchpad and Logo. Geometer's Sketchpad is more common in middle and high school and has been shown to help children to understand the concepts of proof and constructions.

Extensive research has been done on children's learning using Logo. Logo is a computer programming language that was developed at MIT in the 1960's. Logo entails moving a turtle (triangle) around the computer screen to create designs. It was designed to introduce children to computers and computer programming. Those who advocate the use of Logo believe that children who use Logo will gain a better understanding of geometry, increase their spatial abilities, and develop logical thinking (Clements et al., 2001). By writing a program to draw a shape, children make explicit their intuitive notions of the shape. Once written and viewed, such a program enables children to reflect upon their thinking (Papert, 1980). Children learn geometry through active manipulation of their environment, i.e., working with actual shapes and solids. Logo also provides a means for children to be actively involved in a computer environment.

Research has shown that in order for children to make gains in their geometric understanding, their work with the computer must be connected with the geometric ideas (Clements et. al, 2001). Children working on Logo where an attempt has not been made to connect their programming to their learning of mathematics have not improved their mathematical understanding. Activities with interactive software should be well planned and sequenced. The activities should also encourage children to predict and reflect and offer ample opportunities for child/teacher and child/child interaction. Specifically, work with Logo has been shown to help children in their development of the concept of angle, angle measure, length concepts, symmetry, conceptualization of the properties of geometric shapes, measurement, number concepts, and motion geometry with proper instruction (Clements, 2003; Clements, Sarama, & Battista, 1998). The key to using Logo successfully is to encourage connections with geometric ideas!

In addition, work with Logo encourages children to be more analytical rather than visual in their thinking (Clements and Battista, 1992a). Finally, work in computer environments is intrinsically motivating for students; it often provides them with non-threatening feedback and can encourage them to reflect on their geometric thinking (Clements, Battista, & Sarama, 2001). Note how Logo is an improvement over just showing children pictures. With Logo, children are able to symbolically manipulate shapes and pictures, which they cannot do by just looking at pictures. There are many different commercial versions of Logo available such as Geo-Logo. However, a free version, MSW Logo, is available at: www.softronix.com.

8.2   Problems and Exercises

Solve the problems first and then consider some data on how children solved the problems found in the **Children's Solutions and Discussion of Problems and Exercises** section.

1.   Other than the standard name, what other name might children give to each shape?

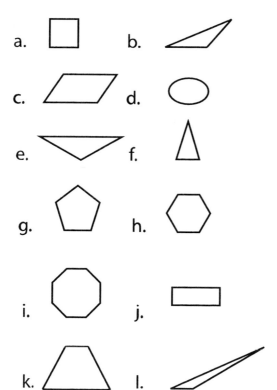

2.   Which of the following shapes are triangles? Why?

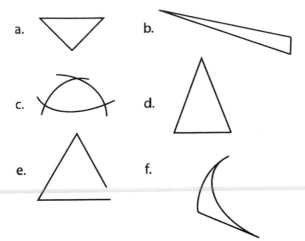

a.   b.

c.   d.

e.   f.

3.   Put these six shapes together to make a hexagon.

4.   A convex polygon has "all sides pushed outward" (*Everyday Math*). Which shapes are not convex? Why?

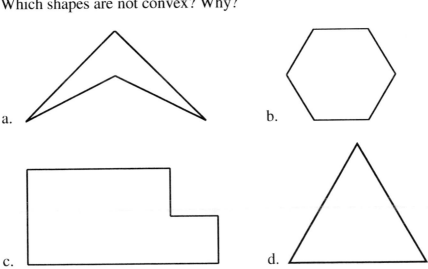

a.   b.

c.   d.

5.   Is a circle convex? If a shape did not have to be a polygon to be convex, would a circle now be convex?

   b. Is a crescent moon a convex shape?

6.   How many squares are in this shape?

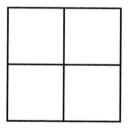

7.   Why do some children call this shape an "upside down triangle?"

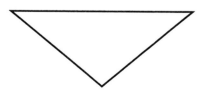

8.   Define a kite.

9.   Alan says that if a figure has four sides, it must be a rectangle. Gina does not agree. Which of the following figures shows that Gina is correct (NAEP, 2003)?

   a.   b.   c.   d.

10. In the space below, draw a rectangle 2 inches wide and 3½ inches long (NAEP, 1992).

11. A triangle that has sides with lengths 6, 6, and 10 is called

    a. acute   b. right   c. scalene   d. isosceles   e. equilateral (NAEP, 2003)

12. Draw 2 straight lines on this rectangle to divide it into 1 rectangle and 2 triangles (TIMSS, 2003).

13. Draw a triangle in the grid so the line AB is the base of the triangle and the two new sides are the same length as each other (TIMSS, 2003).

8.2   Questions for Discussion

1.   What "concept image" do many young children have of a <u>rectangle</u>?
2.   As a fifth-grade teacher, what might you do to help children change their concept image of a rectangle?
3.   At what van Hiele level would a child be working if he thinks of the definition of a rectangle as: A quadrilateral with 4 right angles?
4.   How would you help children develop the concept of <u>invariance of shape</u>?
5.   What geometric concepts do you think children learn by using computer construction tools such as Logo?
6.   How would you attempt to connect geometry concepts on triangles with children working with interactive software involving triangles?
7.   How might Logo and Geometer's Sketchpad encourage analytical thinking?
8.   Why does precision matter in formal geometry and how might the *Everyday Mathematics* definition of 'convex' lead to misunderstandings?

8.2   Children's Solutions and Discussion of Problems and Exercises

1.   Some responses given by children of various ages:
    a. box
    b. see-saw
    c. slanted square
    d. egg
    e. upside down triangle
    f. ice cream
    k. triangle with the top cut off

2.   A four and one-half year old said that b. was a shooting star and c. was an oval. Second graders gave the following explanations for why certain shapes are triangles: "They have 3 sides and 3 corners," "They have 3 pointy sides," and "It looks like the top of a house."
    Following are the number of children in a fourth and fifth grade split class of 17 who indicated each shape was a triangle:
    a. 17
    b. 11
    c. 0
    d. 17
    e. 8
    f. 2

6.   Some children *only* see 4 squares. One fourth grade student said, "I see 10 squares because if you take the lines away …."Can you explain his thinking?

    This problem was given to third graders and 14 out of 37 indicated that there were 5 squares in the figure.

9.   69% of fourth graders gave the correct answer d. as compared to 85% of eighth graders on the 2003 NAEP test.

10.   Only 18% of fourth graders gave a correct response as compared to 58% of eighth graders (NAEP, 1992). Below are some fourth grade incorrect responses.

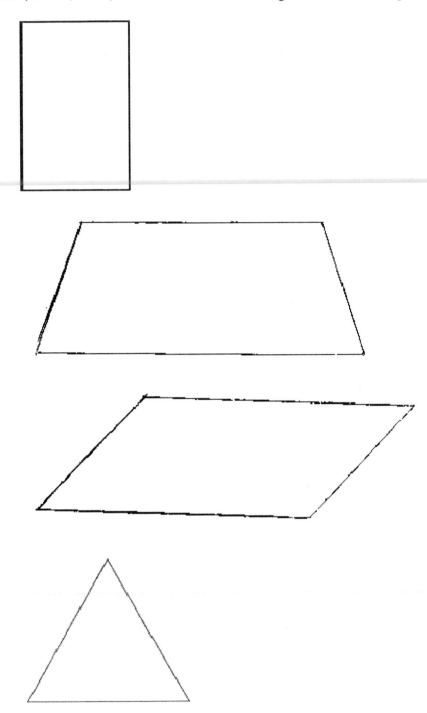

11.   43% of eighth graders gave the correct response d. (NAEP, 2003).
12.   In the United States, 34.5% of fourth graders successfully divided the rectangle (TIMSS, 2003).
13.   In the United States, 59.3% of girls and 67.0% of boys in fourth grade successfully drew the isosceles triangle (TIMSS, 2003).

8.3   Angles

Angle Measurement

Children often look at the length of the rays or line segments of two angles to determine the larger angle. This measurement activity is one of the few where some children may be at the first stage of measurement, perception (See Chapter 10: Measurement for more details.).

Consider the following angles: Which is larger? What do you think children might say and why?

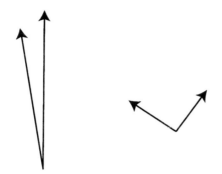

Children have many different conceptions about angle. Some view angle as:

- A corner
- A turn
- A shape
- A side of a figure
- The union of two lines
- A direction (Clements and Battista, 1990).

For some children, it is as if the angles are not part of the figure or shape. For example, we say that a triangle is made up of three line segments. The definition says nothing about a triangle being made of three angles, yet every triangle has three angles and the word *triangle* literally means *three angles*.

In addition note how children copy shapes. Are the lengths of the segments more accurate or are the angles?

What if a child called this, ∟, a right angle and this, ⅃, a left angle? Further, what if they said these two angles are not equal in measure?

Supplementary and Complementary Angles

What is the biggest difficulty that children have with **complementary** (two angles with a sum of 90°) and **supplementary** (two angles with a sum of 180°) angles?

They mix them up!

Common Problems Children have Measuring with a Protractor

In using some protractors, children may align the bottom of the protractor with one ray or side of the angle instead of using the cross hairs.

On most protractors there are two scales of numbers. Children are often confused about what number to use (Tzur & Clark, 2006). When angles are larger or smaller such as 30°, it is not too difficult for children to realize that the angle will be 30° and not 150°. However when the angle is close to 90°, for example 89°, the scales show either 91° or 89°. Children may not be as efficient with their estimation skills in these instances. You can help children avoid such problems by having children look at the initial side and start from 0° to determine the number of degrees.

Children are often not accurate when they have to extend line segments to measure an angle. This fact often leads to inaccuracy.

8.3   Problems and Exercises

Solve the problems first and then consider some data on how children solved the problems found in the **Children's Solutions and Discussion of Problems and Exercises** section.

1.   Which angle is larger? Why?

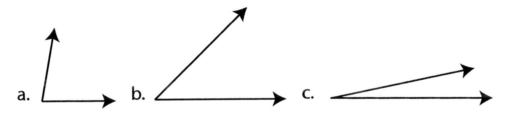

2.   Which angles are right angles? Why?

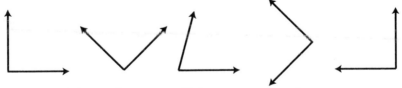

3.   How would you determine if these two triangles are congruent? Would you look at the sides or the angles? Why?

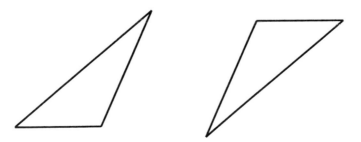

4.   A child measured this angle and found it to be 41° when it should be 45°. What do you think his error was?

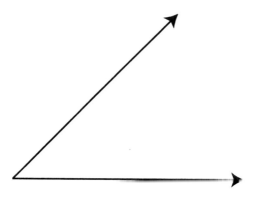

6.   A child measured this angle and found it to be 100° when it should be 80°. What do you think her error was?

7.

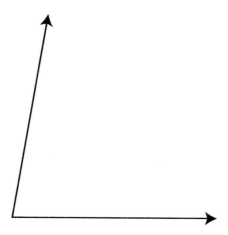

6.   A child measured this angle and found it to be 33° when it should be 30°. Below is his work. What do you think his error was?

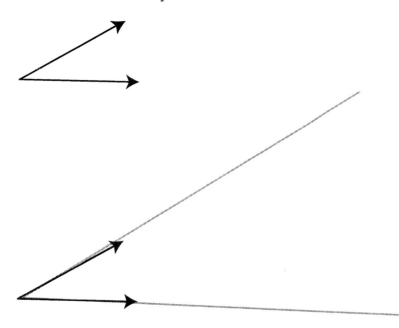

7.   How many angles are in this figure?

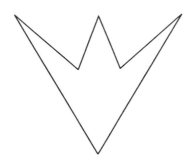

8.   In the space below, draw an angle that is <u>larger</u> than 90° (NAEP, 2003).

9.   In the space below, draw a closed figure with 5 sides. Make 2 of the angles right angles (NAEP, 2003).

9.   In the space below, use your ruler to draw a square with two of its corners at the points shown.

10.

11.   A cow is tied to a post in the middle of a flat meadow. If the cow's rope is several meters long, which of the following figures shows the shape of the region where the cow can graze?

        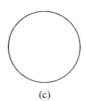

(a)   (b)   (c)   (d)

12.   How many of the angles in this triangle are smaller than a right angle (NAEP, 2005)?

    a.   None
    b.   One
    c.   Two
    d.   Three

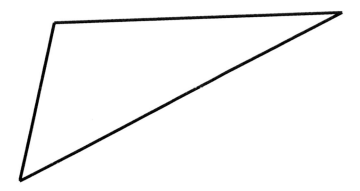

13.   The figure is a regular hexagon. What is the value of x (TIMSS? 2003)?

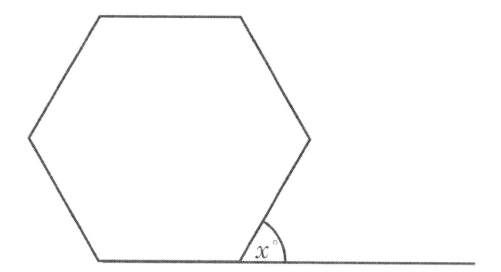

14. In the figure, the measure of ∠POR is 110°, the measure of ∠QOS is 90°, and the measure of ∠POS is 140°. What is the measure of ∠QOR (TIMSS, 2003)?

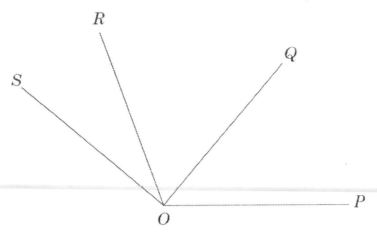

8.3   Questions for Discussion

1. How might a child describe what an angle is?
2. What are some of children's conceptions of angles?
3. How might you help children avoid confusing supplementary and complementary angles?
4. Why is it important to know about common mistakes that children may make when measuring with a protractor?

8.3   Children's Solutions and Discussion of Problems and Exercises

2. What follows is data from a fifth grade class of 13 for number of children who indicated the figure was a right angle:
   a. 12/13
   b. 8/13
   c. 3/13
   d. 6/13
   e. 10/13

7. In a third grade class, 1 child said 1 angle, 2 children said 2 angles, 5 children said 4 angles, and 8 children said 6 angles.

8. Only 28% of fourth graders and 71% of eighth graders successfully drew an angle greater than 90° (NAEP, 2003).

9.   27% of fourth graders gave a correct response as compared to 74% of eighth graders (NAEP, 2003). The following are some incorrect responses:

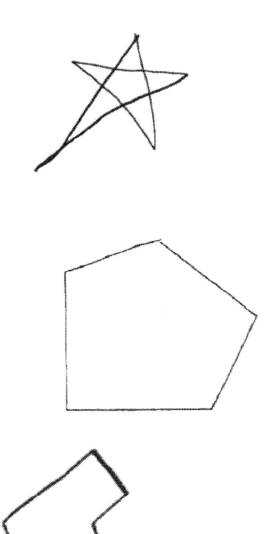

10. 40% of fourth graders gave a correct response as compared to 67% of eighth graders (NAEP, 1992).

    The following are some responses from fourth graders. Which ones would you count as correct?

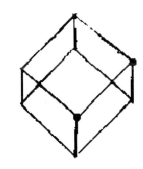

11. Surprisingly, only 30% of fourth graders gave the correct response c. (NAEP, 2003).

12. In the United States, 44% of eighth graders indicted that there were 2 acute angles in the figure (NAEP, 2005).

13. Only 20.1% of eighth graders in the United States indicated that x was 60° (TIMSS, 2003).

14. Only 22.1% of eighth graders in the United States indicated the angle was 60° (TIMSS, 2003).

8.4   Proof/Mathematical Reasoning/Justification/Argumentation

Traditional high school geometry classes using proofs and constructions are amazingly similar and follow the same basic sequence as Euclid's book the *Elements*. The main difference is that modern geometry courses are less rigorous and rely less on constructions. Of all mathematics, Euclidean geometry has changed the least over the last 2,300 years!

One of the main emphases of the NCTM Standards (2000) is on proof and mathematical reasoning. What does this mean for elementary school mathematics? Are elementary teachers to teach proofs like those in the *Elements* or high school geometry?

Studies have shown that most high school students who take traditional high-school geometry have no real concept of proof. Many simply play a guessing game, filling in the blanks of a standard two column proof with reason #1 as always "given" and throwing in a 'SAS' somewhere. We definitely want elementary school children to reason geometrically, but formal proof may not be the best way to help them do this.

Unfortunately, a common mindset is if children do not understand something in high school, then we should introduce it in elementary school! Rather than talk about proof with children, we might talk about a convincing argument or "How do we know or how do we convince someone else that something will always work?" With children, we might talk about different levels of convincing:

- Convince yourself.
- Convince a friend.
- Convince an enemy.
- Create and convince an internal enemy.

One area of focus in elementary school mathematics is a concentration on mathematical reasoning. What does this mean? Mathematical reasoning is a very important goal for elementary school mathematics because "Reasoning is the process through which someone learns" (Yackel & Hanna, 2003). Reform efforts are suggesting that greater emphasis needs to be placed on students' explanations and justifications of their mathematical thinking. One reason for this emphasis is the hope that later in high school mathematics the concept of proof might develop naturally out of children's justifications and explanations (Maher & Martino, 1996).

Consider the following activity for the sum of the measures of the angles of a triangle. This activity may also be in your textbook. As you are doing the activity consider:

- Would you use the activity with children? Would you change it at all?
- What is the purpose of this activity?
- Does this activity promote mathematical reasoning and justification?

The sum of the measures of the angles of a triangle

1.   With ruler or straight edge make a large triangle on a piece of paper, heavier stock paper or a large index card works best.
2.   Cut out the triangle.
3.   Compare your triangle to other students in the room. Note that they are all different.
4.   Label the three angles (1, 2, & 3).
5.   Tear off the three angles. Be careful not to tear off pieces that are too small. (**Do not cut the angles as it is easy to mix up which angles you are working with.**)
6.   Put the three original angles together with the sides touching.
7.   What have you made?
8.   What can you conclude about the sum of the measures of the angles of a triangle?

Is this a justification or an informal proof that the sum of the measure of the angles of any triangle is 180°? For you, what level of a convincing argument is this activity?

Similar justifications can be given to illustrate the sum of the measures of quadrilaterals, pentagons, etc., by dividing the quadrilateral, pentagon, etc., into triangles to find the sum of the measures of all the angles. The textbook gives the formula $(n-2)*180°$ to find the sum of the measures of the angles of an "n" sided figure. The key question is, **what is the nature of the understanding that college students and children should have?** Do we want children and college students to just know the formula or do we want them to understand the conceptual nature of the formula?

Is drawing the triangles in each shape to find the sum of the measures of the angles more meaningful than just using the formula? Would you do this sum of the angles of a triangle activity with children? Why?

8.4   Problems and Exercises

Solve the problems first and then consider some data on how children solved the problems found in the **Children's Solutions and Discussion of Problems and Exercises** section.

1.   How would you convince yourself, a friend, and a child who does not believe that the sum of the measures of the angles in every pentagon is 540°?

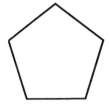

2.   How would you convince yourself, a friend, and a child who does not believe that a diagonal of every rectangle cuts the rectangle into two congruent triangles?

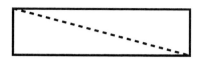

3.   A child told his teacher that if you take any triangle, copy it and flip it over you will always get a rectangle. He gave the following figure to support his argument. How would you convince yourself whether the statement is true?

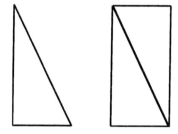

5.   Think carefully about the following questions. Write a complete answer for each. You may use drawings, words, and numbers to explain your answer. Be sure to show all of your work.

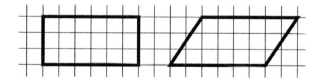

In what ways are the figures above alike? List as many ways as you can.
In what ways are they different? List as many ways as you can
(NAEP, 1996).

6.   What is the value of x (NAEP, 2003)?

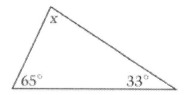

    a. 65°
    b. 82°
    c. 90°
    d. 92°
    e. 98°

6.   In square EFGH, which of these is FALSE (TIMSS, 2003)?
     a. ΔEIF and ΔEIH are congruent.
     b. ΔGHI and ΔGHF are congruent.
     c. ΔEFH and ΔEGH are congruent.
     d. ΔEIF and ΔGIH are congruent

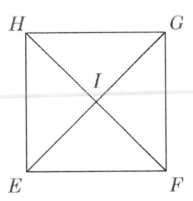

7.   ABCD is a trapezoid. Another trapezoid GHIJ (not shown), is congruent (the same size and shape) to ABCD. Angles G and J each measure 70°. Which of these could be true (TIMSS, 2003)?
     a. GH = AB
     b. Angle H is a right angle.
     c. All sides of GHIJ are the same length.
     d. The perimeter of GHIJ is 3 times the perimeter of ABCD.
     e. The area of GHIJ is less than the area of ABCD.

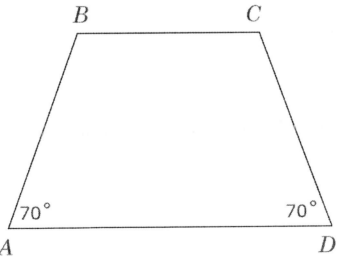

8.   Of the following, which is NOT true for all rectangles (TIMSS, 1999)?
     a. The opposite sides are parallel.
     b. The opposite angles are equal.
     c. All angles are right angles.
     d. The diagonals are equal.
     e. The diagonals are perpendicular.

8.4   Questions for Discussion

1.   As a student in a mathematics class, you mainly have to convince yourself. As a teacher, you will likely have to convince your class. Take an example and discuss how your role would be different as a teacher.
2.   Why would you have children explain and justify their mathematical thinking?
3.   When you took geometry, what did you do when you were asked to construct a proof? How might thinking of proof as argument have helped you?

8.4   Children's Solutions and Discussion of Problems and Exercises

4.   Very few fourth graders, 0% due to rounding, gave a correct extended response; 11% gave a satisfactory response; 29% gave a partial response; and 31% gave a minimal response (NAEP, 1996). A correct response must include 2 reasons for both questions as shown below:

In what ways were the figures alike? List as many ways as you can.

They have 4 sides. They have parallel sides.

In what ways are they different? List as many ways as you can.

One has square corners. One is more slant.

5.   51% of eighth graders gave the correct response of 82° (NAEP, 2003).
6.   In the United States, 55.3% of eighth graders correctly identified answer b. as incorrect (TIMSS, 2003).
7.   In the United States, 72.3% of girls and 65.6% of boys in eighth grade selected the correct response a. (TIMSS, 2003).
8.   In the United States, 46% of eighth graders chose the correct response e. (TIMSS, 1999)

8.5   Three-Dimensional Geometry

Elementary school geometry typically focuses on two-dimensional shapes, yet we live in a three-dimensional world. Given the early grades' emphasis on two-dimensional geometry it is not surprising then that children have more difficulty with three-dimensional geometry.

Upper elementary grade children have difficulty naming three-dimensional figures or solids, let alone thinking about their characteristics and relationships (Carpenter, Coburn, Reys & Wilson, 1976). One activity that has proven helpful in developing children's understanding of three-dimensional geometry is the manipulation of solids in computer environments (Sachter, 1991).

Another excellent activity to help children with three-dimensional figures involves the use of nets (Niewoudt & van Niekerk, 1997). A net is a two-dimensional layout which when folded up becomes a three-dimensional figure. One net activity for both children and college students is to find the 11 nets to a cube.

- If you were to give this activity to children, what else might you do or give them?
- What visualization skills are you using in this activity?

An additional net activity that some textbooks offer is to have elementary school children construct the five regular Polyhedra from nets. What do you think children are learning by doing this activity?

What is important in three-dimensional geometry?

Consider a typical true/false question.

> True or False:
> A line perpendicular to one of two parallel lines is perpendicular to the other.

Why are true/false questions in your college textbook? Do you think you will be giving true/false questions like these to children?

For children it is not the specific mathematics that is important here but the ability to visualize and think in three-dimensions. Consider various occupations and activities that use three-dimensional reasoning. The most obvious careers would be those of architects and engineers, but others less obvious ones include hairdressers, auto mechanics, marching bands, etc. In real life, people use three-dimensional visualization and thinking all the time. One of the goals of this section is not just to solve specific problems, but also to develop the ability to visualize in three-dimensions and to think three-dimensionally. All the children you will be teaching will need this ability when they study geometry in high school. Many of the children you will teach will take calculus and will need to visualize three-dimensional shapes, such as a finding the surface area of a doughnut cut in half. They will have to know the formulas, but the formulas will do no good unless they can visualize the figure.

Prisms

How do children understand prisms? Many are at van Hieles' **Visual** level where they can recognize what is and what is not a prism, but they have difficulty defining it in mathematical terms. They have a *concept image* of a prism. What is your college textbook's definition of a prism? Do you think this definition will make sense to children? Yet, prisms are frequently discussed in fourth and fifth grade.

Euler's Formula

Euler's Formula, for any convex polyhedron, the number of vertices and faces together is exactly two more than the number of edges or $F + V - E = 2$, is sometimes taught in fifth and sixth grade. Problems 3 through 7 in section 8.5 provide some interesting extensions of Euler's Formula. With all problems involving Euler's formula, consider what spatial abilities you and children will be applying while working on them.

Mobius Strips

Your textbook likely contains a Mobius strip activity. Would you do this activity with children? What geometric concepts does it illustrate? Does the activity help children in their three-dimensional visualization skills?

8.5   Problems and Exercises

<u>Solve the problems first</u> and then consider some data on how children solved the problems found in the **Children's Solutions and Discussion of Problems and Exercises** section.

1.   It is interesting to try to imagine higher dimensions, what is the fourth dimension? What is the fifth dimension?

2.   How are a square and a prism similar? Different? How are a circle and a sphere similar? Different?

Euler's formula is an accepted mathematical truth! Does it work for **all** polyhedrons? Does his formula work if the solid has a hole in it? From topology, a solid with no holes is a solid of genus (Here, genus refers to the group of solids with similar characteristics.) zero, a solid with one hole is a solid of genus one, a solid with two holes is a solid of genus two, etc.

3.   Consider a cube of genus one with a square, i.e., a prism cut out of the middle. Consider that the side with the square cut out as being made up of 4 trapezoids. We may want to think of the front and back as being raised; otherwise we will have difficulty determining the number of faces. See the drawing.

The front face looks like this. The back face will look the same.

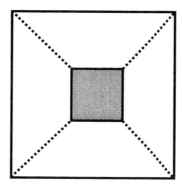

What is F + V – E = _____ ?

Try 4, a triangle cut out of a triangular prism, 5, a triangle cut out of a cube, 6, two squares cut out of a cube, and for fun, 7, two squares cut out of a cube that intersect.

Hint: Draw the edges on the front faces.

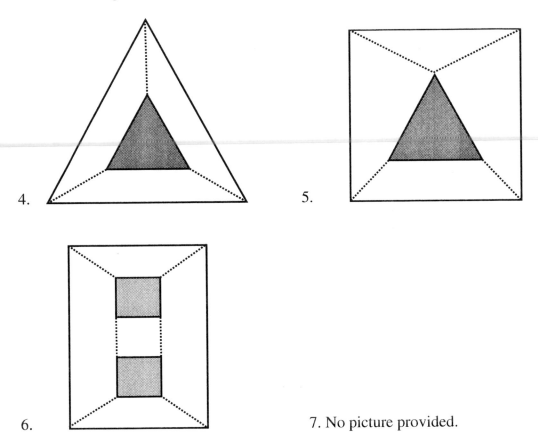

4.   5.

6.   7. No picture provided.

This mathematics is typically done at the graduate level!

8.   Conic Sections. This activity is a very challenging. However, it relates to the mathematics that children will be using when they reach high school and study Advanced Algebra (Algebra II). Two right cones are connected point to point extending infinitely in opposite directions. What are all the ways that a plane could intersect the cones? Draw a picture of the actual intersection for each possibility (cross section). (You do not necessarily have to draw the cone and the plane, just what the intersection itself will look like.) You may want to make a cone to investigate. There are seven conic sections.

9.   Which of the following has the same shape as a cylinder (NAEP, 1990)?

     a. An egg   b. A book   c. A basketball   d. A can of soup

10.   The squares in the figure represent the faces of a cube which has been cut along some edges and flattened. When the original cube was resting on face *X*, which face was on top (NAEP, 1992)?

a. A   b. B   c. C   d. D

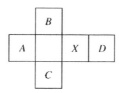

11.   Which of the following could NOT be folded into a cube (NAEP, 2003)?

a.   b.   c.   d.

 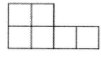 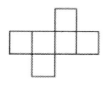 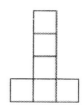

12.   The figure will be turned to a different position.

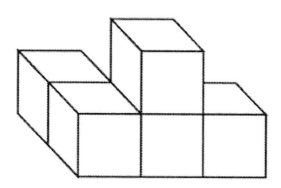

Which of these could be the figure after it is turned (TIMSS, 2003)?

(A)   (B)   (C)   (D)

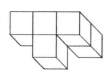  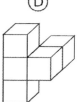

13.   This picture shows a cube with one edge marked. How many edges does the cube have altogether (TIMSS, 1995)?
a. 6
b. 8
c. 12
d. 24

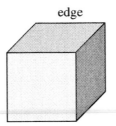

edge

8.5   Questions for Discussion

1.   Why is three-dimensional geometry important?
2.   What difficulties might children have in working in three-dimensional geometry?
3.   What are some activities that might foster the development of three-dimensional geometry and spatial imagery?

8.5   Children's Solutions and Discussion of Problems and Exercises

1.   Albert Einstein contributed to our understanding of the fourth dimension.
A musical group from the sixties was called the *Fifth Dimension.*
In string theory there are 11 dimensions!

3-7.   For one hole, F + V - E = 0
For two holes, F + V - E = -2
For two holes that intersect F + V – E = -4

9.   62% of fourth graders gave the correct answer d. (NAEP, 1990).
10.   This was a challenging problem as 22% of fourth graders gave the correct response a. as compared to 55% of eighth graders (NAEP, 1992).
11.   38% of fourth graders and 71% of eighth graders gave the correct answer b. on the 2003 NAEP test.
12.   In the United States, 38.6% of fourth graders chose the correct figure a. (TIMSS, 2003).
13.   Internationally, 34% of third graders and 40% of fourth graders indicated that the cube has 12 edges (TIMSS, 1995).

Chapter 8   References

Burger, W. F. & Shaughnessy J. M. (1986). Characterizing the van Hiele levels of development in geometry. *Journal of Research in Mathematics Education, 17,* 31-48.

Carpenter, T.P., Coburn, T., Reys, R., & Wilson, J. (1976). Notes from national assessment: recognizing and naming solids. *Arithmetic Teacher, 23,* 62-66

Clements, D. (2004). Geometric and spatial thinking in early childhood education. In D. Clements & J Sarama (Eds.) *Engaging young children in mathematics*. 267-298. NJ. Lawrence Erlbaum Associates.

Clements, D. (2003). Teaching and learning geometry. In J. Kilpatrick, G. Martin, & D. Schifter (Eds.), *A research companion to the principles and standards for school mathematics*. 151-178. Reston, VA: NCTM.

Clements, D. & Battista, M. (1992). Geometry and spatial reasoning. In D. Grows (Ed.), *Handbook of research on mathematics teaching and learning*. 420-464. New York: Macmillan.

Clements, D. & Battista, M. (1990). The effects of Logo on children's conceptualizations of angle and polygons. *Journal for Research in Mathematics Education 21*, 356-371.

Clements, D. & Battista, M., & Sarama, J. (2001). *Logo and geometry. Journal for Research in Mathematics Education*, Monograph Series, 10.

Clements, D. Sudha, S., Hannibal, M.A., & Sarama, J. (1999). Young children's conception of shape. *Journal for Research in Mathematics Education 30*, 192-212.

Fuys, D. J. & Liebov, A. K. (1993). Geometry and spatial sense. In R. J. Jensen (Ed.) *Research Ideas for the Classroom: Early Childhood Mathematics*. 195-222. Reston, VA: NCTM.

Geddes, D. & Fortunato, I. (1993). Geometry: Research and classroom activities. In D. T. Owens (Ed.) *Research Ideas for the Classroom: Middle Grades Mathematics*. 199-222. Reston, VA: NCTM.

Klausmeier, H.J. (1992). Concept learning and concept teaching. *Educational Psychologist, 27*, 267-286.

Klein, A., Strakey, P., & Wakeley, A. (1999, April). *Enhancing pre-kindergarten children's readiness for school mathematics*. Paper presented at the meeting of the American Educational Research Association, Montreal.

Lehrer, R., Jenkins, M., & Osana, H. (1998). Longitudinal study of children's reasoning about space and geometry. In R. Lehrer & D. Chazan (Eds.) *Designing learning environments for developing understanding of geometry and space*. 137- 167. Mahwah, NJ: Lawrence Erlbaum and Associates.

Maher, C.A., & Martino, A.M. (1996). The development of the idea of a mathematical proof: A 5-year case study. *Journal for Research in Mathematics Education, 27*, 194-214.

Mansfield, H.M., & Happs J.C. (1992). Using grade eight students' conceptual knowledge to teach about parallel lines. *School Science and Mathematics, 92*, 450-454.

National Assessment of Educational Progress (NAEP). (2003). U.S. Department of Education, Institute of Educational Sciences, National Center for Educational Statistics Mathematics Assessment.

National Council of Teachers of Mathematics. (2000). *Principles and standards for school mathematics*. Reston, VA: NCTM.

Nieuwoudt, H.D., & van Niekerk, R. (1997, March). The spatial competence of young children through the development of solids. Paper presented at the meeting of the American Educational Research Association, Chicago.

Piaget, J. & Inhelder, B. (1967). *The child's conception of space*. (F.J. Langdon & J.L. Lunzer, Trans.) New York: W. W. Norton.

Porter, A. (1989). A curriculum out of balance: the case of elementary school mathematics. *Educational Researcher, 18*, 9-15.

Senk, S. L. (1985). How well do students write geometry proofs? *Mathematics Teacher, 78*, 448-456.

Tzur, R. & Clark, M. R. (2006). Riding the mathematical merry-go-round to foster conceptual understanding. *Teaching Children Mathematics, 12*, 388-393.

Vinner, S. & Hershkowitz, R. (1980). Concept images and common cognitive paths in the development of some simple geometric concepts. In R. Karplus (Ed.), *Proceeding of the Fourth International Conference for the Psychology of Mathematics Education*. 177-184. Berkeley: University of California.

Yackel, E. & Hanna, G. (2003). Reasoning and proof. In J. Kilpatrick, G. Martin, & D. Schifter (Eds.), *A research companion to the principles and standards for school mathematics*. 227-236. Reston, VA: NCTM.

CHAPTER 9: MORE GEOMETRY

Chapter 8 focused on two and three dimensional shapes and objects, their properties, and characteristics. Chapter 9 will look at both moving these shapes and objects and changing them in different ways, e.g., making them bigger or smaller. Children and perhaps yourselves, often find these ideas challenging. Nonetheless, movement and transformations are essential aspects and vital to understanding geometry. Another central topic of this chapter is constructions. However, these shapes are constructed with certain restrictions, e.g., a ruler is not allowed. These restrictions may seem unnecessary, but they are essential in developing geometry as a logical, well-defined enterprise. Constructions are like proofs.

9.1   Transformations or Rigid Motions

Mathematical Name	Children's Name
1. Translation	1. Slide
2. Rotation	2. Turn
3. Reflection	3. Flip

As a future elementary teacher, it is important that you have a thorough understanding of the rigid motions because many children have difficulty with them. Young children, K-2, have limited understandings of motions (Clements, 2004). They understand slides better than flips and turns (Perham, 1978). Young children can learn some of the basic mathematics of motions, such as recognizing them, but they typically cannot mathematically describe a motion. Elementary and middle school children may have difficulty with motions because it requires formal operational thought (Kidder, 1976).

Work with motions is important because it can help children improve their spatial visualization skills (Clements, et al, 1997). Computer applications, such as the previously mentioned Logo, have proven to be beneficial in helping children understand motions (Clements, 2004).

Your college textbook may take a formal approach to motions. However, most upper elementary school textbooks take a more informal or general approach to motions. Children are frequently asked to identify motions from a drawing or draw simple motions on grid or dot paper. Children can construct more complicated reflections by simply using tracing paper and folding the paper on the line of reflection.

More on Congruence

Why are they called **rigid** motions? Rigid motions provide another perspective on congruence. Two figures are congruent if you can move one on top of the other through combinations of motions. When two figures are congruent, their corresponding parts are congruent. Children are likely to think informally about congruence in this way!

Tessellations

A common elementary school application of rigid motions is the study of tessellations. Tessellations are created by covering a plane with a repeated shape. Many children enjoy constructing and coloring their tessellations. Tessellations are a nice example of the connection between mathematics and art. Consider how a tessellation is in essence a combination of motions.

Vertical Angles and Parallel Lines Cut by a Transversal

Some K-5 textbooks discuss vertical angles. Most K-5 texts do not even mention **alternate interior**, **corresponding**, and **alternate exterior** angles. However, the names and definitions of these angles are very important in high school geometry.

9.1   Problems and Exercises

Solve the problems first and then consider the data on how children solved the problems found in the **Children's Solutions and Discussion of Problems and Exercises** section.

1.   The tessellation begins with the shaded one in the middle. What rigid motion could you use to describe the locations of the other shapes in the tessellation?

2.   Which shapes are congruent to the first one?   Copy the first figure on a copy machine and see if you can show which shapes are congruent.

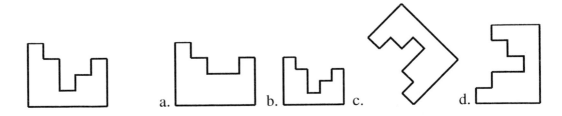

3.   Which rigid motion is illustrated in each picture?

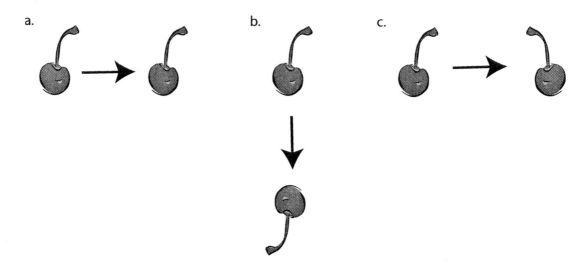

4.   Why is the following motion not just a rotation? How could you describe this motion?   Will copying the first figure on a copy machine help you here? Why or why not?

5.   The figure below is shaded on the top side and white on the under side. If the figure were flipped over, its white side could look like which of the following figures (NAEP, 2003)?

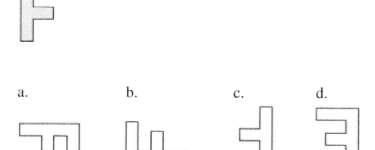

6.   Which of the following shows the result of flipping the triangle over the line; *l* (NAEP, 1990)?

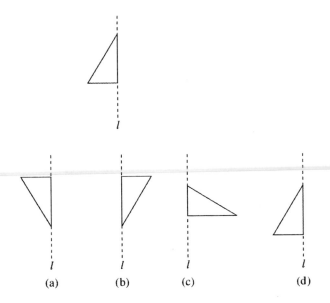

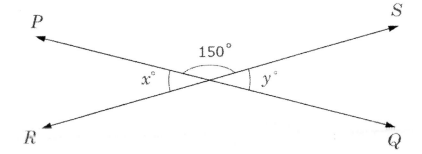

     (a)   (b)   (c)   (d)

7.   In the figure, PQ and RS are intersecting straight lines. What is the value of x + y (TIMSS, 2003)?

a. 15
b. 30
c. 60
d. 180
e. 300

8. In this figure ABC and DEF are congruent with BC=EF. What is the measure of angle EGC (TIMSS, 2003)?

    a. 20°

    b. 40°

    c. 60°

    d. 80°

    e. 100°

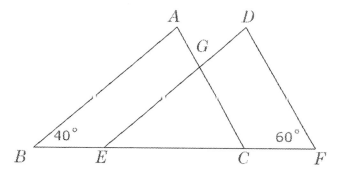

9. In this figure, PQ and RS are parallel. Of the following, which pair of angles has the sum of 180° (TIMSS, 2003)?

    a. $\angle 5$ and $\angle 7$

    b. $\angle 3$ and $\angle 6$

    c. $\angle 1$ and $\angle 5$

    d. $\angle 1$ and $\angle 7$

    e. $\angle 2$ and $\angle 8$

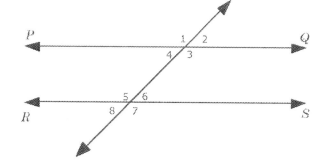

10. Rectangle PQRS can be rotated (turned) onto rectangle UVST. What point is the center of rotation (TIMSS, 2003)?
    a. P
    b. R
    c. S
    d. T
    e. V

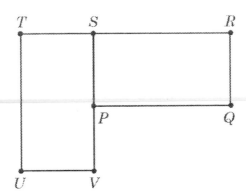

9.1 Questions for Discussion

1. How do tessellations integrate mathematics and art?
2. Escher was a famous artist who combined mathematics and art in his drawings. Find some of his work and describe the motions in some of Escher's drawings.

9.1 Children's Solutions and Discussion of Problems and Exercises

5. On the 2003 NAEP test, 72% of fourth graders and 82% of eighth graders gave the correct answer.
6. 59% of eighth graders gave the correct answer. (NAEP, 1990).
7. In the United States, 47.3% of eighth graders had the correct solution (TIMSS, 2003).
8. In the United States only 36.3%, of eighth graders had the correct solution (TIMSS, 2003).
9. In the United States, 36.9% of eighth graders chose the correct solution (TIMSS, 2003).
10. In the United States, 44.0% of girls and 53.6% of boys in eighth grade chose the correct center of rotation (TIMSS, 2003).

9.2 Constructions

Elementary school children may do simple constructions such as:
1. Copy a line segment
2. Copy an angle
3. Bisect an angle
4. Bisect a line segment
5. Copy a triangle

However, you may be asked to do a few more complex constructions such as:

1.   Construct a parallel line from a point not on the line
2.   Construct a perpendicular line from:
        a.   a point not on the line
        b.   a point on the line.
3.   Trisect a line

You will be better prepared to teach the basic constructions if you can do the more complicated constructions!

Could children do these constructions?
1.   Construct the perpendicular bisector of the sides of triangle and the circumscribed circle.
2.   Construct the angle bisectors of a triangle and the inscribed circle, (incenter).
3.   Construct the medians of a triangle and find the centroid – the balancing point of every triangle.
4.   Construct the altitudes of a triangle and find the orthocenter.

Computer environments, or software such as Geometer's Sketchpad, provide computer tools to do these basic constructions and more complicated constructions. For example, students can instruct the computer to form the angle bisectors of a triangle and the inscribed circle. They can then view the size and shape of the triangle to see what happens to the previous constructions. From creating the same constructions on different size and shapes, they might be able to make generalizations about the constructions. For example, they might generalize that the angle bisectors always give the center of the inscribed circle of any triangle. There is no guarantee what children will create or discover, but they will often find new things that they have never been taught.

9.2   Problems and Exercises

<u>Solve the problems first</u> and then consider the data on how children solved the problems found in the **Children's Solutions and Discussion of Problems and Exercises** section.

     1.   Construct a line parallel to the given line through the given point.

•

⟷

     2.   How is this above construction like a formal geometry proof?

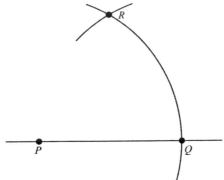

3.   In the figure, an arc of a circle with center p has been drawn to cut the line at Q. then an arc with same radius and center Q was drawn to cut the first arc at R. What would be the size of angle PRQ (TIMSS, 2003)?
a. 30°
b. 45°
c. 60°
d. 75°

9.2   Questions for Discussion

1.   What geometry concepts do you hope children are learning by doing constructions?
2.   Would you use a software program such as *Geometer's Sketchpad* with elementary school children? Why or why not?

9.2   Children's Solutions and Discussion of Problems and Exercises

3.   In the United States, 33.7% of eighth graders chose the correct solution (TIMSS, 2003).

9.3   Symmetry

Preschool age children have intuitive understandings about the concept of symmetry. Children and adults prefer symmetrical figures; they are remembered longer and are easier to discern than asymmetrical ones (Clements, 2004). Line of symmetry is a concept that you teach children in the early grades. Children have an easier time with vertical symmetry than horizontal symmetry (Genkins, 1975). Also, more complicated notions of symmetry, such as rotational symmetry, are not typically understood by children until middle school (Genkins, 1975). Computer environments such as Logo have shown to help children build conceptual understandings of symmetry (Clements, Battista et al., 2001).

The Indiana Mathematics Standards have symmetry as a specific objective in grades 3, 4 and 5.
- **3-Identify and draw lines of symmetry in geometric shapes (by hand or using technology).**
- **4-Identify and draw lines of symmetry in polygons. Example: Draw a rectangle and then draw the lines of symmetry.**
- **5-Identify shapes that have reflectional and rotational symmetry**.

Other states may have similar standards.

Common exercises for children are to find the lines of symmetry for a shape or to complete a drawing halved by a line of symmetry. Sometimes children have difficulty determining the number of lines of symmetry because they count the lines of symmetry twice. For example, on a regular pentagon they sometimes come up with 10 lines of symmetry as opposed to 5.

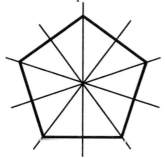

Rotational symmetry is typically taught in the upper elementary grades. Many children have a very difficult time with the technical aspects such as measuring the angle of rotation. Despite the fact that older children often struggle with rotational symmetry, young children are aware of it and refer to it, not by name, when working with manipulatives such as pattern blocks (Sarama, Clements, & Vukelic, 1996).

Symmetry also makes a nice connection to math and art. Many of Escher's drawings contain both rotational and reflectional symmetry.

9.3   Problems and Exercises

Solve the problems first and then consider the data on how children solved the problems found in the **Children's Solutions and Discussion of Problems and Exercises** section.

1.   Which picture shows a line of symmetry?

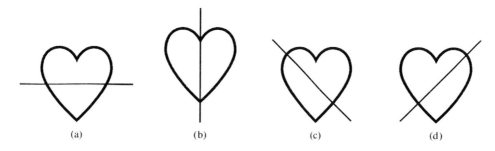

(a)   (b)   (c)   (d)

2.   Write the letters of the alphabet in capital letters. Find all the lines of symmetry for each upper-case letter. For example:

3.   Write the letters of the alphabet in capital upper-case letters. Find all the rotational symmetries for each letter.

4.   Draw a line of symmetry on the triangle below (NAEP, 1990).

5.   Which of these does NOT show a line of symmetry (TIMSS, 1995)?

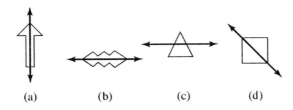

  (a)   (b)   (c)   (d)

6.   Craig folded a piece of paper in half and cut out a shape. Draw a picture to show what the cut-out shape will look like when it is opened up and flattened out (TIMSS, 1995).

fold

7.   The triangle ABC has AB=AC. Draw a line to divide triangle ABC into congruent triangles (TIMSS, 2003).

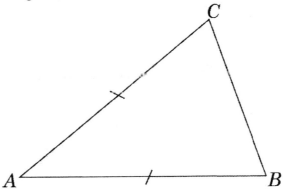

8.   The line *m* is a line of symmetry for figure ABCDE. The measure of angle BCD
is (TIMSS, 1999)
a. 30°
b. 50°
c. 60°
d. 70°
e. 110°

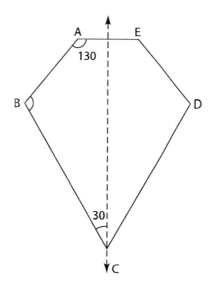

9.3   Questions for Discussion

1.   Why do you think the children using Logo in the study done by Clements, Battista
et al., 2001 did better on tests of symmetry than children who had done freehand
drawings of symmetric figures? Or, why would giving Logo commands for
drawing a symmetrical figure help more than freehand drawings?
2.   Why do you think older children have so much difficulty with rotational
symmetry yet younger children recognize it?
3.   Why do you think children find vertical symmetry to be easier than horizontal
symmetry?

9.3   Children's Solutions and Discussion of Problems and Exercises

4.   37% of fourth graders (see figure that follows) were able to successfully draw the
line of symmetry (NAEP, 1990).
A correct response: An incorrect response:

5.   Internationally, 54% of third graders and 64% of fourth graders identified the shape that was not symmetrical (TIMSS, 1995).
6.   Internationally, 45% of third graders and 59% of fourth graders correctly drew either the shape itself or the exterior of the shape (TIMSS, 1995).
7.   In the United States, 54.2% of eighth graders could divide the triangle into two congruent triangles (TIMSS, 2003).
8.   In the United States, 52% of eighth graders chose the correct solution (TIMSS, 1999).

9.4   Similarity

In some circumstances four and five year olds can identify some similar shapes (Sophian & Crosby, 1998). For example, children may say that the second rectangle is too long to be similar to the first rectangle.

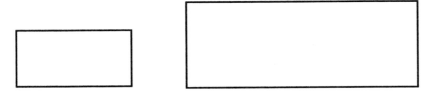

Either enlarging or reducing a shape on a copy machine is a nice illustration of similarity. Given the following triangle and dimensions, what will happen to the length of each side and the angles if the triangle is reduced by 50% on a copy machine? What is the same and what is different in the shape?

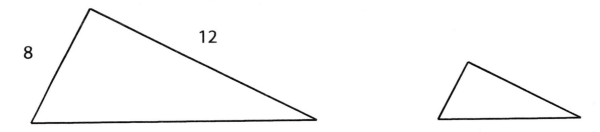

What will happen if the same triangle is enlarged 200% on the copy machine? What is the scale factor (see chapter 7)? The process of enlarging or reducing a shape on a copy machine is called a **dilation** or size transformation. The shapes are similar—the angle measures stay the same and the lengths of the sides all increase or decrease by the same scale factor—the lengths of the sides are related multiplicatively. However, a dilation is different from similarity in that the orientation of the shape must stay the same. Dilations are studied in advanced mathematics.

Shapes other than triangles can also be similar. Often, we only consider similar triangles but other shapes such as: squares, rectangles, etc., can also be enlarged or reduced on the copy machine as well.

Are all squares similar?
Are all rectangles similar?

What is Trigonometry?

One aspect of trigonometry is the study of similar right triangles. Most of the children you will teach will study trigonometry at some point. As their elementary mathematics teacher, it might be helpful to know what trigonometry is. Perhaps you can help children make connections between similarity and trigonometry in elementary school which will help them later in their study of mathematics.

Consider the following right triangle with one angle 30° and the lengths of the sides as given.

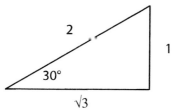

If there is a second right triangle with a 30° angle, are the two triangles similar because one angle is 90° and the other angle is 60°?

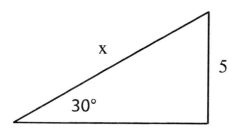

Since the sides of a similar figure are proportional we can find the value of x.

Are all right triangles with a 30° angle similar? Why?

If the 30° angle is our starting point, we can name the lengths of the sides of a right triangle: adjacent (adj.), opposite (opp.), and hypotenuse (hyp.).

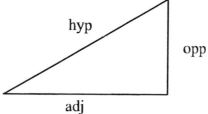

For every similar right triangle with a 30° angle, what is the ratio of the opposite side to the hypotenuse?

No matter how large or how small the triangle, the ratio of the opposite side to the hypotenuse will always be 1/2.

If you are solving problems with a 30° right triangle, you could always make a similar right triangle like the one given with the sides, 1, 2, and √3. However, this construction is not necessary since you will always know the ratio of the opposite side over the hypotenuse of a right triangle with one 30° angle sides. Trigonometry just involves giving the ratio of these sides fancy names:

- sine = opp/hyp.
- cosine = adj/hyp.
- tangent = opp/ adj.

These ratios have been calculated or are able to be computed for every angle of a right triangle, not just one with a 30° angle. Many years ago students just looked up the values for each ratio in a table; the sin of 30° = 0.5, the sin of 31° = 0.515, the sin of 32° = 0.53, etc. Now these ratios are programmed into scientific calculators.

9.4   Problems and Exercises

Solve the problems first and then consider the data on how children solved the problems found in the **Children's Solutions and Discussion of Problems and Exercises** section.

While copying the following figures a child hit the enlarge/reduce button by each of following the percents. Determine the new lengths of the sides.

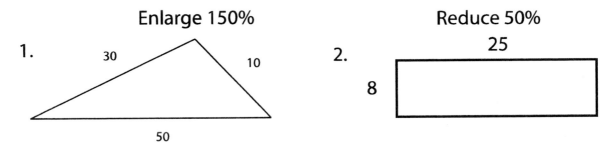

Enlarge 150%   Reduce 50%

1.   30   10   2.   25 / 8

50

3.   Two of the four triangles in the following figure are the same shape but different sizes. Shade in those two triangles (TIMSS, 2003).

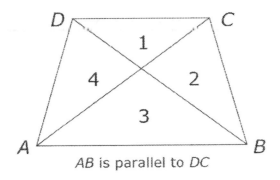

AB is parallel to DC

4.   Which of the following triangles is similar to the triangle shown (TIMSS, 2003)?

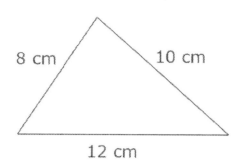

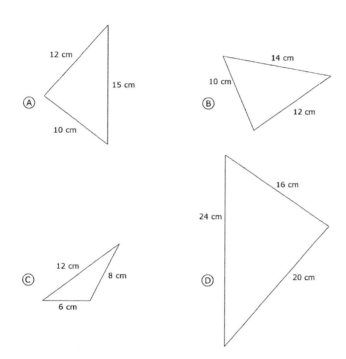

5.   On the map, 1 cm represents 10 km on the land. On the land, about how far apart are the towns Melville and Foley (TIMSS, 1999)?
a. 5 km
b. 30 km
c. 40 km
d. 50 km

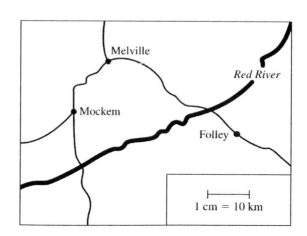

6.   Two of the triangles are similar. Which two triangles are similar (TIMSS, 1999)?
      a. I and II
      b. I and III
      c. I and IV
      d. II and IV
      e. III and IV

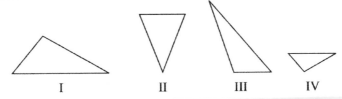

7.   The figure represents two similar triangles. The triangles are shown to scale. In the actual triangle ABC, what is the length of side BC (TIMSS, 1999)?
      a. 3.5 cm
      b. 4.5 cm
      c. 5 cm
      d. 5.5 cm
      e. 8 cm

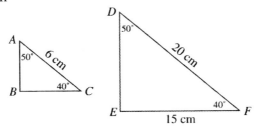

9.4   Questions for Discussion

1.   What is trigonometry?
2.   How is studying similarity laying the groundwork for children's later study of trigonometry?

9.4   Children's Solutions and Discussion of Problems and Exercises

3.   In the United States, 56.7% of fourth graders shaded in the correct triangles (TIMSS, 2003).
4.   In the United States, 46.2% of eighth graders correctly chose the solution. (TIMSS, 2003).
5.   In the United States, 40% of eighth graders chose the correct distance (TIMSS, 1999).
6.   In the United States, 62% of eighth graders had the correct solution (TIMSS, 1999).
7.   In the United States, 36% of eighth graders had the correct solution (TIMSS, 1999).

Chapter 9: References

Clements, D. (2004). Geometric and spatial thinking in early childhood education. In D. Clements & J Sarama (Eds.) *Engaging young children in mathematics*. 267-298. NJ. Lawrence Erlbaum Associates.

Clements, D. & Battista, M., & Sarama, J. (2001). *Logo and geometry. Journal for Research in Mathematics Education*, Monograph Series, 10.

Clements, D. & Battista, M., Sarama, J., & Swaminathan, S. (1997). Development of students' spatial thinking in a unit on geometric motions and area. *The Elementary School Journal, 98*(2), 171-186.

Genkins, E. F. (1975). The concept of bilateral symmetry in young children. In M. F. Rosskopf (Ed.), *Children's mathematical concepts: Six Piagetian studies in mathematics education*, 5-43. New York: Teachers College Press.

Kidder, F.R. (1976). Elementary and middle school children's comprehension of Euclidean transformations. *Journal for Research in Mathematics Education 7*, 40-52.

Perham, F. (1978). An investigation into the effect of instruction on the acquisition of transformation geometry concepts in first grade children and subsequent transfer to general spatial ability. In R. Lesh & D. Mierkiewicz (Eds.), *Concerning the development of spatial and geometric concepts* (pp. 229-241). Columbus, OH: Eric Clearinghouse for Science, Mathematics, and Environmental Education.

Sarama, J., Clements, D. H., & Vukelic, E. B. (1996). The role of computer manipulatives fostering specific psychological/mathematical processes. In E. Jakubuoski & D. Watkins, & H. Biske (Eds.), *Proceedings of the eighteenth annual meeting of the North America Chapter of the International Group for the Psychology of Mathematics Education, 2*, 567-572. Columbus, OH: ERIC Clearinghouse for Science, Mathematics, and Environmental Education.

Sophian, C. & Crosby, M. E. (1998). *Ratios that even young children understand: The case of spatial proportions*. Paper presented at the Cognitive Science Society of Ireland, Dublin.

CHAPTER 10: MEASUREMENT

This chapter will use children's misconceptions and errors of measurement to illustrate what underlying concepts they do not understand. Our intent is not to focus on what they cannot do and how to fix it but rather on what they do not understand!

There is a great deal of technical research which categorizes the underlying concepts necessary for children to understand measurement. We have attempted to synthesize this research into practical information that a teacher could use in the classroom.

10.1   The Concept of Measurement

Measurement is interwoven throughout all grades in elementary school mathematics; approximately 10 to 15% of the mathematics curriculum at every grade level deals with measurement. Since it is an area that everyone will teach, a significant question is: What is measurement? In elementary school, measurement has traditionally been presented as procedures and skills. However, a more careful analysis indicates that measurement is a concept. Teaching measurement entails more than teaching the procedures for measuring, it is also requires helping children understand the concept of measurement. If measurement is just procedures and skills, then this chapter would be very short and just include some discussion of the errors that children make while measuring. However, since measurement is a process, this chapter is rich with children's conceptions and misconceptions about measurement.

Traditional instruction in measurement has focused on "the procedures of measuring rather than the concepts underlying them" (Stephan & Clement, p.3., 2004). This focus on procedures may be due to the fact that measurement is a very physical activity, and it is easier to focus on the activity rather than on children's thinking and conceptualizations of measurement. Measurement is unique in that it combines:

- real world applications with abstract mathematical reasoning
- geometry with arithmetic
- our spatial world in which we live with the mathematical world

Measurement is related to counting, but it is considerably more sophisticated. For example, when we count something such as the children in the classroom, we are not concerned with how old they are or how big they are; we are just concerned with the number of children. When we count the number of potatoes in a sack, we do not take any notice if they are big or small, but when we weigh the potatoes, we use a regular unit of measure such as a pound or a kilogram.

Measurement as a Developmental Process

Children learn measurement developmentally or in stages (Piaget & Inhelder 1948/1956; Piaget et al., 1960). Inskeep (1976) suggested the following stages for children's development of the concept of measurement:

I.   **Pre-measurement (Perception)**

In this stage, children have an intuitive sense of attributes such as length, weight, temperature and time. For the most part, children perceive most types of measurement in pre-school or perhaps kindergarten. Elementary children may be at the perception stage of angle measurement. Children are not always aware of the openness or closeness of an angle, but instead focus on the length of the rays of the angles.

II.   **Measurement as Comparison**

In this stage, children are able to compare two things in terms of measurement. For example, they can say that one student is taller than another or that a brick weighs more than a piece of paper.

III.   **Measurement as the quest for a referent (Nonstandard Units)**

Here, children are developing the idea that they can use a unit to talk and think about measurement. In this stage, children make a comparison to something they know. Often, this is a nonstandard unit but it could also be a standard unit such as 2 liters. Children tend to use child-sized nonstandard units such as their hand or the length of their step. They will also use things that they know, for example the height of their father. Without their father being present, they may say that their father is taller than their teacher.

IV.   **Measurement as a System (Standard Units)**

This is the last stage which is where children learn the US Customary systems (length: inches, feet, miles; weight: pounds; volume: gallons) and the Metric systems (length: centimeters, meters, kilometers; weight: grams, kilograms; volume: milliliters, liters) of measurement. There are other measurement systems such as angle measure (degrees or radians), and time (seconds, minutes, hours, days, weeks, etc.) Within one system, we can operate independently of any other system, usually without too much difficulty. For example, we can change 2 feet to 24 inches. If the systems are measuring the same attribute, we can convert from one system to another, but this is typically more mathematically challenging. Consider the difficulty of converting 24 inches to centimeters.

Stages I and II do not involve any counting. Stages III and IV require that the child use counting, and herein lies the key to understanding how children perceive measurement. They rely on their prior strategies of counting, but now they must also use a suitable unit of measure.

The Metric System

A key to teaching measurement systems, including the Metric System, is to help children develop referents or benchmarks. Human benchmarks, such as the fact that the width of one's little finger is approximately 1 centimeter are valuable. We often use benchmarks we know without realizing it. For example, if the teacher said a person 150 centimeters tall just walked by the door of the classroom, most children (and college students) will have no idea if the person was short, tall or average height. However, if we said that the person was six foot tall, almost everyone in the room would have an idea of the height of the person. Similarly, if we ask how much two liters are, most students would have a good idea because they can relate two liters to a two liter bottle of soda pop. What do you think of for a gallon? Until children, and for that matter adults, develop referents the Metric system will seem difficult to master. Most can picture 100 yards, or 6 feet rather easily because we have developed referents for these measurements. Further, we can use our mental benchmarks to visualize 200 yards. If we had more of these benchmarks for the Metric system, then it would more easily make sense.

Why does the Metric system <u>seem</u> so difficult for American children and adults to learn? Especially since people from other countries say that it is easier! First, the metric system seems more complicated because we do not use it. Second, consider converting between the two systems from children's perspectives. If 1 inch is equivalent to 2.54 centimeters, then in order to convert from one system to another, children will have to multiply and divide by decimal numbers. Elementary children are not proficient with decimals until at least sixth grade and sometimes later. Converting is not amiable to mental math, even for adults. Hence, converting does not contribute to sense-making when teaching the Metric system.

10.1   Problems and Exercises

<u>Solve the problems first</u> and then consider some data on how children solved the problems found in the **Children's Solutions and Discussion of Problems and Exercises** section.

Problem Set A
Measure each of the following.

1.   How many paper clips long is your right little finger? _____
2.   How many arms long is the chalkboard? _____
3.   How many hands high is the bulletin board? _____
4.   How many feet (yours) is the chalkboard? _____
5.   How many pencils long is the table? _____
6.   How many paper clips long is the circumference of your calf? _____
7.   How many paper clips high is the table? _____
8.   How many feet (yours) is the width and length of your classroom? _____
9.   What is the area of the room? _____
10.   How many paper clips does one penny weigh? _____
For 11 through 13, select a box, about the size of a shoe box.
11.   How many dice will fit into the box? _____

12.   How many unifix cubes will fit into the box? _____
13.   If available, how many 1 centimeter cubes will fit into the box? _____
14.   How many full pieces of chalk will fit into a two-pound coffee can? _____
15.   Repeat 1-14 using US Customary measurements; inches, feet, yards, and ounces for weight, e.g., "How many inches long is your right little finger?"
16.   Repeat 1-14 using metric measurements; centimeters, meters, and grams for weight, e.g., "How many centimeters long is your right little finger?"

Problem Set B

1.   A measurement of 60 inches is equal to how many feet (NAEP, 1990)? (12 inches = 1 foot)

2.   The length of a trail that Pat hiked in one day could have been (NAEP, 1992):

   a. 5 milliliters   b. 5 centimeters   c. 5 meters   d. 5 kilometers

3.   Which of the following is usually measured in feet (NAEP, 2003)?

   a. The thickness of a coin   b. The length of a paper clip
   c. The length of a car   d. The distance between New York City
                                      and Chicago

4.   About how many centimeters long is the branch in the figure (NAEP, 2003)?
      a. 5
      b. 10
      c. 25
      d. 100

5.   What is the temperature reading shown on the thermometer (NAEP, 2003)?

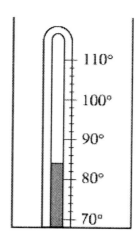

6.   Children were asked to do the following on the NAEP test, metric rulers were
        provided.

        Use your centimeter ruler to make the following measurements to the nearest
        centimeter (NAEP, 1992).
        a.   What is the length in centimeters of one of the longer sides of the
                rectangle?
        b.   What is the length in centimeters of the diagonal from *A* to *B*?"

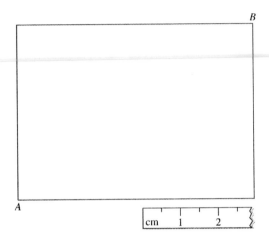

7.   In which of the circles is the diameter less than 1 inch (NAEP, 1992)?

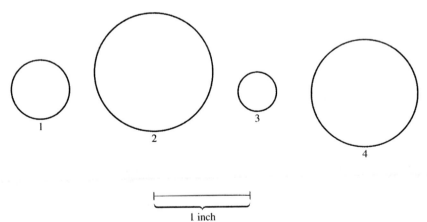

8.   Which of these could be measured with a meter stick (NAEP, 2005)?
        a. The length of a swimming pool
        b. The temperature of water in a swimming pool
        c. The weight of the water in a swimming pool
        d. The number of people in the swimming pool
9.   Which of these could be the weight (mass) of an adult (TIMSS, 2003)?
        a. 1 kg
        b. 6 kg
        c. 60 kg
        d. 600 kg

10. What units would be best to use to measure the weight (mass) of an egg (TIMSS, 2003)?
    a. centimeters
    b. milliliters
    c. grams
    d. kilograms
11. Which of these could equal 150 milliliters (TIMSS, 2003)?
    a. The amount of water in a cup
    b. The length of a kitten
    c. The weight of an egg
    d. The area of a coin

10.1   Questions for Discussion

1. Why would you have children do activities with nonstandard units of measurement?
2. Where might children or adults be at the perception stage of measurement?
3. When asked how tall she was, a little girl responded, "A little above the kitchen table." What stage of measurement is she functioning at?
4. What units do we use to measure light?
5. Why would you have children do problems 1 through 14 and then repeat the same problems using US Customary measurements (#15) and Metric measurements (#16)?

10.1   Children's Solutions and Discussion of Problems and Exercises

Problem Set B

1. 31% of fourth graders gave the correct answer (NAEP, 1990).
2. 60% of fourth graders and 80% of eighth graders gave the correct response on the 1992 NAEP test.
3. 68% percent of fourth graders gave the correct response (NAEP, 2003).
4. On the 2003 NAEP, test 47% of fourth graders gave the correct response.
5. 40% of fourth graders gave the correct answer, while 41% gave the answer of 82°, and 18% gave 85° (NAEP, 2003).
6. For, "What is the length in centimeters of one of the longer sides of the rectangle?" 52% of fourth graders gave the correct answer or any answer between 7.9 and 8.1 which were also considered correct; 11% answered 6 cm; 31% answered 3 cm. (NAEP, 1992). For the question, "What is the length in centimeters of the diagonal from A to B?" 60% of fourth graders gave the correct answer or any answer between 9.9 and 10.1 which were also considered correct (NAEP, 1992).
7. 59% gave the correct response of (NAEP, 1992).
8. On this item, 78% of fourth graders chose the correct solution (NAEP, 2005).
9. In the United States, 54.0% of fourth grader gave the correct solution; however, internationally, 71.7% of fourth graders gave the correct solution (TIMSS, 2003).
10. In the United States, 53.7% of fourth graders gave the correct solution; however, internationally, 68.9% of fourth graders gave the correct solution (TIMSS, 2003).

11. In the United States, 48.4% of fourth graders gave the correct solution. Somewhat surprisingly, 30.2% of fourth graders in the United States indicated b, the length of a kitten. Internationally, 60.9% of fourth graders gave the correct solution (TIMSS, 2003).

10.2 Linear Measurement

Teaching children to measure length using various units of measure is a common elementary school activity as well as a practical everyday life activity. At home, some families keep track of their children's height by keeping written records or marks on the wall. From our adult perspective, measuring may seem obvious; however, children's learning to measure involves some key underlying conceptual understandings that are not obvious. Learning to measure is more complicated than teaching children how to read a ruler. While the method for using a ruler is easy to memorize, children frequently forget the steps or remember them incorrectly. Consider the following example taken from the 1996 National Assessment of Educational Progress (NAEP) test.

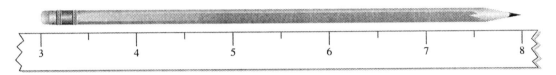

How many inches long is the pencil?

Over 75% of the fourth grade children missed this question. Most children who missed this question answered 8 or 6. Why 6? Children who missed this question answered 8 (the last number to lineup with the end of the pencil) or 6 (the number of hash marks). For these children, measuring length likely has very little meaning outside of a memorized procedure. They do not appear to understand the meaning of the hash marks on the ruler or that the numerals 4 and 5 mark the beginning and end of one *unit* of space. Children are accustomed to *counting* objects such as Unifix cubes and not measuring the distance of the cubes.

Key Concepts of Measurement

Most preschoolers understand that length refers to things that are long or short; it refers to how long something is. They have an intuitive understanding of how big things are without mentally subdividing it into equal parts (Miller & Baillargeon, 1990). Consider the following examples of children's view of measurement and some of their misconceptions. As you read the examples, ask yourself: what are some of the key underlying concepts of measurement? Why are children doing what they are doing?

Iteration/Repeating a unit

One of the most important underlying concepts of measurement is the *building-up* activity of iteration or repeating a unit (e.g., paperclip, inch, or centimeter). Measurement involves learning to *repeat* a unit and the mental ability to place the unit *end-to-end* to measure or represent the length of the object being measured (unit iteration). The fact that the unit can be reused is not obvious to children who do not understand measurement. Children's difficulty with this concept is demonstrated by the fact that:

- Children given meter or yard sticks to measure the room will say they cannot measure the room because they do to have enough meter sticks to go all the way across the room.

One might say that these children cannot *mentally* iterate the units or subdivide the remaining length. How might children measure with a broken ruler? Would they have to understand unit iteration to do so? Again, it is important to emphasize that 4 signifies the space covered by 4 units, not the hash mark next to the 4 or the number of hash marks.

In addition to having difficulty understanding how to repeat units, children are also simply unaware of the consequences of leaving "cracks" in their measuring. First and second grade children frequently leave "spaces" between units without noticing (Horvath & Lehrer, 2000) Also, many young children begin measuring with 1 rather than zero.

To sum up, when it comes to learning the concept of iteration, children may:

- Not understand how to repeat units, e.g. how to measure a room with only one meter stick
- Leave gaps or overlap the units when physically measuring an object (Lehrer et al., 1998)
- Start measuring from 1 on the ruler rather than the zero point – the point on the ruler where measurement begins!

Partitioning/Subdividing

A second key concept is the *breaking-down* activity of partitioning or subdividing. Partitioning is the mental activity of slicing up an object into the same-sized units. Children frequently struggle creating units of equal size (Miller, 1984). For example:

- When asked to make their own rulers, children will draw hash marks at uneven intervals.
- Children mix units to measure an object such as using both small and large paperclips or inches and centimeters.

Accumulation of Distance

A third key concept is accumulation of distance. Accumulation of Distance is the result of placing the unit end to end along side of the object and the fact that the **number of units** signifies the **distance** from beginning to end. Some examples of difficulty with this concept include:

- Children may think that the 4 on the ruler represents 4 hash marks, not 4 equal units.
- A child who is counting his footsteps out loud to measure the length of a table responds, when the teacher asks him what the 7 he just said means,: "7 means the space covered by the seventh foot," not the total distance covered by 7 feet.

An important question to ask to determine if children truly understand Accumulation of Distance is: Are children counting spaces or marks?

Number and Measurement (Measurement is More than Counting)

Another concept that children need to understand when measuring is the relationship between number and measurement. In other words, they need to understand that different numbers can be used to represent the same distance **if** one uses different units of measure. For instance, if one measures a room in meters and then measures a room in yards, one will get two different numbers which both represent the room's size. Measuring is counting the number of iterations one makes. This is an example of the relationship between number and measurement. However, simply counting is not enough. The next examples nicely illustrate why measurement is more than counting:

Which row is longer?

– – – – – – – – – –
— — — — —

- One child responds, "The first row is longer because I counted more segments."
- Mary counted 33 of her footsteps to measure the length of the room; Samuel counted 28 of his footsteps to measure the length of the room. When the teacher asked why they got different answers, Sally said, "Because Mary has bigger feet than Samuel."

Length is not just a matter of counting units, but realizing that different sized units can be used to represent the same length. Children must establish a correspondence between the units and the attribute, such as knowing that one unit on a ruler represents 1 inch. A common misconception is that a rectangle with a side of 7 inches has an area of 7 inches. These relationships may seem transparent to adults but may not be easy for children. As a further illustration, when children mix both inches and centimeters, they reflect their understanding that for them measurement is not significantly different than counting.

Transitivity and Conservation

Two other underlying concepts of measurement are transitivity and conservation. They may not play as significant a role in children's understanding of measurement as the first four (unit iteration, partitioning, accumulation of distance, and relation between number and measurement). However, they still may be necessary for children's understanding of measurement.

It might be easier to understand the concept of transitivity through an example rather than trying to understand the concept through a dictionary definition. Transitivity is: given a relationship between a first and second object, and between a second and a third object, one can find the relationship between the first and the third object and so on. For example, if A=B and B=C, then A=C or if A>B and B>C, then A>C.

As an illustration, put the following five objects in order from shortest to longest without measuring. One could reason that the length of segment D is longer than E but shorter than A; therefore, the lengths of these three segments can be expressed as: A>D>E.

A	B	C	D	E

Another underlying concept of measurement is that of **conservation**. Conservation means that if an object is moved or the parts that make up the object are rearranged, its length does not change.

A Piagetian task is to ask children if the two objects shown are equal in length. Some children will say the bottom rectangle in B is longer. Why?

A.   B.

The child may say that the bottom segment in B is longer because it is farther to the right.

These are some of the concepts that form the foundation of measurement. **Children do not develop them in any specific order, and each child develops them at different rates depending upon different factors such as prior mathematical understanding and measurement experiences.** If a child is having difficulty with measurement, then you might ask yourself, what is the child's understanding of these key underlying concepts? Your assessment of a child's understanding of these concepts will likely be based on his/her errors, and your conversation with the child. From one view of learning, helping the child will entail helping him or her understand these aforementioned underlying concepts.

The Teaching of Linear Measurement

Consider the following approaches or steps to teaching linear measurement and how each relates to how children learn measurement.

- Activities in comparing lengths
  Young children need a variety of experiences **comparing**. These experiences will help in the development of the underlying concepts of measurement (Kamii & Clark, 1997; Lindquist, 1989).

- Activities in measuring using nonstandard units
  A variety of experiences measuring objects in non-standard units is one way for children to learn the concept of measurement and develop referents or benchmarks. When working with nonstandard units it is essential **to connect** this work to standard units of measurement to help children develop a conceptual understanding of measurement.

- Activities measuring with manipulative standard units (i.e., 1 inch strips)
  This suggestion is not agreed upon by everyone. Some believe that using pre-cut units is not that beneficial to children. They point out that often there is only a certain way these manipulatives can fit together and that when children must construct their own units, they often have difficulties that they did not have with the pre-cut units. For example, children will not make all the units the same size or they may overlap them when creating their own units.

- Activities measuring with a ruler
  Clements 1999 and Kamii and Clark 1997 suggest having children measure real life objects, not just pictures or figures in the book or on a paper.

Could these suggestions be adapted to teaching other measurement concepts, such as weight and area?

10.2   Problems and Exercises

<u>Solve the problems first</u> and then consider some data on how children solved the problems found in the **Children's Solutions and Discussion of Problems and Exercises** section.

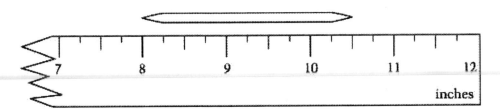

1.   What is the length of the toothpick in the figure above (NAEP, 2003)?
2.   Nancy measured her pencil below and got 6 inches. Is she correct? Why do you think she started measuring from 1?

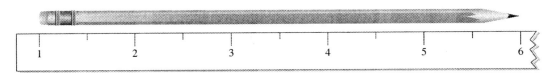

Several children were asked to measure a wall in their classroom using their own footsteps. Below are the children's footsteps and the number below is the number the child said as he or she was counting. Consider what understanding or lack of understanding of the underlying concepts each example suggests. What would you say to each child?

3.   Mary says the wall is 10 steps long.

4.   Sara says the wall is 13 steps long.

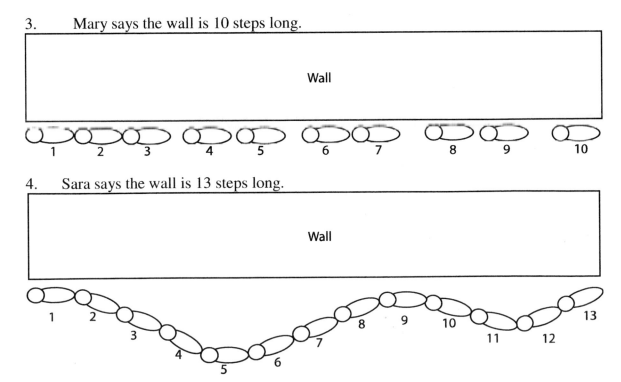

7. Arlene says this wall is 8 steps long. Connie who is working with Arlene says the wall is 8 and ½ steps long.

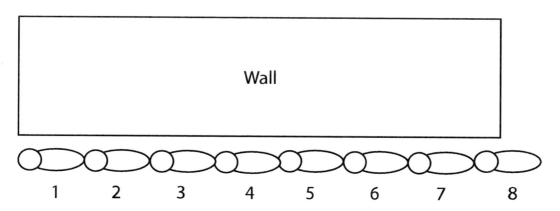

8. Matt says it is 7 and ½ steps long.

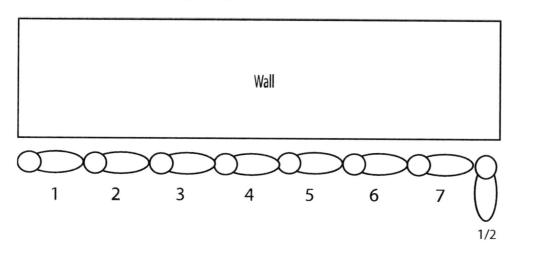

7.   Ted and Martha measured opposite walls in the room which are the same length. Ted says that the front of the room must be shorter than the back wall because Martha counted more steps.

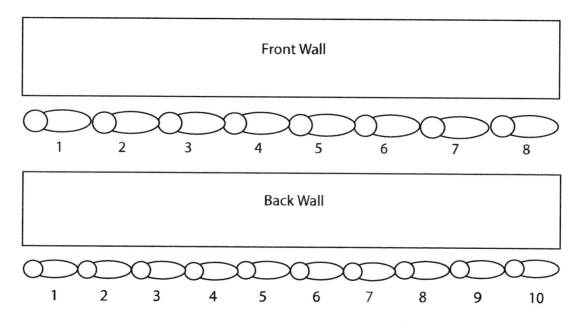

8. Mandy said that she and Mark had the same problem on the side walls. She measured one wall and got 18 steps and Mark measured the opposite wall and got 15 steps. Mandy said, "since I got more steps and the walls are the same my feet must be bigger." Is she right?

9. Andrew measured his pencil and said that it is 5 paper clips long.

10. Sally is shorter than Ronnie. Sally is taller than Michael. Denise's height is between Sally's height and Ronnie's height. Who is the shortest person (NAEP, 2003)?

    a. Denise   b. Michael   c. Ronnie   d. Sally

11. Four children measured the width of a room by counting how many paces it took them to cross it. The chart shows their measurements.

Name	Number of Paces
Stephen	10
Erlane	8
Ana	9
Carlos	7

    Who had the longest pace (TIMSS, 1995)?

12. Here is a paper clip.

    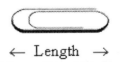

    ← Length →

    About how many lengths of the paper clip is the same as the length of this line (TIMSS, 1995)?

13.   If the string in the diagram is pulled straight, which of these is closest to its length (TIMSS, 1999)?
        a. 5 cm
        b. 6 cm
        c. 7 cm
        d. 8 cm

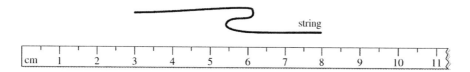

10.2   Questions for Discussion

1.   What do you feel is the most important underlying concept in the teaching of measurement?
2.   Measuring length seems obvious from our adult perspective, why is not so obvious to children?
3.   Below is a formal definition of measurement. Is this definition helpful in helping children understand measurement? Explain your answer.

        The concept of measuring length consists of first, identifying a unit of measurement (i.e., inch, centimeter, or paperclip) and subdividing (partitioning) an object by that unit, secondly physically or mentally placing the unit end to end along side of the object to measure it—iterating the unit (Clements & Stephan, 2004).

10.2   Children's Solutions and Discussion of Problems and Exercises

1.   Only 20% of fourth graders gave the correct response, 20% said it was 3 ½ inches, 23% said it was 10 1/2 inches and 40% said 8 inches (NAEP, 2003).
10.   65% of fourth graders gave the correct response (NAEP, 2003).
11.   Internationally, 21% of the third graders and 32% of fourth graders had the correct solution (TIMSS, 1995).
12.   Internationally, 34% of third grader and 48% of fourth graders had a solution within the appropriate interval of paper clips long (TIMSS, 1995).
13.   In the United States, 39% of eighth graders selected the correct response (TIMSS, 1999).

10.3   Area and Perimeter

Perimeter

Perimeter involves more than just linear measurement. Typically, to find the perimeter children must work with two-dimensional figures and understand that they are taking linear measurements of the sides and combining those. Children sometimes confuse area and perimeter. Some errors that children make finding the perimeter of a shape are illustrated by the following examples:

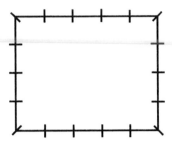

Some children may say the perimeter of the previous figure is 18. Here the child is counting hash marks or points rather than segments.

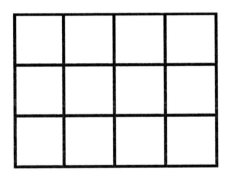

Some children may say the perimeter of this figure is 12. One could say that these children are confusing area and perimeter but a closer investigation may find that some of these children are focusing on the square regions rather than on the *edges* of the square regions.

As a hands-on activity children were asked to find the perimeter using unifix cubes.

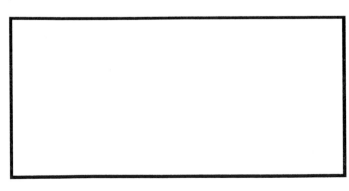

One child did the following:

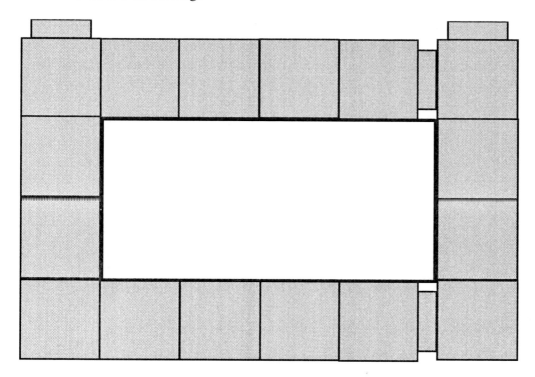

She said the perimeter was 16. This error is similar to the previous one. The child is focusing on the square region rather than on the edge of the unifix cube.

The Concept of Area

It is important for children to develop an understanding of area concepts—not just memorize formulas. **Area is a concept!** Children need to understand the concept of area in order to apply what they know in meaningful ways. The formulas are fairly easy to remember $A = l \times w$, $A = 1/2bh$, etc., but many children and adults do not really understand these formulas and have difficulty applying them in real life or in context.

A bright seventh grade child was working on a worksheet with area problems for rectangles. Some had the picture of the rectangle with the dimensions and others just gave the measurements for the length and width. She had no trouble with the worksheet until she came to an odd shaped figure. Did she understand the concept of area? Only after she was shown how to divide the shape up into rectangles did she see how to solve the problem.

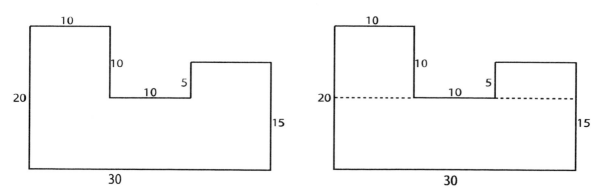

Children's Common Misconceptions about Area

Area measure presents several inherent difficulties for children. First, children must have a good foundation in linear measurement in order to understand area measurement.
Second, children measure the sides of a figure in linear measure and then they must convert that to area measure. Initially, many children say the area of the rectangle below is 8. The sides are one-dimensional, but the solution is two-dimensional! From a child's perspective, how can this be?

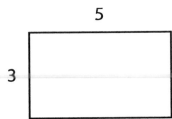

Third, area is about building arrays of units. An array is an arrangement of equal rows and equal columns, like this:

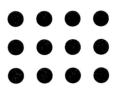

Fourth, reasoning about area formulas requires an <u>understanding</u> of multiplication. Reasoning multiplicatively about area is challenging for children (Simon & Blum, 1994). Children are likely learning about area before they have memorized their multiplication facts. Most children rely on repeated addition or simple multiplicative relationships they know to find other more complicated solutions. To find the area of the rectangle with some of it missing below is then problematic because some children cannot visualize the missing part. They cannot create a mental array as mentioned above, and they cannot use multiplication because they cannot count the missing units.

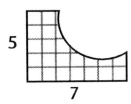

Finally, the formulas for area, and even the act of counting equal rows and columns, seem obvious from our adult perspective. However, an emphasis on formulas and counting square units one at a time can prevent children from developing a conceptual understanding of area. If we always show the grids or have children make the grids to find the area, they may just be counting without understanding. The above problem seems obvious to us; we may be tempted to simply tell children to multiply the two numbers, but will children really understand what they are doing if we take this approach?

Mud Puddle Problem

Consider the children's understanding of area from the two suggested methods for the mud puddle problem. If area is more than just formulas then how might children initially think about area without using formulas? Consider how you might solve the following problem and how children might solve it. Find the area of the mud puddle:

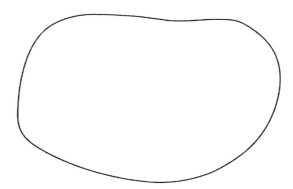

Two ways children have suggested for solving the problem are: take a piece of string and outline the mud puddle, then make the string into a rectangle of similar shape and find the area of the rectangle. Make the shape in cookie dough, cut out squares from the cookie dough, then take the rest and roll it flat and cut out squares again. Repeat the process until one can no longer make squares.

Key Concepts of Area

Like linear measurement, children's understanding of measurement can be traced to some key underlying concepts. Children who have not developed these concepts will naturally make errors based on their prior understandings.

Partitioning/Subdividing

Partitioning is the mental activity of slicing up a two-dimensional, bounded figure into two-dimensional units (typically squares). Given the length and width of a rectangle, it is not obvious to children to make it into an array of equal square units. Can children cover or more appropriately draw square units so that they a have equal rows and columns?

How might a child draw in the squares to find the area for the following rectangle?

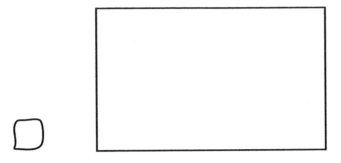

Unit Iteration/Repeating a Unit

Unit Iteration is the activity of covering a two-dimensional region with units (typically squares) **with no gaps or overlapping units**. Also, children are not to mix units such as using squares and triangles to cover a region.

Some children say that the area of the triangle on the geoboard is 10.

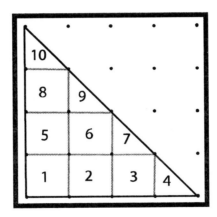

Conservation

Understanding conservation requires knowing that when a region is cut up and rearranged to form another shape, its area does not change. Conservation may be more important in understanding area measurement than in understanding linear measurement. Some children think the following two shapes do not have the same area!

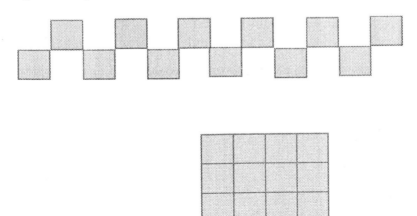

Hence, area of separate figures is additive; the separate pieces of the previous figure shown can be added or put together to make the same area as the bottom figure.

Structuring an Array

Structuring an array requires the ability to think of a rectangle region as being subdivided into rows and columns and to recognize that there are an equal number of units in each row and column. Again, these concepts may seem obvious from our adult perspectives. Consider how children find the area of a subdivided rectangle. Do they count one square at a time or are they able to make a row a composite unit and count that same number repeatedly? Can they count the rows when some of the rows are covered? Children's use of manipulative square tile units to find area may mask their true understandings (Outhred & Mitchelmore, 2000; Doig, Cheeseman, & Lindsay, 1995). For example, it is not easy to overlap plastic tiles. It may be more difficult for children to draw in the same square units repeatedly. They must figure out how to make the units fit together. In their drawings, they do not have equal rows and columns (Batista, et al., 1998). If you ask children to find the area of a rectangular shape, first by drawing in squares and then by using pre-cut square units, they will be more successful with the pre-cut shapes. How many squares will fit in this rectangle?

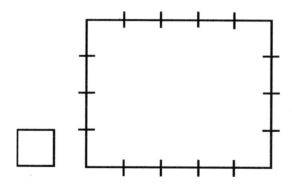

<u>The Teaching of Area Measurement</u>

In elementary school, area is predominantly taught as a covering and a counting process (Outhred & McPhail, 2000). For example, children are often asked to count the squares on a geoboard to find the area. This activity is important for children to do, and this activity is also an illustration of the nonstandard-unit stage. However, when the figure is not cut into perfect squares units, children may use triangles or some other shape to find the area. They will divide the figure into triangles, when the triangles are no longer half of a square, they may use their intuitive sense and decide that ¼ and ¾ pieces fit to make a square. They may also use the idea that the diagonal of a rectangle or parallelogram divides the figure in half. Thus, a one by two rectangle cut in half is equivalent to one square.

Children do not have to think in square units to think about area. In the geoboard example repeated below, some children will combine triangles 4 and 7 to make a square unit and 9 and 10 to make another. Here, area can be thought of as triangle units or square units.

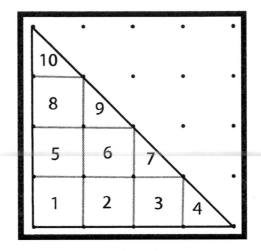

Kamii (2004) has argued that children may not be ready to think of area as square units until they reach the formal operational stage of development, e.g., seventh or eighth grade. Several studies have illustrated that children will often pick a unit that *resembles* the initial shape. For example, to find the area of a triangle, some children use triangles, to measure the area of a circle, children may use circles, and for an outline of their hand, they may pick jelly beans, but not square units. Secondly, while children pay close attention to the boundaries and try not to violate the boundaries of the closed figure, they frequently leave gaps or overlap their units.

Area Formulas

Children's understanding of the concept of area can be used to help them grasp some other basic area formulas beyond that of a rectangle. Area formulas are not magic! As a future teacher, you may have to explain the formulas for a rectangle, parallelogram, and triangle.

How would you explain the formula for the area of a rectangle: **A = lw,** to a class of fourth or fifth grade children?

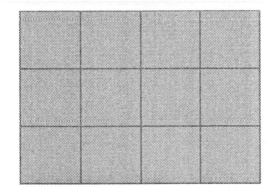

Many hands-on activities such as working with geoboards or filling in a rectangle with smaller squares can be used to explain this formula to children.

How would you explain the formula for the area of a parallelogram: **A= bh,** to a class of fifth grade children?

If we cut off a triangle on the left using the dotted line for the height shown and paste it on the right side, we will have a rectangle with the length, b, and the width, h. This explanation will not work if the parallelogram is too long and skinny (very mathematical terms) but it works for most parallelograms.

How would you explain the formula for the area of a triangle is: **A=(1/2)bh** to a class of fourth grade children?

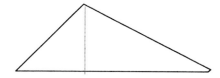

If we copy the triangle, flip it over, rotate it 180 degrees, and connect it to the original triangle, we will have a parallelogram with the same base and height as the triangle. The side, connecting the triangle, is the diagonal of the parallelogram. The diagonal of any rectangles or parallelogram will cut the shape in half. So, if the area of the parallelogram is bh, then the area of the triangle is bh/2 or (1/2)bh.

Area of a Circle

Use the grid to find the area of the circle by counting squares and combining pieces to make squares.

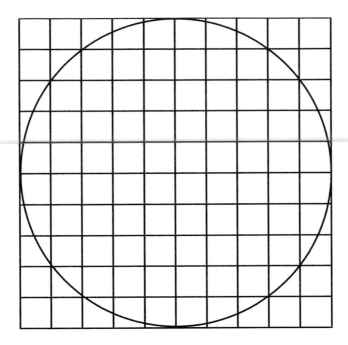

In the formulas for both the perimeter and area of a circle, where does π, (pi) come from? A good class activity is to take string and have the class measure the circumference and diameter of various circles using string. Then have them divide each circumference by the diameter. For the figure above:

1. Use a piece of string to find the circumference of the circle and then divide the circumference by the diameter (10). What did you get?

2. Find the area of the circle by counting squares and divide it by the radius squared (5^2). What did you get? Should you get the same answer as in 1?

An approximation for the formula for the area of a circle can also be developed by cutting the circle into small pie-shaped sections and then rearranging the sections to make a parallelogram.

10.3   Problems and Exercises

<u>Solve the problems first</u> and then consider some data on how children solved the problems found in the **Children's Solutions and Discussion of Problems and Exercises** section.

1. Find the area of each figure without using formulas.

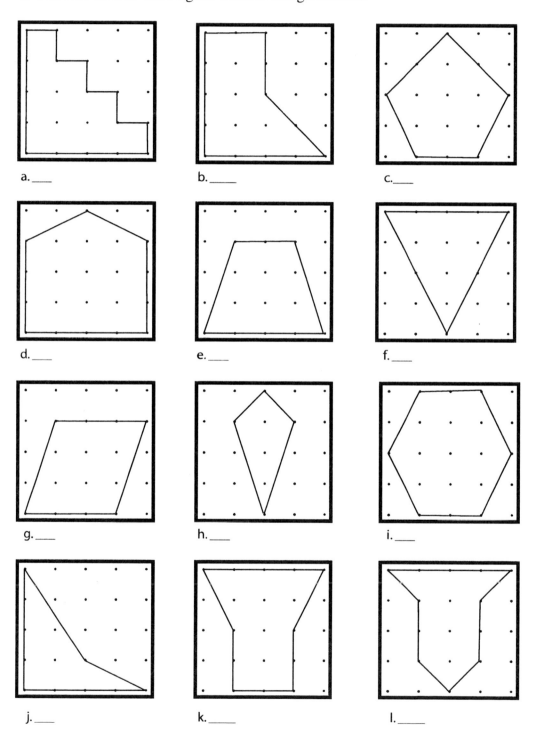

a. ____   b. ____   c. ____

d. ____   e. ____   f. ____

g. ____   h. ____   i. ____

j. ____   k. ____   l. ____

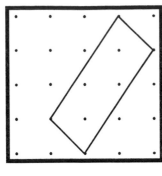

m. ___

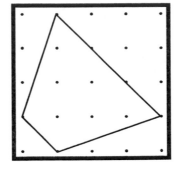

n. ___

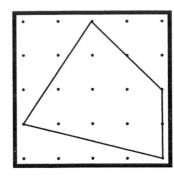

0. ___

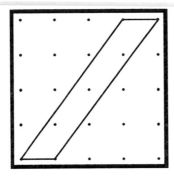

p. ___

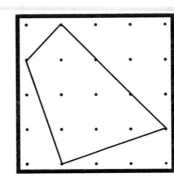

q. ___

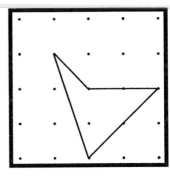

r. ___

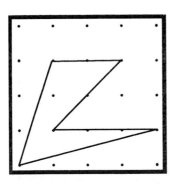

s. ___

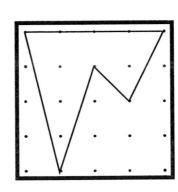

t. ___

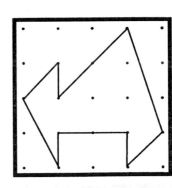

u. ___

Consider the following four problems and how children understand or misunderstand the concept of area.

2.   If these were two chocolate bars, and I asked you to choose the bigger one that has more to eat, which one would you chose? I want you to choose one of these and then count whatever way you need to count to prove to me that it really has more to eat. (Kamii, 2004). (Note that the word area was never mentioned in the question.)

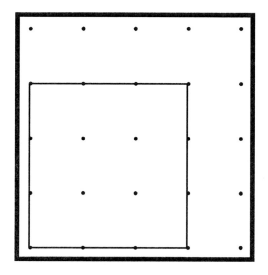 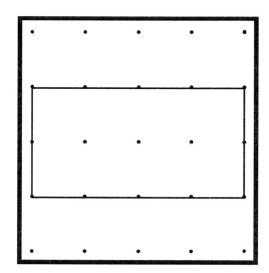

3.   What is the area of this shape (Kamii, 2004)?

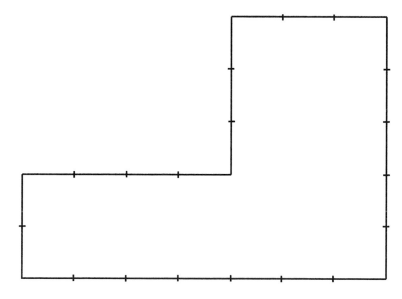

Children gave the following solutions. Can you explain each one?
a.   23
b.   18
c.   23 or 24
d.   24

4.   What is the area of each shape? Are they the same area (Kamii, 2004)?

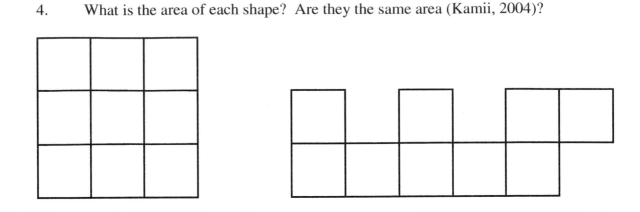

5.   Draw a straight line on the second grid to show where a straight cut would have to be made to make the strip have exactly the same amount of space as the 3 x 6 rectangle.

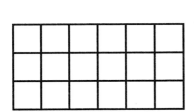

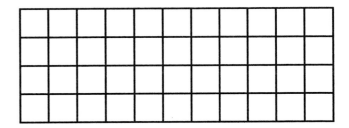

6.   How many feet of fencing would it take to go around the garden shown (NAEP, 1992)?

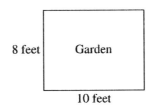

   a. 18
   b. 28
   c. 36
   d. 80

7.   What is the distance around the rectangle shown (NAEP, 1990)?

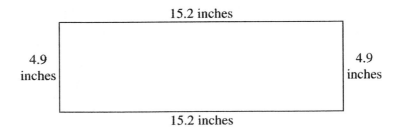

8.   If both the square and the triangle above have the same perimeter, what is the length of each side of the square (NAEP, 2003)?
    a. 4
    b. 5
    c. 6
    d. 7

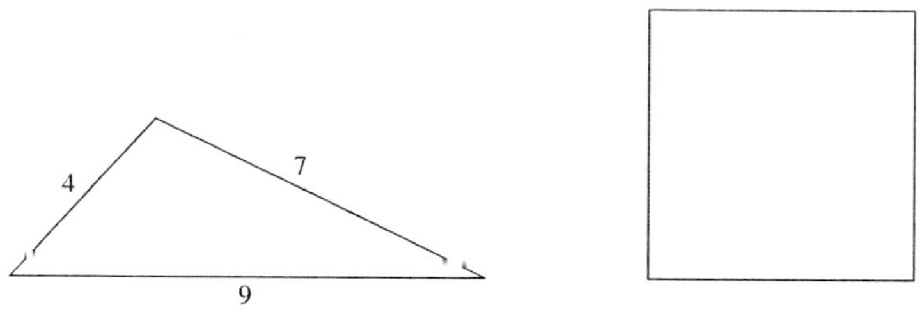

9.   A rectangular carpet is 9 feet long and 6 feet wide. What is the area of the carpet in square feet (NAEP, 1992)?

    a. 15
    b. 27
    c. 30
    d. 54

10.   Which figure has the <u>least</u> area (NAEP, 1992)?

    a. A
    b. B
    c. C
    d. D

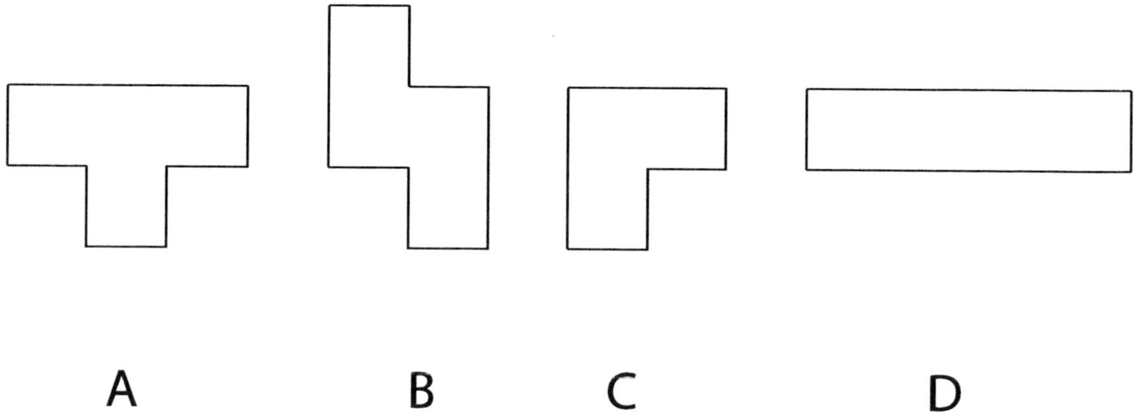

A   B   C   D

11. On the grid below, draw a rectangle with an area of 12 square units (NAEP, 1992).

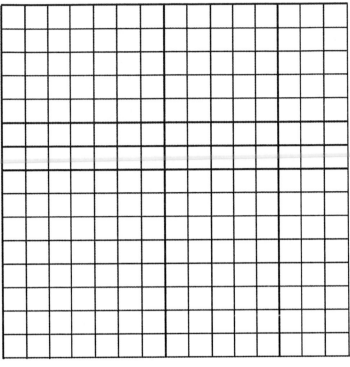

☐ = 1 square unit

12. What is the area of the shaded figure (NAEP, 2005)?
    a. 9 square centimeters
    b. 11 square centimeters
    c. 13 square centimeters
    d. 14 square centimeters

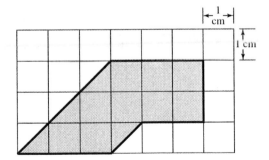

13.   Here is a rectangle with length 6 centimeters and width 4 centimeters. The distance right around its shape is called its perimeter. Which of these gives the perimeter of the rectangle in centimeters (TIMSS, 2003)?
    a. 6 + 4
    b. 6 x 4
    c. 6 x 4 x 2
    d. 6 + 4 + 6 + 4

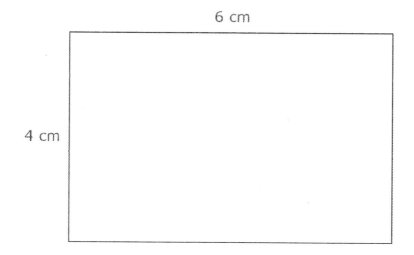

14.   The squares in the grid have areas of 1 square centimeter. Draw lines to complete the figure so that it has an area of 13 square centimeters (TIMSS, 2003).

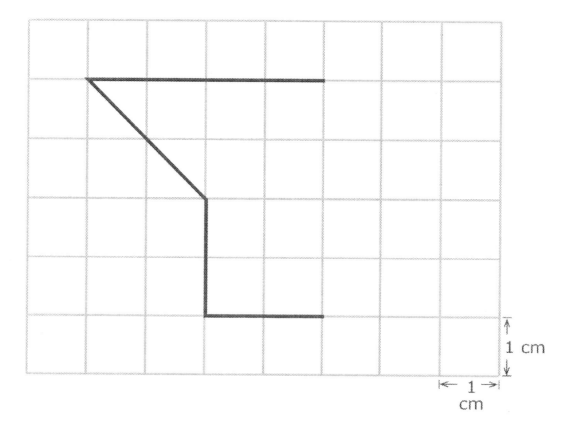

15. A thin wire 20 centimeters long is formed into a rectangle. If the width of this rectangle is 4 centimeters, what is its length (TIMSS, 1995)?
    a. 5 centimeters
    b. 6 centimeters
    c. 12 centimeters
    d. 16 centimeters
16. The triangle represents one tile in the shape of a triangle.

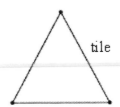

How many tiles will it take to cover the figure below? Use the figure to show how you worked out your answer (TIMSS, 1995).

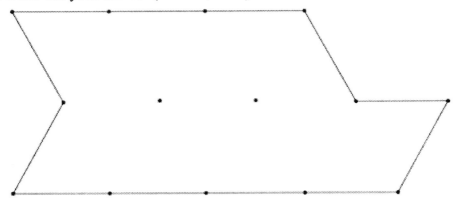

10.3 Questions for Discussion

1. Do you understand area as a procedure or a concept? Explain.
2. What are some difficulties children have with area? Why do they have these difficulties?
3. What activities helped you or might help children understand area better? Why?
4. Consider the following formal definitions of area. Are they useful in helping children understand area?

Area: a process of covering and counting or as a process of subdividing a region into equal two-dimensional units (Outhred, et al, 2004)

or

the amount of two-dimensional surface that is contained within a bounded region and that can be expressed in a numerical form (Baturo & Nason, 1996)

or

the act of finding area is mentally or physically, tiling or partitioning the region with a fixed two-dimensional unit (Stephan, 2004), typically, square units.

10.3   Children's Solutions and Discussion of Problems and Exercises

2.   When this question was asked to fourth through eighth graders, most children counted the pegs on the geoboard rather than squares. In fourth grade, only 16% counted squares, 56% in sixth grade, and in advanced eighth grade (those taking algebra), 83% counted squares (Kamii, 2004).

3.   Of 60 eighth graders (Kamii, 2004):
      a.   23 (counted squares)   43%
      b.   18(counted hash marks)   24%
      c.   23 or 24 (counted hash mark and all or some corners) 23%
      d.   24 (perimeter)   10%

4.   67% of the eighth graders indicated that the two shapes have the same area (Kamii, 2004).

5.   On this task, 6% of the eighth graders drew a line between the fourth and fifth line, and 87% said the task was impossible because it would have to be a zigzag line (Kamii, 2004).

6.   46% of fourth graders gave the correct answer (NAEP, 1992).

7.   31% of fourth graders gave the correct answer (NAEP, 1990).

8.   Only 26% of fourth graders gave the correct answer (NAEP, 2003).

9.   On the 1992 NAEP test, 19% of fourth graders, and 65% of eighth graders gave the correct answer.

10.   72% of fourth graders gave the correct response as compared to 74% of eighth graders (NAEP, 1992).

11.   If only 42% of fourth graders and 66% of eighth graders gave a correct response (NAEP, 1992), what do these facts indicate about children's understanding of the concept of area?

12.   On this item, 47% of fourth graders gave the area (NAEP, 2005).

13.   In the United States, 64.4% of fourth grader gave the correct solution. Internationally, 51.1% of fourth graders gave the correct solution (TIMSS, 2003).

14.   In the United States, only 24.4% of fourth graders could successfully draw lines to give a figure with an area of 13 (TIMSS, 2003).

15.   Internationally, only 21% of third graders and 23% of fourth graders chose the correct length (TIMSS, 1995). This same problem was given to eighth graders in 2003, and 39.2% had the correct solution (TIMSS, 2003).

16.   Internationally, 36% of third graders and 50% of fourth graders indicated the figure could be divided into the correct number of tiles (TIMSS, 1995).

10.4   Volume and Surface Area

Children conceptualize volume in two ways (Wilson & Rowland, 1993). One way is by considering the capacity of a container. For example they may ask themselves, how many cubes will fit into a box? The other way children conceptualize volume is by thinking about the space as occupied. For example, they might ask: how much space does a book occupy?

Young children cannot fully understand volume until they can *conserve*. Conservation of area was illustrated in the previous section. Conservation of volume can be illustrated by Piaget's task of taking equal amounts of water and placing each into two glasses: a tall, skinny glass and a shorter, wider glass. Children who cannot conserve will say that the tall skinny glass has more water in it even though they know they started with the same amount of water. By third grade, most children can conserve (Wilson & Rowland, 1993).

Children in the middle grades have difficulty understanding volume. When given a three dimensional solid such as the large cube shown, which is made up of smaller cubes, many children will count the faces of the smaller cube. For example, what is the volume of the following large cube?

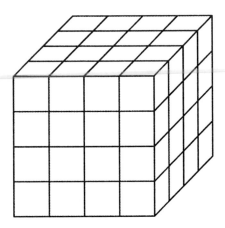

A child may say the large cube has a volume of 54 or is made up of 54 smaller cubes. The child is counting some cubes more than once and is not counting any cubes in the interior of the shape. In one study, only 20% of third graders could find the volume of a solid like this, but in fifth grade over half were able to think about the cube in layers and determine the volume as 27 small cubes (Batista & Clements, 1998). Visualization skills are invaluable in helping children and adults understand volume. Children must be developmentally ready to visualize the interior of a three-dimensional figure, or think of it in layers, in order to understand volume.

Finding volume is similar to finding area in that children must employ the process of constructing composite units (typically cubes), but it is more challenging than area because they are working in three dimensions, and two-dimensional pictures do not show the interior of a solid (Outhred et al., 2003).

Surface Area of a Three-dimensional Figure

Surface area can be thought of as wrapping paper. If there is no waste, how much wrapping paper will it take to wrap a box? In the previous example of volume, the child found the surface area but it is unlikely that the child actually understood 54 to be the surface area. The number 54 was the count of the faces of the cubes. Does the child understand that the large cube could be covered with 54 squares the size of one face of the small cube?

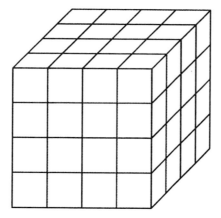

In fifth grade children may be asked to find the surface area of a cube, rectangular prism, or cylinder. Again, one's spatial visualization skills play a large part in understanding surface area.

Consider how a teacher might try to explain how to find the surface area of a rectangular prism without using the formula, or explain what each part of the formula represents to a fifth grade class? The formula is: SA= 2lw + 2lh + 2 wh. Dividing the figure into surfaces such as the front/back, top/bottom, and the two sides corresponds to the formula. Children need an understanding of area and the spatial abilities to visualize the faces of all the sides of the figure.

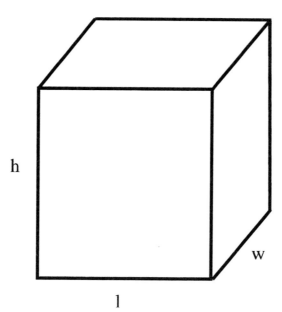

10.4   Problems and Exercises

<u>Solve the problems first</u> and then consider some data on how children solved the problems found in the **Children's Solutions and Discussion of Problems and Exercises** section.

1.   In this figure, how many small cubes were put together to form the large cube (NAEP, 2003)?

       a. 7
       b. 8
       c.12
       d. 24

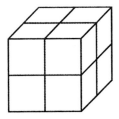

2.   Linda had three large boxes all the same size, and three different kinds of balls as shown above. If she fills each box with the kind of balls shown, which box will have the fewest balls in it (NAEP, 1990)?

       a. The box with the tennis balls
       b. The box with the golf balls
       c. The box with the rubber balls
       d. You can't tell

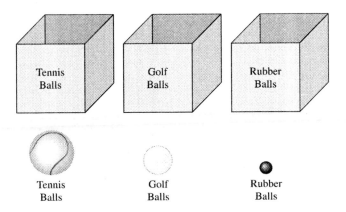

3.   Jasmine made a stack of cubes of the same size. The stack had 5 layers and each layer had 10 cubes. What is the volume of the stack (TIMSS, 2003)?
       a. 5 cubes
       b. 15 cubes
       c. 30 cubes
       d. 50 cubes

4.   All the small blocks are the same size. Which stack of blocks has a different volume from the others (TIMSS, 2003)?

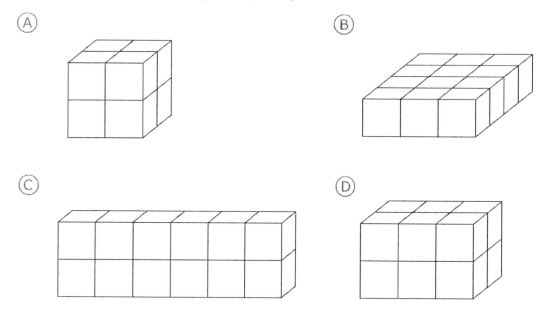

10.4   Questions for Discussion

1.   How do the underlying concepts of area apply to understanding volume?
2.   Explain how to find the surface area of a cylinder.

10.4   Children's Solutions and Discussion of Problems and Exercises

1.   47% of fourth graders gave the correct response (NAEP, 2003).
2.   70% of fourth graders gave the correct answer (NAEP, 1990).
3.   In the United States, 67.4% of fourth graders gave the correct response (TIMSS, 2003).
4.   In the United States, 44.8% of eighth grade girls and 56.1% of eighth grade boys selected the correct response (TIMSS, 2003).

10.5   Time

Teaching children about measuring time, something that they cannot see or touch, involves more than just teaching them how to read a clock (Kamii & Long, 2003). Time is inherently more challenging for children to understand than other forms of measurement, such as linear measurement. First, they cannot see time, but they can see an object when measuring length. Secondly, Kamii and Long point out that children need to have three conceptual orientations in order to understand the measurement of time: transitivity, unit iteration, and the conservation of speed (2003).

The first two concepts are similar to those used in linear measurement but only in reference to time. *Transitivity* implies that children can use a time they know is fixed to compare two other times. For example, if recess is 20 minutes each day, they might be able to compare that with a game of hopscotch or football to determine which takes longer.

Unit iteration is similar to other areas of measurement children must be able to mentally divide time into equal units. In the standard time system we think of seconds or minutes, but we could also use a sand timer to measure time. More specifically, children need to realize that when they flip the sand time over and the sand runs out that they are measuring the same amount of time each time they flip the timer.

Conservation of speed is a bit more challenging to describe. As an illustration, a child is asked to do something as slow as possible, such as put marbles in a bowl while a sand timer or water timer is running. Next, they are asked to do something as fast as they can such as put marbles into a bowl with the sand or water timer running. A child who does not have the concept of conservation of speed, when asked, "When did the water or sand move faster?" will say that when they were doing the task as fast as they could the sand or water was moving faster than when they were doing the task slowly. These children cannot conserve speed. In a study of 30 fourth grade and 30 sixth grade children, only 30% of the fourth grade children understood the concept of conservation of speed, and it was not until sixth grade that 83% understood the conservation of speed (Kamii & Long, 2003). The conservation of speed is one reason why measuring time is so different from measuring length or volume.

The conceptual nature of time is an important issue to consider when teaching time to children. Some ways to address the issue are by relating problems with time to real life situations, such as asking, "How much longer until recess?" and "How many days until the science fair?" Children can also make their own nonstandard time measuring devices, such as water or sand timer.

10.5   Problems and Exercises

<u>Solve the problems first</u> and then consider some data on how children solved the problems found in the **Children's Solutions and Discussion of Problems and Exercises** section.

1.   If you add the digits on a digital clock, what time will give the <u>largest</u> sum?
2.   If you add the digits on a digital clock, what time will give the <u>smallest</u> sum?
3.   Ted went to the beach at 10:30 a.m. and came home at 2:00 p.m. How many hours was he gone (NAEP, 2003)?
    a. 8 ½
    b. 4 ½
    c. 3 ½
    d. 2 ½
4.   Which of the following is the most reasonable distance for a person to walk in one hour (NAEP, 1990)?
    a. 2 miles
    b. 2 yard
    c. 2 inches
    d. 2 feet

5.   Jo's recipe says to bake a cake for 25-28 minutes. About how long is this (NAEP, 2005)?
    a. A quarter of an hour
    b. Half an hour
    c. An hour

d. An hour and a half

6.   Simon wants to watch a film that is between 1½ and 2 hours long. Which of the following films should he choose (TIMSS, 2003)?
   a. a 59-minute film
   b. a 102-minute film
   c. a 121-minute film
   d. a 150-minute film

7.   Which of these is the LEAST amount of time (TIMSS, 2003)?
   a. 1 day
   b. 20 hours
   c. 1800 minutes
   d. 90000 seconds

8.   Kris begins her homework at 6:40. If it takes Kris three-quarters of an hour to do her homework, at what time will she finish (TIMSS, 2003)?

10.5   Questions for Discussion

1.   Why is understanding time so difficult for children?
2.   Einstein showed that as one approaches the speed of light, time slows down (see chapter 8 section 3)! Is this idea relevant to teaching children about time? Why or why not?
3.   Is the nature of time important in teaching time? Explain your answer.

10.5   Children's Solutions and Discussion of Problems and Exercises

3.   40% of fourth graders gave the correct response (NAEP, 2003).
4.   79% of fourth graders gave the correct response (NAEP, 1990).
5.   Only 50% of fourth graders selected the correct time (NAEP, 2005).
6.   In the United States, 33.8% of fourth graders the correct response (TIMSS, 2003).
7.   In the United States, 47.3% of eighth graders chose the correct response, but 34.3% chose d (TIMSS, 2003).
8.   In the United States, 49.9% of eighth grade girls and 61.1% of eighth grade boys had the correct item (TIMSS, 2003).

Chapter 10: References

Battista, M. T., & Clements, D. H. (1998). Students' understanding of three-dimensional cube arrays: Findings from a research and curriculum development project. In R. Lehrer & D. Chazan (Eds.), *Designing learning environments for developing understanding of geometry and space* (pp. 227-248) Mahwah, NJ: Erlbaum.

Battista, M. T., Clements, D. H., Arnoff, J., Battista, K., & Can Auken Borrrow, C. (1998). Students' spatial structure of 2D arrays of squares. *Journal for Research in Mathematics Education, 29,* 503-532.

Clements, D. (1999). Teaching length measurement: Research Challenges. *School Science and Mathematics,* 99, 5-11.

Clements, D. (2004). Geometric and spatial thinking in early childhood education. In D. Clements & J Sarama (Eds.) *Engaging young children in mathematics*. 267-298. NJ. Lawrence Erlbaum Associates.

Clements, D. (2003). Teaching and learning geometry. In J. Kilpatrick, G. Martin, & D. Schifter (Eds.), *A research companion to the principles and standards for school mathematics*. 151-178. Reston, VA: NCTM.

Horvath, J., & Leherer, R. (2000). The design of a case-based hypermedia teaching tool. *International Journal of Computers for Mathematical Learning, 5*, 115-141.

Inskeep, J. (1976). Teaching measurement to elementary school children. In D. Nelson & R. Reys (Eds.), *NCTM 1976 Yearbook: Measurement in School Mathematics*. 60-86. Reston, VA: National Council of Teacher of Mathematics.

Kamii, C., & Clark, F. B., (1997). Measurement of length: The need for a better approach to teaching. *School Science and Mathematics, 97*, 116-21, 299-300.

Kamii, C., & Long, K. (2003). The measurement of time. In D. H. Clement & G. Bright (Eds.), *NCTM 2003 Yearbook: Learning and Teaching Measurement*. 168-179. Reston, VA: National Council of Teacher of Mathematics.

Lehrer, R., Jenkins, M., & Osana, H. (1998). Longitudinal study of children's reasoning about space and geometry. In R. Lehrer & D. Chazan (Eds.), *Designing learning environments for developing understanding of geometry and space* (pp. 137-167) Mahwah, NJ: Erlbaum.

Lindquist, M. (1989). The measurement standards. *Arithmetic Teacher, 37* (1), 22-26.

Miller, K. F. (1984). Child as a measure of all things: Measurement procedures and the development of quantitative concepts. In C. Sophian (Ed.), *Origins of Cognitive Skills* (pp. 193-228). Hillsdale, NJ: Erlbaum.

Miller, K. F., & Baillargeon, R. (1990). Length and distance: Do preschoolers think that occlusion bring things together? *Developmental Psychology, 26*, 103-114.

Outhred, L. N. & McPhail, D. (2000). A framework for teaching early measurement. In J. Bana & A. Chapman (Eds.), *Proceedings of the 23rd Annual Conference of the Mathematics Education Research Group of Australasia, Fermantle, Australia*. 487-494. Sydney, Australia: MERGA.

Outhred, L. N., & Mitchelmore, M. C. (2000). Young children's intuitive understanding of rectangular area measurement. *Journal for Research on Mathematics Education, 2*, 144-167.

Outhred, L. N., Mitchelmore, M. C., McPhail, D., & Gould, P. (2003). Count me into measurement: A program for the early elementary school. In D. H. Clement & G. Bright (Eds.), *NCTM 2003 Yearbook: Learning and Teaching Measurement*. 81-99. Reston, VA: National Council of Teacher of Mathematics.

Piaget, J. (1946). The Child's Conception of Time. Translation, London: Routledge & Kegan Paul.

Piaget, J. & Inhelder, B. (1948/1956) The child's development of space. London: Routledge & Kegan Paul.

Simon, M. A., & Blume, G. W. (1994). Building and understanding multiplicative relationships. *Journal for Research in Mathematics Education, 25*, 472-494.

Stephan, M., & Clement, D. H. (2003). Linear, Area, and Time Measurement in Prekindergarten to Grade 2. In D. H. Clement & G. Bright (Eds.), *NCTM 2003 Yearbook: Learning and Teaching Measurement.* 3-16. Reston, VA: National Council of Teacher of Mathematics.

Wilson, P. S. & Rowland, R. E. (1993). Teaching measurement. In R. J. Jensen (ed.) *Research Ideas for the classroom: Early Childhood Mathematics.* 171-194. Reston, VA: National Council of Teacher of Mathematics.

Chapter 11: Statistics/Data Analysis

In recent years, the most significant change in the K-12 mathematics curriculum is the increased emphasis on statistics at every grade level. State and national mathematics standards are advocating for an increased emphasis on statistics. Children as young as preschool and kindergarten are engaged in studying data analysis or statistics. K-6 mathematics textbooks also include sections on statistics. These sections are no longer the last sections of the textbook, but more often the first sections to be covered. Understanding statistics is important in our modern society because as we encounter more and more statistics, an understanding of statistics is necessary for an educated citizenry to make informed decisions. Further, some would suggest that an understanding of statistics provides opportunities for higher education and opens the gate for educational equity for all!

To this point, CMET has been concerned primarily with mathematics. It is now important to point out that there are some key differences between mathematics and statistics. Mathematics is about decontextualizing information. For example, to find the sum of $3 + 4$, it does not matter whether one is adding apples or computers, the answer is 7. However, in statistics the numbers 3 and 4 are meaningless unless we know something about what these numbers represent. Mathematics attempts to strip away the context in order to abstract and generalize, whereas statistics always depends on the context for meaning. This point should become clearer in this chapter as we discuss children's understanding of statistics, starting with graphing, continuing with average and variation, and concluding with statistical samples.

11.1   Data Analysis and Statistical Graphs

Statistically generated data provides useful information about and can help us understand what is being investigated. However, children often do not understand data as information. Instead, children may view data, i.e., the numbers generated, as equivalent to the event or events about which the data describes. It is important to help children realize that data is not the same as the event (Russell, 2006).

Data analysis can be broken down in many different ways, but from a child's perspective, we might use the following categories:

- Ask a question
- Collect information (sorting and classifying)
- Organize and represent the data
- Communicate and interpret results

Ask a Question

Foremost, it is essential that children work with questions that are of interest to them. Young children are very capable of generating questions. Some questions generated by children are:

- Can you tie your shoes?
- Do you have a pet?
- Do you a have a computer?
- What month is your birthday?
- (At Halloween) What are you scared of?
- (Food) What is your favorite flavor of ice cream?

Children may need assistance in formulating questions or the teacher can suggest a question and the children may reformulate it into one that is more interesting to them. For example, rather than asking, "Do you have a pet?", children may be more interested in asking, "What kind of pet do you have?" or "How many pets do you have?" When helping children develop questions, there are two things we might suggest to them. First, we want to help them develop a question that all people will interpret in similar ways. Second, we want to help children to ask questions that will provide information that is of interest to children (Russell, Schifter, & Bastable, 2002).

Often children's first attempt at formulating a question is too general. For example, asking, "When is your birthday?" may not produce data that is easily usable. Instead asking, "What month is your birthday?" may produce results, i.e., data, with similarities and differences that children can organize in meaningful ways. Children often need guidance in developing a more specific question that can be answered with data and/or that can generate quantifiable answers. By revising their questions, children are learning how to change a general question into a statistical question.

Collect information (sorting and classifying)

After children create a question, their next step is to gather information or collect data. One method that some teachers have used to involve children as young as kindergarten in data collection is to provide them with a clipboard for collecting data. Children walk around the room with the clipboard and ask each other questions. However, turning observations, which in this case are children's responses to a survey question, into data requires higher order thinking, i.e., abstraction (Lehrer & Romberg, 1996).

Kinds of higher order thinking that underlie data analysis include sorting and classifying. Children can work on these concepts independently by simply sorting and classifying without considering the other aspects of data analysis. Children who are sorting pattern blocks, buttons or coins, and classifying them by color, shape, or some other characteristic, are engaged in a valuable activity that will serve as the <u>foundation</u> for future data analysis.

Children may make their own classifications which may be different than the way adults organize the information. For example, second graders classified "ghosts, skeletons, rats, demons, goblins, bats, maggots, and Dracula" under the category of "Haunted House" (Russell, 1991). What would be some things you might list under the category "Haunted House?" Unless young children have the opportunity to formulate their own questions and classify data in a way that is meaningful to them, they will have difficulty in the upper grades constructing representations and interpreting statistical graphs of others.

Organize and Represent the Data

Organizing and representing data poses some interesting challenges for young children. First, they may not be readers and therefore may not be able to give a word description to a response. Likewise, they may have difficulty recording numeric data (numbers) as well. However, they can often come up with their own unique solutions to these problems. Consider how two kindergarten children and a fourth grade child represented data in ways that were significant to them.

- One 4 year old preschooler used unique methods for recording his data for the question, "Can you tie your shoe?" He recorded an 'X' if a fellow preschooler could complete the first part of the process of crossing their laces, a loop if they could complete the second part, and a zero for one child who was unwilling to participate (Whitin, 1997).
- Another child drew a dog, cat, or fish for children's response to, "Do you have a pet?" and if they had more than one pet, he drew overlapping pictures (Whitin, 1997).
- A fourth grader asked, "How many people are in your family?" She made a pictograph by putting a stick figure for each person's response above the number in their family. However, she gave the stick figure long hair if the response was from a girl and short hair if it was from a boy (Russell, Case #3, 2002). In this example, the child is not differentiating between the event and the data. The data, in this case the picture, is a 'pointer' to the event itself, that is who answered this question. (Russell, 2006). The picture reminds the child who they asked.

However, organizing and displaying data, even as a pictograph, may be problematic for young children. Even first and second graders may not yet be at the developmental stage where they realize the pictures must be spaced evenly and be the same size. For instance, the same problems that children have when measuring such as leaving gaps (see chapter 10) can occur when they create pictographs. This difficulty when coupled with Piaget's notion of conservation, found in Chapter 3, can cause problems for children. For example, a non-conserver sees the following two rows of paperclips as being the same:

Consider how children with similar concepts might create a pictograph. Nonetheless, children should still be encouraged to organize and represent their data in ways that make sense to them (Russell, 1991). Later in their development, they will create more standard forms of data representation such as pictographs and bar graphs.

Communicate and interpret results

A valuable skill in data analysis is being able to make some kind of interpretation based on the displayed or representation of data. The creator of a graph is attempting to communicate his or her results. What can be learned by looking at the data? There are always multiple ways of representing data, and no one way can provide all the information. In the representation of the overlapping pets, one child noted that now he can tell who had more than one animal to feed (Whitin, 1997). Children typically have difficulty making a general conclusion about a set of data. They are likely to give more specific conclusions, "Now I know who likes red", instead of the more general conclusion: "Red was the class's favorite color." Children have difficulty talking about an entire set of data; they tend to focus on individual events. They have even more difficulty when comparing two sets of data (Russell, 2006).

Statistical Graphs

Statistical graphs and tables are ways of organizing and representing data. It is common to have elementary school children construct and interpret graphs that are already made. However, data collection is a more meaningful activity to children if connected to real problems in the class or connected to what children really want to know. For example, in a Kindergarten class in which a number of children didn't know how to tie their shoes, the children were always relying on their teacher to help them. The children decided it would be better if they knew which children in the class could tie their shoes, so they could help those that could not. This idea led to a survey, tally, a display of the collected data, and a solution to a problem that was meaningful to the children in the class. They asked a question, sorted the information, made a representation of the data, and communicated the results to other children. Children will need support in interpreting their own and other's data representations and graphs.

Graphs of Real Objects

In the early grades, graphs of actual objects are one possible starting point for organizing and representing data. For example, to answer the question, "Who wore tennis shoes and who wore leather shoes today?", children can actually take off their shoes, sort the shoes, and compare them. The piles of shoes become the representation. Next, the children might put the shoes in rows and compare the length of the rows. Another graph involves children rather than the actual objects. For instance, in answering the question "What is your favorite juice?" each child could stand in a line representing his or her favorite juice.

Pictographs

A natural progression from graphs of real objects to more abstract graphs could be made through the use of pictographs. In answering the question, "How did you get to school?" second graders drew wheels to show they rode to school and feet to show they walked to school. Notice how we can make the natural progression from a graph of real objects to a pictograph. For the question, "Are you a boy or a girl?" the children could form lines, and then draw their own picture on a chart. If children are having difficulty representing data evenly, the chart can be lined so that children can more easily space their pictures. Children often have difficulty with icons that represent more than one unit.

Children are interested in graphs that relate to them and that can be referred to over the course of the school year, such as a birthday month graph. Some teachers use a tooth graph where children put their name on a larger tooth if they lose a tooth that month. One second grader came home with a loose tooth in late May and insisted that his dad pull out his tooth. When asked why, the child indicated that if he did not lose his tooth soon then he would not get his name on the graph. While pictographs may not seem like the most efficient way to represent data from an adult perspective, pictographs may help children make connections between the data and the actual objects or events so that they can think about the data in the appropriate context (Konold & Higgins, 2003).

However, in interpreting this data, it is very common for young children to associate the specifics with each data value rather than making a generalization about the data. For example, children may communicate their interpretation of results as, "Now I know Mary rides to school and Martha walks to school" rather than making the generalization that more children walk to school. One way to help children make the leap to generalization is to ask them to consider the graphs from someone else's point of view. For instance, "Suppose the other second grade teacher, Mrs. B, comes into the room, What would she know by looking at this chart?" Note that in the shoe tying survey, it was important to know who could and could not tie his or her own shoes so that each child unable to tie his or her shoes could get help. It did not matter if more or fewer children could tie their shoes; this information would not help them in getting their shoes tied! The children's purpose for collecting information makes a difference in the ways that the results of data analysis are interpreted and communicated.

Even older children cannot always make this leap to generalization. After fifth graders had collected data about their classmates' personal interests, e.g., favorite sport, etc., the older children thought it was not meaningful to ask a new question. For example, when asked to, "Come up with questions about the data," they thought they should survey again to ask any further questions (Lehrer & Romberg, 1996).

Bar Graphs

Bar graphs are one of the many graphs that children and adults encounter in our technological society. In many cases, children can more accurately compare the bars on a bar graph than they can the sections of a pie graph (Friel, Curcio, & Bright, 2001). In bar graphs, children are comparing the lengths of the bars and in pie graphs, children are comparing proportions—a more advanced mathematical topic.

In the upper primary grades, children typically will construct and investigate already constructed bar graphs. Some math educators have suggested that in traditional instruction children are learning "how to graph," but they are not learning what graphs are used for or why they are used (Disessa, Hammer, Sherin, & Kolpaksoski, 1991). Instead, graphs can be used in the context of making sense of data (Cobb, 1999). When children are working with graphs, they are performing several mental processes including making comparisons and arithmetical computations.

Stem-and-leaf Plots

A stem-and-leaf plot is like a bar graph with more information provided. Keep in mind that initially children focus on specifics, and therefore, the stem-and-leaf plot may have too much information. Stem-and-leaf plots can be confusing when children first encounter them.

Histograms, while in your college textbook, are not typically covered in elementary school. However, they are important in the development of more complex statistical concepts that are used to assess children such as the bell shape curve and normal distributions!

To give an idea of how children might progress in their development and use of graphs, we have modified the following table from Friel, Curcio, and Bright, (2001). There is certainly an overlap; graphs introduced in an early grade are frequently revisited again in an upper grade. There is also a difference, developmentally, in reading or interpreting a graph and actually constructing the same kind of graph. For instance, children in fifth and sixth grade will be working with bar graphs. Children may be taught how to read a simple circle or pie graphs in third and fourth grade, but do not construct them until fifth or sixth grade. This table might be helpful in learning what type of graphing children are typically taught at different grade levels but also how a normal progression of graphs is developed.

Grades PK-K	Grades 1-2	Grades 3-4	Grades 5-6
Object Graphs Pictographs Tables	Line Plots Bar Graphs	Line Graphs Double Bar Graphs Pie Graphs (read)	Stem and Leaf Plots Pie Graphs (construct) Box Plots

11.1   Problems and Exercises

Solve the problems first and then consider some data on how children solved the problems found in the **Children's Solutions and Discussion of Problems and Exercises** section.

1.   What are some statistical survey questions that might be of interest to children?
2.   How might a child graph the following data? Illustrate your answer by making the graph.
   a.   Kindergarten: What is your favorite shape?
        Square – 4, Circle – 3, Triangle – 7, Kite – 1
   b.   Second Grade: What is your hair color?
        Black – 4, Brown – 9, Blonde – 6, Red – 2, Undecided – 1
3.   According to the graph below, how many cartons of eggs were sold altogether by farms *A, B,* and *C* last month? (NAEP, 2003)

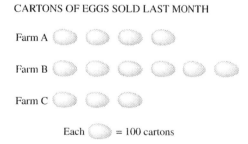

CARTONS OF EGGS SOLD LAST MONTH

a. 13
b. 130
c. 1,300
d. 3,000

4. Each boy and girl in the class voted for his or her favorite kind of music. Here are the results:

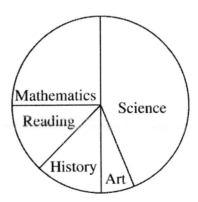

What kind of music did most children in the class prefer (NAEP, 1996)?
a. Classical
b. Rock
c. Country
d. Other

5. The pie graph below shows the portion of time Pat spent on homework in each subject last week. If Pat spent 2 hours on mathematics, about how many hours did Pat spend on homework altogether (NAEP, 2003)?

a. 4
b. 8
c. 12
d. 16

6.   Ms. Chen's class earned how many more points from the read-a-thon than from the math-a-thon (NAEP, 1992)?

POINTS EARNED FROM SCHOOL EVENTS

Class	Mathathon	Readathon
Mr. Lopez	425	411
Ms. Chen	328	456
Mrs. Green	447	342

7   a.   Use the information in the table to complete the bar graph. (NAEP, 1992)

FINAL TEST SCORES	
Score	Number of Students
95	50
90	120
85	170
80	60
75	10

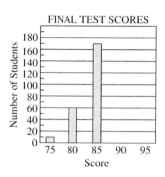

b.   Of the two responses given by children below, which is correct? How do you think the incorrect response was arrived at by the child?

Student A

Student B

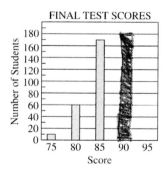

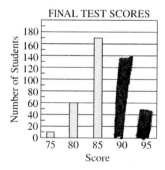

8.   This question refers to pieces *N*, *P*, and *Q*.

 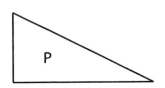 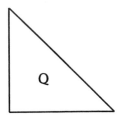

In Mr. Bell's classes, the children voted for their favorite shape for a symbol. Here are the results (NAEP, 1996).

	Class 1	Class 2	Class 3
Shape *N*	9	14	11
Shape *P*	1	9	17
Shape *Q*	22	7	2

Using the information in the chart, Mr. Bell must select one of the shapes to be the symbol. Which one should be selected and why? The shape Mr. Bell should select: _____   Explain:

9.   The following graph shows how many of the 32 children in Mr. Rivera's class are 8, 9, 10, and 11 years old. Which of the following is true (NAEP, 1992)?

   a. Most are older than 9.
   b. Most are younger than 9.
   c. Most are 9 or older.
   d. None of the above is true.

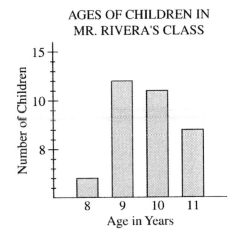

AGES OF CHILDREN IN
MR. RIVERA'S CLASS

10. The graph shows 500 cedar trees and 150 hemlock trees (TIMSS, 1995).

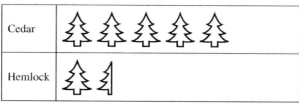

How many trees does each ⟨tree⟩ represent?

11. This table shows the ages of the girls and boys in a club.

Age	Number of Girls	Number of Boys
8	4	6
9	8	4
10	6	10

Use this information in the table to complete the graph for ages 9 and 10 (TIMSS, 1995).

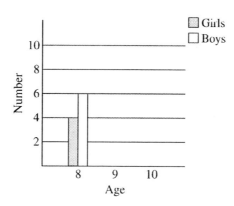

11.1   Questions for Discussion

1. How can teachers help children turn a general question into a statistical question? What are some questions that teachers might ask?
2. How is *sorting and classifying* data analysis?
3. Describe how different graphs about the same data might be used to encourage children's natural progression of graph development.
4. Do you think stem-and-leaf plots initially make sense to children? Why or why not?
5. Why do you think it is so difficult for children to make general statements about a set of data or a graph? Why do they often focus on specific responses instead?

11.1   Children's Solutions and Discussion of Problems and Exercises

1.   A kindergarten class came up the following questions:
      Who is your favorite singer: Lizzie McGuire or Britney Spears?
      Is your dog nice or mean so I can pet it?
      Do you have a 4-wheeler?
      Do you like Legos or blocks?
      What is your favorite animal?
      Who is your best friend in class?

2b.   A second grade class used Unifix cubes to graph each child's hair color.
      However, one boy insisted that his hair was brown, but the class thought it was
      black.

3.   Nationally, 61% of fourth grade children in 2003 gave the correct response
      (NAEP). How might children incorrectly arrive at each the other three answer
      choices?

4.   Nationally, 59% of fourth grade children gave the correct response (NAEP, 1996).
      Answer a is also correct! Why?

5.   Nationally, 51% of fourth children in 2003 gave the correct answer (NAEP).
      How might children incorrectly arrive at each the other three answer choices?

6.   Nationally, 49% fourth grade children in 1992 gave the correct response (NAEP).
      How might children incorrectly arrive at each the other three answer choices?

7.   Nationally, 73% of fourth grade children in 2003 gave the correct bar graph
      (NAEP). To obtain the correct bar graph, a child must select the appropriate
      values from the table, determine the correct height of the bars representing scores
      of 90 and 95, and then draw the bars on the graph. How might children incorrectly
      arrive at each the other three answer choices?

8. Nationally, 32% of children gave a correct response (NAEP, 1996). Some examples of student responses follow.

The shape Mr. Bell should select: _N_

Explain:

more votes $-\dfrac{\begin{array}{c}N\\\hline 14\\19\\9\end{array}}{34}$ $\dfrac{\begin{array}{c}P\\\hline 17\\9\end{array}}{27}$ $\dfrac{\begin{array}{c}Q\\\hline\\\\\end{array}}{31}$

The shape Mr. Bell should select: _U_

Explain: Because if you combine the classes results N is the largest!

The shape Mr. Bell should select: _Shape Q_

Explain:

more students voted for it

The shape Mr. Bell should select: _Q_

Explain:

It has 32

The shape Mr. Bell should select: _U_

Explain: Because if you combine the classes results N is the largest!

9. Nationally, 49% of children gave the correct response. How might children incorrectly arrive at each the other three answer choices?

10. Internationally, 49% of fourth graders and 34% of third graders indicated that each picture of a tree represented the correct number of trees (TIMSS, 1995).

11. Internationally, 41% of fourth graders and 24% of third graders were able to successfully complete this double bar graph.

11.2 Statistical Deceptions and Examining Statistics Critically

Children are frequently not aware of many of the common deceptions/abuses of statistical graphs because they in fact unknowingly make many of the same mistakes. Some children may:

- Start from 0 with the scale
- Change the scale, e.g., mark off units of 5 and then switch to 10's
- Use percents improperly
- Use biased questions
- Leave out the number surveyed

Children will typically study statistical deceptions in middle and high school.

A more important aspect of statistics is what orientations or attitudes children have and are developing about statistics.

- Do children believe every statistics they read or hear? Some children, and perhaps a few adults, believe if a fact is a statistic, then it must be true!
- Do children ignore some statistics because they cannot understand them?
- Do children disbelieve all statistics they see or read? This cynical view may be more prevalent among adults than children.
- Are children critical thinkers about the statistics they see or read?

Thinking critically about statistics is a tool that children and adults need to develop so that they can make good decisions based on any given set of statistics. More importantly, critical thinking can help us from being misled or swayed by the improper use of statistics. To encourage critical thinking of statistics Whitin (2006) offers the following suggestions:

- Questioning the question
- Examining what the data do not say
- Analyzing the categories for the data
- Identifying the background knowledge and experience of the sample population

These points can also be helpful in the process of collecting and analyzing data as previous examples in section 11.1 illustrate. For example asking, "What month is your birthday?" was a more statistical useful question than asking, "When is your birthday?" The shoe tying question does not statistically indicate how well the children are able to tie their shoes nor how many times they have to be retied! The way children categorized scary things under "Haunted House" is interesting but not how adults might find the information to be useful. In all the examples given in section 11.1, it is important to know what population was surveyed: a kindergarten class, a fourth grade class, etc.

Statistics are created by people and are always connected to a context. We want to develop attitudes and beliefs in children so that they can competently question statistics and use them in informative and intellectually honest ways.

11.2   Problems and Exercises

<u>Solve the problems first</u> and then consider some data on how children solved the problems found in the **Children's Solutions and Discussion of Problems and Exercises** section.

1. There are 20 students in Mr. Pang's class. On Tuesday <u>most</u> of the students in the class said they had pockets in the clothes they were wearing. Which of the graphs most likely shows the number of pockets that each child had? Explain why you chose that graph. Explain why you did not choose the other graphs (NAEP, 1992).

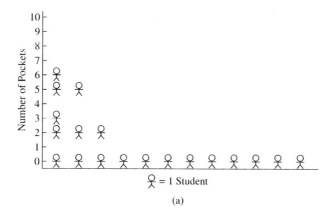

(a)

2.   The pictograph shown is misleading. Explain why (NAEP, 1992).

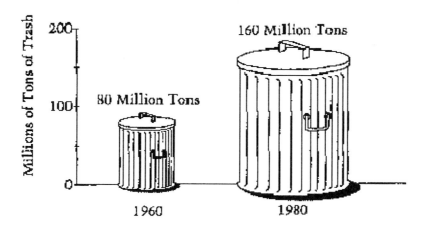

11.2   Questions for Discussion

1.   Why do you think most children unintentionally make deceptive graphs?
2.   Why are some children unaware of a deceptive graph?
3.   How can teachers help children avoid making unintentionally deceptive graphs?

11.2   Children's Solutions and Discussion of Problems and Exercises

1.   Nationally, 48% of the children chose pictograph B (NAEP, 1992). An extended (or exemplary) response was given by only 3% of the children who chose B. These children gave explanations dealing with both the number of students in the class and the fact that most of them have pockets. In order are some children's responses starting with what was considered an exemplary response to responses with the incorrect solution and reasoning.

I.

Which of the graphs most likely shows the number of pockets that each

child had? _____ B _____

Explain why you chose that graph.

I chose graph B because I could read it better and at the top it said that most of the kids had pockets in their clothes graph C had a whole bunch of kids who didn't have pockets - I think graph B explained it better

Explain why you did not choose the other graphs.

I did not chose the other graphs because graph C had too many kids in the graph and graph A had to many kids who didn't have pockets in their clothes.

II.

Which of the graphs most likely shows the number of pockets that each child had? _____ B _____

Explain why you chose that graph.

B and had a total not that many people had 0 pockets

Explain why you did not choose the other graphs.

*c. had more people on the chart than in the class
a. had too many people with 0 pockets*

III.

Which of the graphs most likely shows the number of pockets that each child had? _____ B _____

Explain why you chose that graph.

Because that graph had exactly 20 students

Explain why you did not choose the other graphs.

Because the other graphs had more or less than twenty students

IV.

Which of the graphs most likely shows the number of pockets that each child had? _____C_____

Explain why you chose that graph.

Becaus most them

Had pockets

Explain why you did not choose the other graphs.

it wasnt very many

2. Only 8% of eighth grade students successfully explained why the pictograph of trash produced was misleading (NAEP, 1992).

11.3 Mean, Mode, and Median

Mode

Given a set of data, many young children are likely to use their **mode** as their measure of average.   However, for children in many cases the mode is just the "winner." It is not a number that can be used to describe the set. For instance, when kindergarten children are polled about their favorite color, a child whose favorite color is blue, which is the most popular choice of the whole class, may say, "I have the winning color." He does not realize that blue was the class's favorite color; he does not make a generalization about the whole set.   Rather, children are more likely to focus on the specifics, e.g., "Green is my favorite color and Mary's favorite color is red" rather than focusing on the general (Russell et al. 2002, Case 7).   Teachers may have to encourage children to focus on the general or characteristics of the group. When given a choice, many children choose the mode as "their measure of average" and the last thing these children want to give up is the mode (Russell, 2002; Konold & Higgins, 2003).

Ideal Average

Children, and perhaps adults too, tend to want an **ideal average**. For children an ideal average is:

*   The number that occurs most frequently (the mode).
*   It is positioned midway between the highest and the lowest value (midrange).
*   When placed in order, it is the middle number (median).
*   It is not too far from most of the other numbers.

Unfortunately, an ideal average rarely exists!

Midrange

Another number that children sometimes use to describe a set of numbers is the midrange. As an illustration of midrange consider the following problem. Five children had a contest to see how far they could throw a baseball. They threw the ball: 20, 25, 25, 35, and 40 feet. What one number could be used to describe the average distance?

Some children may use 30 to describe this set of data. Why? Note that 30 is in the middle of the highest number 40 and the lowest number 20 or the midrange. It is not the median, mean, or mode.

Median

The median is an important average, especially when you want to diminish the effect of a few exceedingly high or low values in your data (outliers). The median may be a natural way that some children express the average. Like the mode, the median may be a number in the data, and it has many of the characteristics of the ideal average. However, when there is an even number of data values, the median may not be a value in the data.

In certain contexts, some children do think of average as the 'middle' or 'midpoint'. The representation of the median is also symmetrical which some children may be inclined to accept since they think in this patterned way. They may naturally think that half the values are above and below this number. However, they may not think of this middle number of the median as a way of describing the entire set or as a descriptor. In working backwards from the average to construct possible data values, these children had difficulty when they were not allowed to use the average (Shaughnessy, 2006).

Mean

Unlike the median, in many cases, and the mode, the mean is a mathematical abstraction. It is derived from a mathematical procedure and may not even be a number in the data. It may be a number that makes no sense at all in reality. For example, in the previously discussed basketball problem the mean is 7.6. In reality, it is not possible to make 7.6 baskets. The numbers of baskets made must be a whole number. This example illustrates two reasons why the mean, and sometimes the median, may be problematic for children:

- The mean may not equal one of the values of the data set.
- The mean may be physically impossible in reality; e.g., no one can make 7.6 baskets or have 3.2 children.

Often children learn how to compute the mean as a mathematical procedure, add up all the values and divide by the number of values, in the fourth or fifth grade. Children learn to compute the mean but do not really understand it. Many children do not understand the effect when 0 is a value in the data set, and they are asked to compute the mean. For example, when asked to find the mean of 8, 4, 0, 12, 6, many children will ignore the 0 and simply divide the total by 4. They erroneously believe that the 0 has no effect (Bright & Hoeffner, 1993).

Russell (1995) and others have suggested that teaching the procedure for computing the mean should be postponed because teaching this rather simple procedure to find a mean may cause children to lose the meaning for the statistical concept of the mean as one way of describing a set of data. After computing the mean, children do not understand what it represents or how it can be used. Even older children in grades 4-8 have difficulty when they are given an average and told to make up numbers that will give them that average, AND they cannot use the average number in their set of numbers. For instance, children may be asked: if the average price of a movie is $5.00, give 6 possible prices for movies that will give an average of $5.00 without using $5.00 as one of your numbers. Some children will say this problem cannot be done!

When teaching the concept of mean to children, teachers have found that the previously described misunderstandings associated with mean also apply to the concept of median (Russell, et. al., 2002).

Children in second and third grade are capable of finding an average (mean). Consider how these children might solve the following problems.

> Mary checked out 5 books from the library. Sally checked out 2. Paul checked out 4 and Nancy checked out 1. What was the average number of books checked out by the children?

> A third grader might say: "I took 2 from Mary and gave them to Nancy. So they each would have 3, and then if I take one from Paul and give it to Sally, everyone will have 3."

The child in this example has used the fair-share or a redistribution model that was already discussed in Chapter 3.3. Even when some children used this method, they did not develop an understanding of the mean (Russell & Makros, 1996).

Children may also be unable to reverse the process. Children, who think of average as the mode, especially have difficulty working backward from the mean. The following reversal of the previously discussed book example may be much more difficult for children: given an average (mean) of 3 books, what are possible numbers of books that 4 children may have checked out? Do not use the number 3. These children do not see the distribution as an entity in itself; they see only individual data values (Shaughnessy, 2006). As a further illustration, some children who are capable of computing means will say the following problem cannot be done:

> If the average (mean) age of three boys is 10, the average age of two girls is 15, what is the average for the entire group?

These children think of a data set as individual values, and this problem does not fit their conception. College students also have difficulty with weighted mean problems like this one (Bright & Hoeffner, 1993).

The key to understanding mean and median occurs in the middle and high school where children must compare two sets of data using either the median or the mean. These older children have the same difficulty as elementary children; they have difficulty separating <u>average</u> as a **descriptor** of a single group from average as a **representation** of the group. For them, an average is not a measure of the group; it is something that describes the group.

Children simply have difficulty using a single number, whether it is mean, median or mode, to describe an entire set of data (Russell, 2006). Children may be able to compute the mean and find the median and mode in the upper elementary grades, but they have difficulty understanding what these values represent and how to use them in meaningful ways. As several examples have demonstrated, children have difficulty when they are given the mean and then told to work backwards to construct some possible data. Children have even more difficulty using any conception of average, mean, mode, or median when comparing two sets of data.

11.3   Problems and Exercises

Solve the problems first and then consider some data on how children solved the problems found in the **Children's Solutions and Discussion of Problems and Exercises** section.

Try to answer problems 1-3 (Kamii, Pritchett, & Nelson, 1996) WITHOUT using the standard procedure for finding the mean; i.e., adding the scores and dividing by the total number of scores.

1. A third grader received 40 out of 100 on the first test. The teacher indicated that his grade would be the average of this test and the next test. The third grader wanted to know if he could still get a C if he made 100. The grading scale was 70% for a C (Kamii, Pritchett, & Nelson, 1996). How do you think a third grader might solve this problem?

2. Find the average of the following bowling scores: 150, 125, and 200.

3. Find the average of 2, 9, 3, and 6.

4. Beth averaged 150 points per game in the bowling tournament. On her first two games she scored 170 and 110. What was her score on the third game (Zawojewski, 1988)?

5. The mean of five brothers' ages is 4 and the mode is 3. What are some possible ages for the five brothers (Zawojewski, 1988)?

6. Seven 100-point tests were given during the fall semester. Erika's scores on the tests were 76, 82, 82, 79, 85, 25, 83. What grade should Erika receive for the semester (Groth, 2006)?

7. Consider the number of baskets five children made on the basketball court. The five children are labeled here as players A, B, C, D, and E.
   Player A – 12, Player B – 10, Player C – 7, Player D – 5, Player E – 4.
   What one number could you use to describe the <u>average</u> number of baskets made?

8. Joe had three test scores of 78, 76, and 74, while Mary had scores of 72, 82, and 74. How did Joe's average (mean) score compare to Mary's average (mean) score (TIMSS, 2003)?
   a. Joe's was 1 point higher.
   b. Joe's was 1 point lower.
   c. Both averages were the same.
   d. Joe's was 2 points higher.
   e. Joe's was 2 points lower.

9. The prices of gasoline in a certain region are $1.41, $ 1.36., $1.57, and $1.45 per gallon. What is the median price per gallon for gasoline in this region (NAEP, 2005)?

a. $1.41

b. $1.43

c. $1.44

d. $1.45

e. $1.47

10. The table shows the scores of a group of 11 students on a history test. What is the average (mean) score of the group to the nearest whole number (NAEP, 2003)?

Score	Number of Students
90	1
80	3
70	4
60	0
50	3

11.3   Questions for Discussion

1. Why might a child choose the mode as an "average?"
2. When a child is taught how to find the mean of a set of data, why might the child have difficulty accepting his answer – even if it is correct?
3. In solving the problems in 11.3, what problems did you encounter because you could not find the averages in the typical way? Do you think children would encounter similar problems? Why or why not?
4. How does the Problem #6 reflect the real life application of statistics?

11.3   Children's Solutions and Discussion of Problems and Exercises

In problems 1-3, you will see how third and fourth graders "invented" ways to compute averages. None of the children had received any formal instruction in how to compute averages (Kamii, Pritchett, & Nelson, 1996).

1. "I think my average would be 70 and that's a C because half of 40 is 20 and half of 100 is 50. That's a C because 20 plus 50 is 70," he explained (Note: "the teacher was using a grading scale where 70-79 was a C") (Kamii, Pritchett, & Nelson, 1996).

a. Can you explain why Nick's solution/explanation works? How does his explanation compare to the usual way to average two numbers?

b. Does Nick's solution work for the numbers in the set 80, 90, 94, 100?

2.   To find the average of 150, 125, and 200 one third grader began by using 150 as an estimate. The following is a representation of his work.

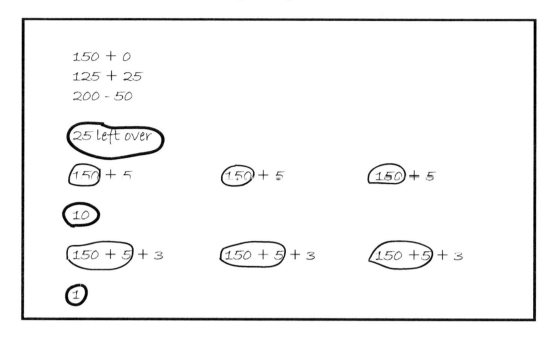

The child's answer was 158 with 1 left over.
Can you explain his thinking?

3.   "The child explained that the average of 2, 9, 3, and 6 is 5 because the midpoint between 2 and 6 is 4, and the midpoint between 3 and 9 is 6. Since the midpoint between 4 and 6 is 5, the average of the four numbers is 5, he asserted" (Kamii, Pritchett, & Nelson, 1996).

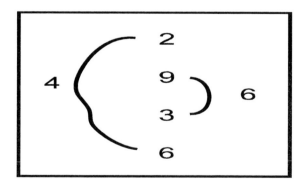

7.   One third grader explained 5 baskets because, "That is the most baskets I would make." Other third graders added all the numbers and responded 38.

8.   In the United States, 74.2% of eighth graders indicated the means were the same (TIMSS, 2003).

9.   In the United States, 51% of eighth graders successfully determined the median (NAEP, 2005).

10.   Only 19% of eighth graders were able to find the mean from the data on the table (NAEP, 2003).

11.4   Variation or Spread

Children typically begin thinking about variation and spread in terms of **range** (high minus low) beginning in third grade. They may also use the **midrange** (average of the high and low) as in the throwing the baseball example in Section 11.3. However, some children do not think of the range as one number, (high minus low) but as a descriptor of all possible values. For example, if children threw a baseball 20, 25, 25, 35, and 40 feet, the distances ranged from 20 to 40 feet. In statistics, range is a single number, in this case 20 feet (40 – 20 = 20).

Children may have some intuitive notions of variability but they often fail to connect these to measures of variations. Consider the following problem. How might children realize that there is a difference in the two machines? Range is one way to measure the variation, but there may be other measures as well.

> In a candy factory, two machines put candy into bags. Five bags were randomly selected from each machine. The bags were opened and counted. The following numbers were obtained:
>
> Machine #1   17, 19, 20, 21, 23
> Machine #2   10, 14, 20, 26, 30
>
> Is there a difference between the two machines? Describe in words why you think there is a difference. How could we measure this difference?

Fifth graders and sixth graders were asked this question. Many of the children focused on the beginning numbers in each set and how the numbers increased. One fifth grader wrote, " Machine #1 has more candy at first but then it gets less and less candy while Machine #2 has a little candy to start but gets more and more candy and it finally passes machine #1." Another child indicated that, "Machine #1 will start off faster but then Machine #2 gets faster…" In one sixth grade class, only one child found the average in both sets, but she indicated that Machine #2 put more candy out! Overall, the children tended to focus on the order of the values and looked for patterns.

To test if the machines are performing properly, find the mean for each machine. What do you find? YES, they have the same mean of 20! They also have the same median, 20, and neither has a mode. Yet, something is wrong with Machine #2, but how can we show it with statistics? What if the differences were not as so obvious? How mathematically can we show that there is a difference between the two machines? One way of measuring variation is by computing the standard deviation, but this computation is a high school activity. However, teachers should have some understanding of measuring variations with standard deviations especially in the use of standardized test scores.

Upper elementary children as well as middle and high school children's intuitive notions of variation may include (Shaughnessy, 2006):

1. Extreme values or outliers. Children focus on the strange values. This view may not be the best, and it may interfere with a more sophisticated understanding of variation.
2. Change over time. Again this notion is like the candy machine problem where children were looking for patterns across time rather than patterns in the variations.
3. Range. Here, some children may have the misconception that all values should occur since they could occur.
4. Likely range. For example, if half of 100 candies are red, and we draw out 10 candies, one might expect to get between 2-8 red candies most times. (Some children believe that if you repeat this process you will likely draw out 5 candies, the expected value, each time.)
5. The distance or difference from a fixed point, usually the mean. An example of when the fixed point might not be the mean or median might be the baseball throwing problem. Here a child might take the largest value, 50 feet, and see how far each person was from it to look at variation.
6. Sum of the residuals. This sum is found by adding up how far away each value is from the mean or median. This sophisticated measure of variation is similar to the development of the standard deviation.

One way to help children develop an understanding of variation is to have them compare different graphs of data or distributions. In these instances, encourage children to look at both average and variation. Children may also look at 'clumps' of data rather than the overall shape of the distribution. This view can lead to useful analysis as well! In some respects, 'looking at clumps' is what you are doing when you are looking at the top or bottom quartile.

11.4   Problems and Exercises

Solve the problems first and then consider some data on how children solved the problems found in the **Children's Solutions and Discussion of Problems and Exercises** section.

1. Compare the midrange for Machine #1 with that of Machine #2 for the data previously described in this chapter. Do these numbers suggest there is something wrong with Machine #2? Why or why not?
2. Compare the range for Machine #1 with that of Machine #2 as previously described in this chapter. Do these numbers suggest there is something wrong with Machine #2? Why or why not?
3. Find the **standard deviation** for Machine #1 and Machine #2. Which machine has the largest standard deviation? Is it Machine #2?

4. The graph shows the daily high and low temperature for a week. On which day is the difference between the high and low temperature the greatest (TIMSS, 2003)?
    a. Monday
    b. Thursday
    c. Friday
    d. Saturday

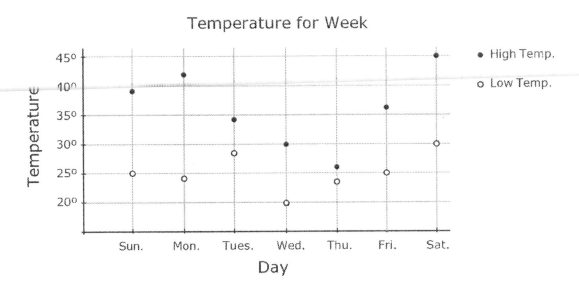

11.4   Questions for Discussion

1. Why is it important for children to learn about the concept of variation and spread?
2. What are some ways that teachers could help children understand this concept?
3. Why do you think that children may be capable of understanding the concept of variation and spread on an intuitive level but not on a mathematical level?

11.4   Children's Solutions and Discussion of Problems and Exercises

4. In the United States, only 38.3% of fourth graders chose the correct day, but 42.4% incorrectly indicated d, Saturday (TIMSS, 2003)!

11.5   Statistical Samples

Sampling is about examining a part of a group (sample) to gather information about the whole group (population). Children may have a few misconceptions about taking statistical samples.

*   Children associate the word sample with customary uses such as a food sample, blood sample, or a free sample of shampoo.
*   Children may believe that it is possible to ask everyone the same question. They typically do not realize how difficult it would be to question everyone, even in a small city (Jacobs, 1999). They believe that you must ask everyone in a group to know about the group.

- Children frequently do not understand how a small sample can represent the entire population.
- Children may be unwilling to generalize from a sample. They may believe that you only know about the ones you surveyed. You cannot sample because populations vary; there are differences. Therefore, you cannot say something that is true about everyone (Metz, 1999).

In contrast some adults believe that small samples provide reliable information about the entire population.

In fact, children often prefer biased samples over unbiased samples. This may be due to their perception of fairness. They especially like voluntary samples because everyone has the opportunity to participate, and no one is forced to participate (Watson, 2004). In addition, some children are attracted to averages and do not look at variation in sampling. Some children try to create a situation to control variation. They want to make sure they get every possible answer. Children's understanding of sampling is dependent on their understanding of average and variation (Reading & Shaughnessy, 2004), and they must be <u>aware</u> of variation in populations and samples (Watson, 2004). Even children who have been actively involved in developing and carrying out their own statistical samples may not be convinced of the power of sampling (Metz, 1999)

<u>Randomness</u>

Children do not see why a sample should be random. They may choose a biased sample rather than unbiased random sample.

- Children may want to sample their friends.
- They might sample the first people they meet. When asked, 60% of sixth graders preferred sampling the first 60 children in line as opposed to the more random method of drawing 60 names out of a hat (Schwartz, Goldman, Vye & Barron, 1998).
- They may want a fair-split to be fair. For example, in a class of 20 boys and 10 girls they may want to sample 5 boys and 5 girls (Schwarz et. al., 1998).
- Children do not think a random sample will work precisely because it is random. "Perhaps the person will draw the names of all girls from the hat."

Children in upper grades are more likely to see the benefits of using stratified-random samples. They may see that different groups are different, and therefore, it may be a good idea to question some from each group. For example, "Girls may think differently than boys" (Jacobs, 1999)!

Children can also struggle with putting the ideas of randomization and stratification together. They may see the need to ask different strata or groups, but they may not see the need to randomize within those groups (Schwartz, et. al., 1998).

Normal Distribution

A central concept related to the statistical concepts of average, variation and sampling is normal distribution. Children are unlikely to ever study normal distributions. However, normal distributions can be used to describe many physical, biological and psychological characteristics. Especially significant to teachers are standardized test scores which are normally distributed. The graph of a normal distribution is a 'bell shaped curve'. Some misconceptions (Batanero, Tauber, & Sanchez, 2004) that adults have about the normal distribution are all scores will be within either +3 or – 3 standard deviations of the mean or there is no restriction on the maximum or minimum values. Also, one single class of children's test scores are typically not normally distributed—an entire state's test scores are approximately normal! Finally, test scores are a finite set and therefore are never exactly a normal distribution. They are approximately normal.

11.5   Problems and Exercises

Solve the problems first and then consider some data on how children solved the problems found in the **Children's Solutions and Discussion of Problems and Exercises** section.

1.   How would you conduct a sample to find out everyone's favorite flavor of ice cream in your school?

2.   A poll is taken at Baker Junior High School to determine whether to change the school mascot. Which of the following would be the best place to find a sample of students to interview that would be most representative of the entire student body (NAEP, 1996)?
a. An algebra class
b. The cafeteria
c. The guidance office
d. A French class
e. The faculty room

3.   From a shipment of 500 batteries, a sample of 25 was selected at random and tested. If 2 batteries in the sample were found to be dead, how many dead batteries would be expected in the entire shipment (NAEP, 1992).
a. 10
b. 20
c. 30
d. 40
e. 50

4.   A survey is to be taken in a city to determine the most popular sport. Would sampling opinions at a baseball game be a good way to collect this data? Explain your answer (NAEP, 2003).

11.5   Questions for Discussion

1.   Why is the concept of using a statistical sample a difficult one for children to grasp?

2.   How could you help children understand the importance of randomization and stratification?

11.5   <u>Children's Solutions and Discussion of Problems and Exercises</u>

1.   Children are likely to want to ask everyone in the school. Is this feasible? When this question was asked of a fifth grade class of 21 children, most indicated how they would record the information, e.g., tally marks, bar graph. Some would have everyone in the school vote. No one suggested taking a sample.

2.   Of eighth graders, 65% correctly chose correctly (NAEP, 1996).

3.   Only 36% of eighth graders and 51% of twelfth graders had the correct solution (NAEP, 1992).

4.   Only 45% of eighth graders could give a written explanation to explain why this survey would be biased (NAEP, 2003).

Chapter 11: References

Batanero, C., Tauber, L. M., & Sanchez, V. (2004). Students' reasoning about the normal distribution. In D. Ben-Zvi & J. Garfield (Eds.) *The challenge of developing statistical literacy, reasoning, and thinking*. 257-276. Dordrecht: Kluwer.

Bright, G. W. & Hoeffner, K. (1993). Measurement, probability, statistics, and graphing. In D. T. Owens (Ed.) *Research ideas for the classroom: Middle grades mathematics*. 78-98. Reston, VA: NCTM.

Cobb, P. (1999). Individual and collective mathematical development: The case of statistical data analysis. *Mathematical Thinking and Learning, 1*(1), 5-43.

diSessa, A., Hammer, D., Sherin, B., & Kolpakowski, T. (1991). Inventing graphing: Meta-representational expertise in children. *Journal of Mathematical Behavior*, 10, 117-160.

Friel, S. N., Curcio, F. R., & Bright, G. W., (2001). Making sense of graphs: Critical factors influencing comprehension and instructional implications. *Journal for Research in Mathematics Education*, 32(2), 124-158.

Groth, R. E. (2006). Engaging students in authentic data analysis. *NCTM 2006 Yearbook: Thinking and reasoning with data and chance*. 41-48. Reston, VA: National Council of Teacher of Mathematics.

Jacobs, V.R. (1999). How do students think about statistical sampling before instruction? *Mathematics Teaching in the Middle School*, 5(4), 240-246, 263.

Kamii, C., Pritchett, M., & Nelson, K. (1996). Fourth Graders invent ways of computing averages. *Teaching Children Mathematics*, 3(2), 78-82.

Konold, C. & Higgins, T. L. (2003). Reasoning about data. In J. Kilpatrick, G. Martin, & D. Schifter (Eds.), *A research companion to the principles and standards for school mathematics*. 193-215. Reston, VA: NCTM.

Lehrer, R., & Romberg, T. (1996). Exploring children's data modeling. *Cognition and Instruction, 14*(1), 69-108.

Metz, K. E. (1999). Why sampling works or why it can't: Ideas of young children engaged in research o f their own design, In F. Hitt & M Santos (Eds.), *Proceedings of the 21ˢᵗ Annual Meeting of the North American Chapter of the International Group for the Psychology of Mathematics Education* (pp. 492-498), Morelos, Mexico.

Reading, C. & Shaughnessy, J. M. (2004). Reasoning about variation. In D. Ben-Zvi & J. Garfield (Eds.) *The challenge of developing statistical literary, reasoning, and thinking.* 201-226. Dordrecht: Kluwer.

Russell, S. J. (2006). What does it mean that "5 has a lot"? From the world to data and back. In G. F. Burill & P. C. Elliot (Eds.) *NCTM 2006 Yearbook: Thinking and reasoning with data and chance.* 17-30. Reston, VA: National Council of Teacher of Mathematics.

Russell, S. J., (1991). Counting noses and scary things: children construct their ideas about data. In D. Vere-Jones (Ed.), *Proceedings of the third international conference on teaching statistics* (Vol. 1, pp. 158-164). Voorburg, The Netherlands: International Statistics Institute.

Russell, S. J., & Mokros, J., (1996). What do children understand about average? *Teaching Children Mathematics*, 2(6), 360-364.

Russell, S. J., Schifter, D., & Bastable, V. (2002). *Developing mathematical ideas: Working with data.* Parsippany, NJ: Dale Seymour Publications.

Shaughnessy, J. M. (2006). Research on students' understanding of some big concepts in statistics. *NCTM 2006 Yearbook: Thinking and reasoning with data and chance.* 77-98. Reston, VA: National Council of Teacher of Mathematics.

Schwartz, D. L., Goldman, S. R., Vye, N. J., & Barron, B. J. (1998). Aligning everyday and mathematical reasoning. The case of sampling assumptions. In S. P. Lajorie (Ed.), *Reflections on statistics: Learning, teaching and assessment in grades K-12.* 233-273. Mahwah, NJ: Erlbaum.

Watson, J. M. (2004). Developing reasoning about samples. In D. Ben-Zvi & J. Garfield (Eds.) *The challenge of developing statistical literacy, reasoning, and thinking.* 277-294. Dordrecht: Kluwer.

Whitin, D. L. (2006). Learning to talk back to statistics. *NCTM 2006 Yearbook: Thinking and reasoning with data and chance.* 31-40. Reston, VA: National Council of Teacher of Mathematics.

Whitin, D. L., (1997). Collecting data with young children. *Young Children*, 28-32.

Zawojewski, J. S. (1988). Teaching Statistics: Mean, mode and median. *Arithmetic Teacher*, 35, 25-27.

Chapter 12: Probability

Probability, like statistics, plays an ever increasing role in our technological society. More and more of our decisions are based on available data and the likelihood of different outcomes. In the real world, most everything is uncertain, and probability is an important <u>tool</u> to help make decisions about uncertain events. To illustrate the importance of probability in everyday adult life, consider a medical study (Schwartz, Woloshin, Black, & Welch, 1997) which found that the ability of a woman to judge data on the effectiveness of mammograms to detect breast cancer was related to her mathematical understanding. The decision to have or not have an important medical test may be based on one's understanding of probability and statistics.

12.1   Basic Notions of Probability

For younger children, probability is looking at what is <u>likely</u>, what is <u>not likely</u>, and the different degrees in between. Children encounter probability in playing games using cards, dice, and spinners. They may wonder, "How likely am I to roll a 2 or draw a jack?" Children develop notions of what will become an understanding of probability through these natural, everyday experiences. These experiences may lead children to solid concepts but also to some possible misconceptions. For example, tossing a coin many times may lead children to believe that a head or a tail is equally likely; however, if they toss several heads in succession they may be more likely to think that the next toss will be a tail.

While young children have the beginnings of an understanding of probability, formal probability is typically not introduced to children until the upper primary grades. These introductions are the foundation for a later, more detailed study of probability in middle and high school. In about third grade, children begin to study basic probability through problems such as: "If a bag has 3 blue marbles and 1 red marble, what is the chance that you will select a red marble?"

<u>The Ratio Concept</u>

One of the difficulties when introducing probability to children is that probabilities are typically written as ratios and most commonly as fractions. For instance, the probability of selecting a red marble in the previous example can be expressed by the fraction 1/4 or by the decimal 0.25. Third graders and many older children do not have a good grasp of fractional concepts (as discussed in detail in chapter 6), and the concept of ratio is typically not covered in detail until the middle school years. In order to better understand the difficulty probability may pose for children, consider the following problem that has been given to children of varying ages:

Two bags have black and white counters.

Bag A: 3 black and 1 white
Bag B: 6 black and 2 white

Which bag gives the better chance of picking a black counter?

A) Bag A
B) Bag B
C) Same chance
D) Don't know

Why?

We might expect only younger children to select Bag B because it has more black counters. However, one study (Green, 1983) found more than 50% of 11-16 year olds (sixth– tenth grade) chose Bag B. The overwhelming reason given by the older children was: "because there are more blacks in Bag B." These children are focusing on the <u>absolute size</u>, (the actual number of black counters) not the <u>relative size</u>, (the ratio of black to white counters). They are adding and not using multiplicative reasoning and fail to realize that the correct answer is A. To grasp this distinction, children must also understand part-whole relations as discussed in Chapter 3.

Children also have more difficulty with probability problems that ask for 'm out of n' rather than '1 out of n' solutions. For instance, in the previous problem the children may have had an easier time finding the probability of drawing a white counter from Bag A than finding the probability of drawing a white counter from Bag B.

As another example of the difficulty that children have with the ratio concept consider the next problem.

An urn has 5 red marbles and 3 white marbles. One red marble is removed from the urn. What is the probability of drawing a red marble?

Many fifth and sixth graders would give incorrect solutions like 5/8; they did not decrease the number red marbles or the total number of marbles (Bright & Hoeffner, 1993). These children do not demonstrate an understanding of part-whole relations (see chapter 3).

Despite the difficulties that children in grades three through six may have in fully understanding probability, it is important that they have early experiences with probability so that they can develop more sophisticated understandings later. These experiences should focus on how likely is an event to happen or not to happen — and not so much on the mathematical probabilities.

Chance

In a traditional math classroom, children typically view mathematics as certain and rule-driven. Their viewpoint is further reinforced by their home lives which also tend to be driven by the routines and rules created by parents or adults. From this traditional mathematics perspective, there is typically only one right answer, and the teacher or the textbook are the sources of these answers. Chance introduces the notion that the outcome (answer) is uncertain and that there is a mathematical way to describe this uncertainty. As such, **probability can be contrary to children's ways of experiencing the world**.

Despite this contradiction, children have some intuitive notions of probability which do not rely on their understanding of the ratio concept. What does **chance** mean to children? Children in kindergarten can distinguish from a certain event (the sun will rise tomorrow) and an uncertain event (in the summer, it will snow tomorrow). They also have some understanding of randomness. For example, a study of 4 and 5 year olds (Metz, 1998) found that they could distinguish between a random occurrence (the color of the gumball from a machine) and a nonrandom occurrence (the gumballs are lined up in the machine, so they can figure out what color they will get next).

Consider children's responses to the following questions about what is *certain* to happen and what is *unlikely* to happen:

- What do you think third and fourth graders might say is *certain* to happen?

    I am <u>really</u> going to the movies.
    I am certain that there are 50 stars on the flag.
    Certain is like a math fact that is true, 12 x 12 = 144.

- What do you think third and fourth graders might say is *unlikely* to happen?

    It means you are really not going to go.
    When you are playing the lottery, you don't know witch [sic] number is coming out.
    Something that you don't usually see.
    You are unlikely to live to be 119.

Children can answer these questions, and think about chance (probability) without an understanding of the concept of ratio (as we already described in section 10.1 in the case of measurement, where children develop through perceptive and comparative stages before using more sophisticated arithmetic).

Next, consider how third grade children might answer these questions that require some understanding of ratio:

- If I flip a quarter, what is the *chance* it lands on heads?

    Half because you can not count on getting heads all the time.
    50%
    You will get heads half the time.
    It will probably be half and half.
    ½ because a quarter has 2 sides
    If you do it 10 times the chance it land on heads is I think 5/10 1 out of 2 chances

- I have a bag with 3 green chips and 2 blue chips. If I pick 1 chip from the bag without looking, what is the *chance* that it will be green?

> I think it will be green because green is more than blue. 3/5 because there are more green chips than blue chips
>
> Other answers: 3/4, 2/3, 5/6

Intuitive Understanding of Probability

Another difficulty children and adults have when considering probability problems is that they tend to rely on their personal preferences and experiences when developing an answer. The next three examples demonstrate the ways personal preference and experiences might influence one's understanding of probability.

> If I have 2 red chips and 1 blue chip in a bag and ask a child what color of chip I would be most likely to draw, a child may say, "Blue." When asked why, the child may say, "Blue is my favorite color." This child's answer is subject to personal preference and not based on mathematical reasoning.

> If a child puts a quarter in a gumball machine, receives a red gumball and is then asked to estimate the probability of obtaining a red gumball, in what ways will the child's experience influence his mathematical thinking? Given his experience, he is likely to overestimate the probability of receiving a red gumball. A second child, who received a gumball other than red, is more likely to underestimate the probability of receiving a red gumball.

> While one is on vacation in a distant city, it rains everyday of the vacation. This person is likely to overestimate the frequency of rain in that city. In contrast, a person who visits the same city at another time and has beautiful weather throughout her vacation may likely underestimate the frequency of rain.

Our personal experiences in any given situation may influence our ability to estimate probabilities in that situation. Personal preference, or what one wants to happen, may influence one's thinking about probability. These estimates may cause one to question correct theoretically determined probabilities and ignore theoretically determined probabilities which seem unrealistic. For example, consider the probabilities for the sum of two dice. A child may have the **misconception** that since there are 11 different outcomes (2,3,4,5,6,7,8,9,10,11,12) the probability of rolling a 7 is 1 out of 11, or 1/11. However, the theoretical probability of rolling a sum of 7 with two dice is actually 6/36 or 1/6.

In addition, children may not understand the nature of the mathematics of probability. For instance, if two children are each given a different spinner where one spinner has an unfair advantage of landing on the desired color, such as the case where Spinner A's surface is 1/8 blue and Spinner B's surface is 3/4 blue, children may believe that Spinner A will never land on blue (Metz, 1998).

Given a random event such as flipping a coin or rolling a die, children may believe that with practice or by some trick the desired outcome can be achieved. Children may believe that a person can flip a head on a coin if he or she 'really wants to'. Some adults may also erroneously believe that they can control adult dice games to their advantage as well!

Equally Likely Outcomes

Children frequently believe in 'equal probability' (Le Coutre, 1992) or that all outcomes have an equal chance of happening. Children have a fundamental sense of *fairness*, and equate fairness with the idea that all outcomes must have an equal chance of happening. In addition, children sometimes believe that in order for something to be *random*, the events must have the same probability of occurring; they must be *equally likely* (Le Coutre, 1992). Children have better success at understanding the concept of equally likely than other probability concepts.

What we know about children's understanding of probability is not always clear. In contrast to what we have just described, some children do not believe that the probability of each outcome of the roll of a single die has equal probabilities. They have an intuitive belief, probably through playing games with dice, that one number will come up more than another number (Watson & Moritz, 2003). The number rolled depends on how or who rolls the die.

Simulations

One way to help children realize that some of their intuitive notions of probability are incorrect is through conducting simulations. From a child's perspective, a simulation is acting out of the problem or conducting an experiment. Again consider the sum of two dice. There are 11 different outcomes (2,3,4,5,6,7,8,9,10,11,12); therefore, some children may incorrectly believe that the probability of rolling a 7 is 1 out of 11 or 1/11, that is all the sums are equally likely. To test the notion that the probability of rolling any one of the possible sums with two dice is 1/11, a simulation could be conducted by rolling two dice 36 times and comparing the number of each sum rolled. A child is likely to notice that one rolled many more 6's and 7's than 2's and 12's. Simulations have been shown to be useful in helping children gain a better understanding of some probability concepts (Bright & Hoeffner, 1993).

Randomness

Randomness is an exceptionally difficult concept for children and adults. When third graders were asked, "What things happen in a random way?" some responses were earthquakes and the lottery. Surprisingly, 78% of third graders in this study did not even attempt to answer the question (Moritz, Watson, & Pereira-Mendoza, 1996). Longitudinal studies (covering 4 years) found that children do not make much progress in their understanding of randomness, especially when compared to their understanding of other probability concepts such as average and sampling (Watson & Caney, 2005). Randomness requires the coordination of the processes of uncertainty with patterning.

Children and adults are not very good at estimating or generating random events (Shaughnessy, 2003). It is our nature to look for patterns, even when none exist.

When looking for randomness, children tend to pick sequences with more switches or those that alternate back and forth. For example, they would likely say that a two color pattern of Red (R) and Blue (B) like the following is random:

RBRBRBRB

In contrast they may say that the following sequence is not random, or not as random:

RRRBBRRB

In fact, both sequences could be random, and in reality sequences with several repetitions of the same symbol happen very often.

The concept of randomness was also introduced in random samples (see chapter 11). As described in the previous chapter, children want to make sure that 'everything can happen'. Consequently, they may not use random techniques and instead may purposely make selections so that 'everything will happen.' If all things can happen then all things should happen! For example, a child drawing out different colored marbles from a bag may continue selecting marbles until he gets at least one blue one because he knows that there are blue marbles in the bag.

Sample Space

A key to understanding probabilities is the ability to generate all possible outcomes. A listing of all possible outcomes is the sample space. An understanding of ratios is not required to generate all possible outcomes. Generating all possible outcomes is also a useful skill in algebraic reasoning (see chapter 13). When finding the probability of the sum of two dice, children who can find all 36 possible outcomes are more likely to determine the correct probabilities. Here, the difficulty for children is not understanding basic probability or understanding ratios, but in generating all outcomes.

Generating sample spaces, all possible outcomes, can be done through tree diagrams, and *counting* principles can also be used to determine the number of possible outcomes. Order typically matters in a sample space; in flipping two coins, HT is different from TH. A variety of experiences creating sample spaces (listing the set of all possible outcomes) will help children in their understanding of probability (Shaughnessy, 2003).

If children are able to construct sample spaces, they may be more likely to understand *variability*. One cannot get a sense for the *variability* of outcomes if one does not have all the possible outcomes.

Despite the importance of generating a sample space, one study found that children in grades 1 through 3 were not able to list all the possible outcomes of an event such as rolling one die even after instruction (Jones, Langrall, Thornton, & Mogill, 1999). Determining the sample space for rolling two dice is more problematic for children, even in the upper elementary grades.

12.1   Problems and Exercises

<u>Solve the problems first</u> and then consider some data on how children solved the problems found in the **Children's Solutions and Discussion of Problems and Exercises** section.

1.   What is the probability of rolling a "3" on a fair die? What is the probability of rolling a "7" on a fair die?

2.   Bag A has 1 red marble and 2 blue marbles. Bag B has 1 red marble and 5 blue marbles.   Which bag has the greatest chance of drawing a red marble?

3.   A bag has 3 green chips and 8 white chips. What is the probability of drawing a green chip?

4.   In a bag of marbles, 1/2 are red, 1/4 are blue, 1/6 are green, and 1/12 are yellow. If a marble is taken form the bag without looking, it most likely is (Zawojewski & Heckman, 1997):
a. Red
b. Blue
c. Green
d. Yellow.

5.   There are 3 fifth graders and 2 sixth graders on the swim team. Everyone's name is put in a hat and the captain is chosen by picking one name. What are the chances that the captain will be a fifth grader? (NAEP, 1996)
a. 1 out of 5
b. 1 out of 3
c. 3 out of 5
d. 2 out of 3

6.   Think carefully about the following question. Write a complete answer. You may use drawings, words, and numbers to explain your answer. Be sure to show all of your work (NAEP, 2003).

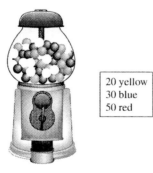

20 yellow
30 blue
50 red

The gumball machine above has 100 gumballs; 20 are yellow, 30 are blue, and 50 are red. The gumballs are well mixed inside the machine. Jenny gets 10 gumballs from this machine. What is your best prediction of the number that will be red?

Answer: _____ red gum balls. Explain why you chose this number.

7.   Jan's Snack Shop has 3 flavors of ice cream: vanilla, chocolate, and strawberry. The ice cream is served in a dish, a sugar cone, or a regular cone (NAEP, 2003).

There are 9 people who chose 1 scoop of ice cream in a dish, or in a sugar cone, or in a regular cone, and all of their choices are different. List or show the 9 different choices. Could another person have a choice that is different from one of these 9 choices? Why or why not?

8.   A bag contains red and blue marbles. Two marbles are selected from the bag. List all the possible outcomes (NAEP, 1996).

9.   There is one red marble in each of these bags.
Without looking in the bags, you are to pick a marble out of one of the bags. Which bag would give you the greatest chance of picking a red marble (TIMSS, 1995).
a. The bag with 10 marbles
b. The bag with 100 marbles
c. The bag with 1,000 marbles
d. All bags would give you the same chance.

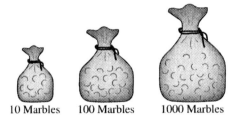

10.   The balls in this picture are placed in a box and a child picks one without looking. What is the probability that the ball picked will be one with dots (NAEP, 2003)?
a. 1 out of 4
b. 1 out of 3
c. 1 out of 2
d. 3 out of 4

11.   There are 15 girls and 11 boys in a mathematics class. If a student is selected at random to run an errand, what is the probability that a boy will be selected (NAEP, 1990)?
a. 4/26
b. 11/26
c. 11/15
d. 15/11

12.1   Questions for Discussion

1.   What is the difference between *fairness* and *bias*?
2.   What are some experiences that may influence your abilities to accurately estimate probabilities?
3.   How are children's experiences deterministic? How might these experiences influence how they think about probabilities?
4.   Why are sample spaces so important in helping children understand probability?
5.   Why is it important for children to conduct experiments or simulations in determining probabilities?
6.   How would you explain to your fourth grade class that making a tree diagram generates the sample space?

12.1   Children's Solutions and Discussion of Problems and Exercises

1.   In a fourth grade class only 10%, 2 out of 20, indicated that the probability of rolling a 3 on a fair die was 1/6; however, 40%, 8 out of 20, indicated that there was no chance of rolling a 7.
2.   In a fifth grade class, 13 out of 17 or 76.5% indicated that bag A had the greatest chance, no one indicated Bag B, and the rest either said neither or both.
3.   In the same fifth grade class as reported in question #2, 56% or 10 out of 18 children indicated the probability would be 3/11.
4.   In fourth grade, 25% answered the question correctly, but by eighth grade, 73% of the children answered the same question correctly (Zawojewski & Heckman, 1997).
5.   Nationally, only 31% of fourth graders correctly answered this question.
6.   The following are some children's responses given on the NAEP test. They are in order, starting with what were considered exemplary responses to responses with the incorrect solution and reasoning.
I.

Answer. ____5____ gum balls

Explain why you chose this number.

____Be cause there are more red gumballs. Also because there are 50 red gumballs, 20 yellow gumballs and 30 blue gumbal

II.

Answer: _____6_____ gum balls

Explain why you chose this number.

I got that answer because there
are more reds so more changes
of getting it.

III.

Answer: _____5_____ gum balls

Explain why you chose this number.

I picked that one because I wanted
to put the number that was in font
the 0.

IV.

Answer: _____red_____ gum balls

Explain why you chose this number.

Red has the most the most
colored gum balls

V.

Answer: _____40_____ gum balls

Explain why you chose this number.

becase it she got 10 red
that makes 10 fess
then have 40.

7.   Solution:
- Dish, vanilla ice cream
- Sugar cone, vanilla ice cream
- Regular cone, vanilla ice cream
- Dish, chocolate ice cream
- Sugar cone, chocolate ice cream
- Regular cone, chocolate ice cream
- Dish, strawberry ice cream
- Sugar cone, strawberry ice cream
- Regular cone, strawberry ice cream or

No, these are the only ways to order 1 scoop with these flavors and containers; or Yes, if they have two scoops, etc.

The following are some children's responses given on the NAEP test. They are in order, starting with what was considered exemplary responses to responses with the incorrect solution and reasoning.

I.

① Vanilla and dish
② Vanilla and Sugar cone
③ Vanilla and regular cone
④ chocolate and dish
⑤ chocolate and sugar cone
⑥ chocolate and regular cone
⑦ strawberry and dish
⑧ strawberry and Sugar cone
⑨ Strawberry and regular cone

Could another person have a choice that is different from one of these 9 choices? Why or why not?

No, they couldn't. Those are all the choices possible. If they ordered 2 scoops or if they combined them they could, but if they won a dip, those are all the possible choices.

II.

III.

1 Vanilla with a dish
2 chocolate with a sugar cone
3 strawberry with a Regular cone
4 vanilla with a sugar cone
5 Chocolate with a regular cone
6 Strawberry with a dish

IV.

Incorrect (28%):

dish
sugar cone
regular cone

Could another person have a choice that is different from one of these 9 choices? Why or why not?

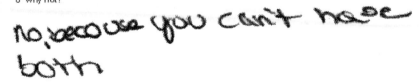

No, because you can't have both

8.   On the 1996 NAEP test, only 24% of fourth graders could successfully list the sample space for a problem like this. Of eighth graders, only 59% could list all possible outcomes.

9.   Internationally, 40% of third graders and 51% of fourth graders correctly selected 'the correct bag (TIMSS, 1995).

10.   Of fourth graders, 66% chose correctly (NAEP, 2003).

11.   Only 38% of eighth graders chose the correct answer (NAEP, 1990).

12.2 More Sophisticated Concepts of Probability

Multistage Probability

Many of the concepts used in multi-stage probability are not explicitly taught to children; however, some ideas are implicitly introduced. This section will provide a few illustrations of the difficulties older children face with probability in order to give you an idea of where children are going in their study of probability so that you might consider your own understanding.

Some of the basic notions of probability in the first section involved multi-stage probability such as selecting two marbles from a bag. One way to help children understand these problems and generate a sample space is to use a tree diagram. Tree diagrams can also be used to develop an understanding of *counting* principles. The number of branch ends in a tree diagram is the total number of outcomes in an experiment.

Some children and some adults have what is referred to as the "gambler's fallacy." They believe that probability has to even out eventually. For example, if one flips 3 heads in a row the fourth flip of a coin is more likely to be a tail.

Independent and Dependent Events

When two cards are drawn from a deck of cards with replacement, the events are independent, i.e., the first drawing does not affect the probability of the second. When two cards are drawn from a deck of cards without replacement, the events are dependent, i.e., the first drawing does affect the probability of the second drawing. High school and even college school students have difficulty figuring out if events are statistically independent or dependent (Shaughnessy, 2003). While this concept may not be directly taught to elementary children, we can certainly ask children if not replacing a marble after the first drawing in a bag affects the likelihood of what happens in the second drawing.

The next problem illustrates older students misunderstanding of probability.

> The two fair spinners shown below are part of a carnival game. A player wins a prize only when <u>both</u> arrows land on black after each spinner has been spun once.

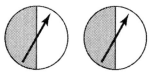

> James thinks he has a 50-50 chance of winning. Do you agree? Justify your answer.
> (NAEP 1996)

Only 8% of 12th graders disagreed and correctly said that the probability of obtaining two blacks was 1/4 (Zawojewski & Shaughnessy, 2000). (See Problems and Exercises, Exercise #2 for examples of students' work.)

While most high school seniors cannot answer this question, it might be helpful if elementary school children develop an intuitive understanding of these more complex concepts of probability. One way to foster this intuitive sense is to conduct *simulations* in which individual or small group results are taken all together. We might give children two spinners, as previously described, have them spin them many times, and determine the experimental probability. In other situations, we could have them toss coins, draw marbles from a bag, or roll two dice and find the sums. Children have lots of 'hunches' about probability and enjoy investigating their hunches in *simulations* or experiments (Shaughnessy, 2003).

Middle school children do better on probability tasks that involve 'with replacement' (independent events) than those involving 'without replacement' (dependent events) (Fischbein & Gazit, 1984). For example, children's performance is better on determining the probability of drawing two kings from a deck of cards with replacement than drawing two kings from a deck of cards without replacement. In another study, 38% of third and fourth graders believed that tossing one coin three times would have different probabilities than tossing three coins simultaneously (Fischbein, Nello, & Marino, 1991). They believed that the outcomes of the tosses could be 'controlled' perhaps in how one tossed the coins.

Mutually Exclusive Events

The language and meaning of mutually exclusive events is often confusing to children and adults. *Mutually exclusive* events cannot happen at the same time. Because the definition of mutually exclusive events focuses on what is <u>not</u> possible, it becomes an especially confusing concept to understand.

A second difficulty experienced with mutually exclusive events is that they are frequently thought of in terms of intuitive notions of probability. For example, if the probability that a person has brown hair is 1/4 and the probability that a person has brown eyes is 1/4; is the probability that a person has brown hair or brown eyes 1/4 + 1/4 = 1/2? Since these two events are not mutually exclusive (they can happen at the same time), the probabilities cannot be added. Further, it "seems intuitively natural" that the probability of a person having brown eyes and brown hair should be 1/2! Why isn't the probability 1/2? As previously discussed, a person might also respond to this problem based on personal experience by considering the people that they know with brown hair and/or brown eyes.

However, if the probability of brown eyes is 1/4 and the probability of blue eyes is 1/4, the probability of a person having brown eyes or blue eyes is 1/4 + 1/4 = 1/2. These events are mutually exclusive, so their probabilities can be added.

Expected Value

Expected value has different meanings—statistical and literal. Statistically, expected value is: the sum of the probability of each outcome times its value. Expected values cannot be used to determine a value for a single event but rather to predict the value of repeated events.

Children may interpret expected value as the value that one would most likely expect for an event—the outcome with the highest probability. For example, if a bag has 3 blue, 1 red, and 1 green marble, the most likely marble drawn out the bag would be blue. So if they drew one marble out of the bag they might expect that it would be blue. This literal meaning of expected value is not what is meant statically by expected value and may cause confusion.

A literal definition more closely related to expected value is the expected number of outcomes of an event that is repeated. For example, if the event of drawing a marble out of the bag just described was repeated 5 times, a child might expect to draw a blue marble 3 times. Children are unlikely to study the statistical expected value, but they may experience activities that examine the expected number of outcomes of a repeated event. Children can compare this expected number of outcomes with results from their own *simulations*.

However, some children do not think of what will occur more often when an experiment is repeated several times. Instead they believe that they are predicting what will happen <u>for each single experiment</u> (Konold, 1991). Therefore, in predicting the sum of two dice rolled, they might change their guess after each roll rather than sticking with one guess that has a greater chance of occurring. This belief in prediction illustrates that children are more capable of considering the probability of a single event as opposed to the distribution of a series of events. Children focus on each event individually and not on the series of events or expected number of outcomes.

Odds

If the odds against drawing a blue marble from a bag are 8 to 1, many erroneously think that the probability of drawing a blue marble from the bag is 1/8 when if fact it is 1/9. Here constructing the *sample space* may help children see the relationship between odds and probability. However, when working with probabilities and odds on a horse race where the odds against my horse winning are 10 to 1, the *sample space* is more difficult to determine.

Children are better able to compare two odds when they share a number in common. For instance, children can more easily answer a question such as: which are the better odds, 1:5 or 3:5? Children have more difficulty comparing odds when all the numbers are different as is the case in the question: which are the better odds, 2:3 or 3:4 (Metz, 1998)? An understanding of ratio concept is crucial here.

12.2 Problems and Exercises

<u>Solve the problems first</u> and then consider some data on how children solved the problems found in the **Children's Solutions and Discussion of Problems and Exercises** section.

1. If I flip two coins, which result is most likely to happen?
    a) HH
    b) HT
    c) TH
    d) TT
    e) All results are equally likely.
2. A boy has two quarters. What is the probability that he will get one "heads" and one "tails' if he flips them? Explain (Ruble, 2006).
3. What is the probability of getting two 'heads' on a toss of two coins?

4.   The two fair spinners shown below are part of a carnival game. A player wins a prize only when <u>both</u> arrows land on black after each spinner has been spun once.

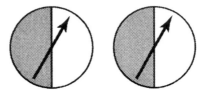

James thinks he has a 50-50 chance of winning. Do you agree? Justify your answer (NAEP, 1996).

5.   A package of candies contained 10 red candies, 10 blue candies, and 10 green candies. Bill shook up the package, opened it, and started taking out one candy at a time and eating it. The first 2 candies he took out and ate were blue. Bill thinks the probability of getting a blue candy on his third try is 10/30 or 1/3. Is Bill correct (NAEP, 2005)?

6.   A box contains 3 chips numbered 1 through 3. One chip is taken at random from the box and then put back into the box. Then a second chip will be taken from the box. In the space provided, list all possible pairs of chips (NAEP, 2003).

Number on First Chip	Number on Second Chip

12.2   Questions for Discussion

1.   How might one's personal experience influence one's understanding of independent/dependent events?

2.   How can we help children look at a series of events as a distribution rather than considering each event individually?

3.   How do all the branches in a tree diagram illustrate the counting principle or generate all possible outcomes?

4.   If the probability that a person has brown hair is 1/4 and the probability that a person has brown eyes is 1/4, is the probability that a person has brown hair or brown eyes 1/4 + 1/4 = 1/2? Why or why not?

5.   Consider problems #2 and #3 and the descriptions given in the children's solutions and discussion for these problems. What implications might these problems have for just looking for correct solutions or looking at children's explanations of their solutions—both correct and incorrect?

12.2   Children's Solutions and Discussion of Problems and Exercises

1.   If the question were changed to "least likely," we are likely to get different results (Konold, et al., 1993). In a fifth grade class 42% (8 out of 19) incorrectly chose either b. HT or c. TH, no one chose HH or TT, and 58%, 11 out of 19, indicated that 'All the results are equally likely.'.

2.   Out of 173 children in grades 5, 7, 9, and 11, 54% gave the correct response. However, some children came to the correct conclusion through incorrect reasoning: "It's a 50 percent chance each so he has an even chance of getting both." Or "because there are two outcomes there is a 50 percent chance of getting any of the outcomes concluding two heads." On the same question, 23% said 1/3. One high school student explained "… two heads, two tails, and one tail and one head. So one out of three." Some respondents interpreted the problem as 'a head followed by a tail' and they gave 1/4 as their response. They had reasonable mathematical thinking but used an alternative interpretation (Rubel, 2006).

3.   In a different study, only 18% of 13 year olds responded correctly and 58% responded incorrectly with 1/2 (Bright & Hoeffner, 1993).

4.   Only 8% of twelfth graders had this problem correct. What follows are some student responses.

I.

   ⓐ Yes   ● No

Justify your answer.

He only has a ¼ chance because you must multiply the 2 ½ chances from each individual spinner.

II.

   ⓐ Yes   ⓑ No

Justify your answer.

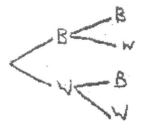

Ⓐ Yes ● No

Justify your answer.

She has a 25% chance because there are now a total of 4 halves because there are 2 circles.

III.

Ⓐ Yes ● No

Justify your answer.

they start at the same place but it depends on how hard or light each spinner was spun

5. Of eighth graders, 48% gave a correct solution and 30% gave a partially correct solution to explain why the probability was not 1/3 (NAEP, 2005).
6. Only 18% of eighth graders could successfully list the sample space (NAEP, 2003).

Chapter 12: References

Bright, G. W. & Hoeffner, K. (1993). Measurement, probability, statistics, and graphing. In D. T. Owens (Ed.) *Research ideas for the classroom: Middle grades mathematics*. 78-98. Reston, VA: NCTM.

Green, D. R. (1983). A survey of probability concepts in 3000 pupils aged 11-16 years. In D. R. Grey, P. Holmes, V. Barnett, & G. M. Constable (Eds.), *Proceedings of the First International Conference on Teaching Statistics* (pp.766-783). Sheffield, England: Teaching Statistics Trust.

Fischbein, E., & Gazit, A. (1984). Does the teaching of probability improve probabilistic intuitions? *Educational Studies in Mathematics, 15*, 1-24.

Fischbein, E., Nello, M. S., & Marino, M. S. (1991). Factors affecting probabilistic judgments in children and adolescents. *Educational Studies in Mathematics, 22*, 523-549.

Jones, G. A., Langrall, C. W., Thornton, C. A., & Mogill, A. T. (1999). Students' probabilistic thinking in instruction. *Journal for Research in Mathematics Education, 30*, 487-519.

Konold, C. (1991). Understanding students' beliefs about probability. In E. von Glasersfeld (Ed.), *Constructivism in mathematics education*. (pp. 139-156). Dordrecht, the Netherlands: Kluwer.

Konold, C., Pollatsek, A., Well, A., Lohmeier, J. & Lipson, A. (1993). Inconsistencies in students' reasoning about probability. *Journal for Research in Mathematics Education, 24,* 392-414.

LeCoutre, V. P., (1992). Cognitive models and problem spaces in "purely random" situations. *Educational Studies in Mathematics, 23,* 557-568.

Metz, K. E. (1998). Emergent ideas of chance and probability in primary-grade children. In S. P. Lajorie (Ed.), *Reflections on statistics: Learning, teaching and assessment in grades K-12*. Mahwah, NJ: Erlbaum.

Moritz, J. B., Watson, J. M., & Pereira-Mendoza, L. (1996). *The language of statistical understanding: An investigation in two countries.* Paper presented at the annual conference of the Australian Association for Research in Education: Singapore.

Rubel, L. H. (2006). Students' probabilistic thinking revealed: The case of coin tosses. In D. Ben-Zvi & J. Garfield (Eds.) *The challenge of developing statistical literacy, reasoning, and thinking.* 49-60. Dordrecht: Kluwer.

Schwartz, L., Woloshin, S., Black, W. C., & Welch, H. G. (1997). The role of numeracy in understanding the benefit of screening mammography. *Annals of Internal Medicine, 127,* 966-972.

Shaughnessy, M. J. (2003). Research on Students' Understanding of probability. . In J. Kilpatrick, G. Martin, & D. Schifter (Eds.), *A research companion to the principles and standards for school mathematics.* 216-226. Reston, VA: NCTM.

Watson, J. M. & Caney, A. (2005). Development of reasoning about random events. *Focus on Learning Problems in Mathematics, 27,* 1-42.

Watson, J. M. & Moritz, J. B. (2003). Fairness of dice: A longitudinal study of students' beliefs and strategies for making judgments. *Journal for Research in Mathematics Education, 34,* 270-304.

Zawojeski, J. S., & Shaughnessy, J. M. (2000). Data and chance. In E. A. Silver & P. A. Kenney (Eds.), *Results from the Seventh Mathematical Assessment of the National Assessment of Educational Progress* (pp. 235-268). Reston, VA: National Council of Teacher of Mathematics.

Chapter 13: Algebraic Reasoning

Elementary school children do not typically study algebra, but they do study many of the underlying concepts of algebra or what is often referred to as *algebraic reasoning*. These fundamental concepts include: the concept of variable, expressing generality, function, graphing, and equality. This chapter will describe these fundamental concepts and how to engage children in algebraic reasoning. However, it should be noted that in most elementary school mathematics lessons, algebraic reasoning is not typically the main focus of study but rather an extension that can be added on to arithmetic activities.

There are several perspectives on what algebra is and, more importantly, on what algebraic reasoning entails. Foremost, this chapter presents a view of algebra as *generalized arithmetic*. This view point can be contrasted to the algebraic reasoning that occurs in high school algebra where algebra is primarily presented as the manipulation of symbols. Some examples of this high school perspective include: solving equations, factoring, and simplifying expressions. These activities can be described as transformational activities, but they are not and should not be a main focus of elementary school level mathematics. Based on the National Research Council book, *Adding it Up* (2001), we offer our own perspective of what algebraic reasoning should entail in the elementary school. One way to categorize algebraic reasoning at the elementary level is by the types of activities that children engage in. These activities include but are not limited to:

- **Representational Activities:** These activities include representing a number, relationship, or operation. Children might use a letter of the alphabet, a box, or even a question mark to represent an unknown number in a problem. Children may represent a relationship in a problem using symbols such as N + 5 to represent the fact that John has 5 more marbles than his friend. They can also represent an operation such as doubling with the expression 2N. However, representation is more than the symbolic notation; it is also the mental ability to represent a number, relationship, or operation.

- **Generalizing a Specific Problem:** Children generalize a specific problem into a general case. For example, a specific case might involve the problem, "How many eyes and ears do three goats have?" and a general case might be, "How can we express the number of eyes and ears, if we do not know the number of goats or if there are 'N' goats?" Another common example is the generalization of a pattern.

- **Generalizing about a Principle or Property:** Children can generalize about a principle or a property of numbers such as the commutative property of addition, which can be expressed as: a + b = b + a. This type of generalization often involves children in justifying or explaining why they think the sum of any two numbers added together will be the same regardless of the order of the numbers. A mathematics relationship that children might generalize is the sum of any two odd numbers is always an even number (National Research Council, 2001).

In addition to these activities, children study the algebraic concepts of function, graphing, and equality. The concept of function is often introduced through various generalizing activities.

Graphing is one way of representing such functions. Equality is a concept relevant to both arithmetic and algebra. The concept of equality may at first seem straightforward and easily understood by children, but it is not.

13.1   The Concept of Variable

Children begin thinking symbolically early in their development. For example, in play children will represent one object for another such as pretending that a block is a phone. Similarly, in algebra a letter may stand for a number. Both of these activities are representational activities.

The concept of variable is a complex one, and it is important to note that a variable is more than a letter used in place of a number or a place holder. However, many children and older students have this narrow view of variable. To address complex nature of the concept of variable, consider the following "What's My Rule" activity. Note that with elementary school children the primary purposes of this activity include problem solving and practice with computation. Algebraic reasoning is simply an extension that can be added to this activity, and it is also a long term goal that develops after doing the activity many times. This activity is a common elementary school activity, and there are many different variations and names for it.

What's My Rule?

Mathematical Purpose:

> This activity has short and long term purposes. Its short term purposes include providing children with the opportunity to practice problem solving and computation. Its long term purpose emerges as the activity is done throughout the school year. After repeated use, the long term goal is to help children develop algebraic reasoning, specifically the concepts of variable and of function.

Suggestions:

- This activity is a good introductory or warm-up activity.
- Carry out this activity for 10 - 15 minutes.
- This activity should be a mental math activity.
- Children should not use paper or pencil.

Tell children you are thinking of a rule and that when you apply the rule to the first number you get the second number. Write <u>at least two pairs</u> of numbers that fit the rule on the board or overhead. Ask the children to give you two other numbers that they think may fit the rule and record the solution on the chalkboard or overhead.

Hint: If children are unable to generate appropriate pairs, give them more than two examples;

It is very important <u>not</u> to let the children tell you the rule or yell it out before you ask for it.

The teacher must tell children if their pair of numbers fit the rule.
The teacher might say, "Yes, that fits my rule" or "No, that doesn't fit my rule."

Try to give the majority of the class the opportunity to figure out the rule. You may ask everyone who thinks they know the rule to raise their hand without telling you the rule. If most raise their hands and have had an opportunity to give a pair of numbers, ask a child to give the rule. **Finding the rule is an important step in developing algebraic reasoning, so as many students as possible should be given a chance to develop the rule on their own.** Ask if anyone thought of the rule in a different way. If the rule is just addition, there may be only one way to think about the rule, but as the rules involve more than one operation, there may be several ways to look at the rule.

Write down the rule or rules <u>in words</u>. Talk about how you might write down the rule using mathematical symbols. For example if the rule were "Add 2", you might record, "Add 2" and a shorter, symbolic version might be "+ 2".

Possible rules for second, third, and fourth grade include:

<u>Add 3</u>	<u>Subtract 2</u>	<u>3N</u>
2,5	3,1	2,6
6,9	8,6	7,21

Once upper elementary school children have tried this activity several times and are familiar with multiplication, the following rule is designed to encourage algebraic thinking. It is very important here to write the rule in words and then, usually with your help, engage children in writing the rule symbolically!

The teacher writes the following pairs of numbers on the board:

5,9
8,15

The class is likely to generate correct solutions like the following (there will be some incorrect solutions that are not recorded here):

5,9
8,15
4,7
10,19
6,11
100,199
2,3
1,1
23,45

Ask for the rule <u>in words</u>. Children may say something like one of the following:

Double the first number and subtract one.

Multiply the first number by 2 and subtract 1.

Add the first number, and the number 1 less than the first number.

With the help of the class ask or suggest how these written rules can be expressed in a shorter more precise way:

Here is an important point, when children are finding a value of the second number (9, __), they are doing arithmetic. However, when children have the rule in their head and express it in written words, or express it in symbolic notation, they are doing **algebra**! Most would agree that the symbolic notation is algebra, but so are the words and so is <u>thinking</u> or knowing the rule.

When the rules are expressed in words, they are different, especially the first and the last one. The power of algebra is showing that these rules are the same (or mathematically equivalent):

$$2N - 1 = N + (N - 1).$$

In our notation, we used "N." We could have used any letter, a box, or most any symbol. We say that "N" is a variable. In this activity notice how the value of "N" truly does vary. It can be any number! The fact that a variable can vary and be any number is a concept of variable that we want children to develop.

Contrast the "What's My Rule?" activity to the following examples:

$N + 4 = 7$

$X - 3 = 5$

$4 + \square = 9$

How are the "letters used as numbers" in these equations different from "What's My Rule?"

One of the most common problems in teaching algebra at a higher level is that students do not have an understanding of the concept of variable. They think of a variable as a specific number and have difficulty reasoning abstractly about an entity, which has an unknown value or many values, but when solved has a known value or many values.

For children, N in the equation, $N + 4 = 7$, does not vary and is a "place holder" for the missing number. How do children view N, in $N + 4 = 7$? Do they view it as a variable or as a replacement? Or is N a constant that varies from equation to equation (for example, $N + 4 = 7$; $6 - N = 4$; $5 + N = 9$)? A place holder is different than a variable. In "What's My Rule?," N is variable because it changes. For $N + 4 = 7$, N does not change. It is just a number that children may or may not be able to find, but once they do find it, N is fixed and is not a variable.

In addition, consider how equations like $N + 4 = 7$ are to be solved algebraically: one would subtract 4 from both sides of the equation. However, most children would not solve this problem like that. A child might say, "I know that $3 + 4$ is 7, so $N = 3$!" Or a child may say, "I can count on from 4 to get 7 with my fingers, so N is 3!"

One final note for "What's My Rule?" is that its primary educational purpose is not the development of algebraic reasoning. This concept is interwoven within arithmetic as children attempt to change from specific thinking to general thinking.

13.1   Problems and Exercises

Solve the problems first and then consider some data on how children solved the problems found in the **Children's Solutions and Discussion of Problems and Exercises** section.

1.   a. In the following formulas, which letters or symbols represent a variable?

$A = \pi r^2$ $E = mc^2$

b. For a child, what is the difference between a variable and a constant?

2.   Combinations of three different shapes were weighed three different times. From the information below find the weight of each shape.

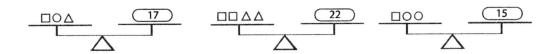

3.   What does the * indicate one should do to the numbers on either side of it in the following number sentences?
4 * 5 = 17
7 * 3 = 18
1 * 3 = 0

4.   The table below shows some number pairs. The following rule was used to find each number in column B. (NAEP, 1990)

Rule: Multiply the number in column A by itself and then add 3.

Find the missing number, using the same rule.

	A	B
Example:	2	$7 = (2 \times 2) + 3$
	3	12
	5	28
	8	?

5.   ☐ represents the number of magazines that Lina reads each week. Which of these represents the total number of magazines that Lina reads in 6 weeks (TIMSS, 2003)?
a. 6 + ☐
b. 6 x ☐
c. ☐ + 6
d. (☐ + ☐) x 6

6. Ali had 50 apples. He sold some and then had 20 left. Which of these is a number sentence that shows this (TIMSS, 2003)?
   a. ☐ -20 = 50
   b. 20 - ☐ = 50
   c. ☐ - 50 = 20
   d. 50 - ☐ = 20

7. N stands for the number of hours of sleep Ken gets each night. Which of the following represents the number of hours of sleep Ken gets in 1 week (NAEP, 2005)?
   a. N + 7
   b. N – 7
   c. N x 7
   d. N ÷ 7

8. Graham has twice as many books as Bob. Chan has six more books than Bob. If Bob has x books, which of the following represents the total number of books the three boys have (TIMSS, 2003)?
   a. 3x + 6
   b. 3x + 8
   c. 4x + 6
   d. 5x + 6
   e. 8x + 2

9. For all numbers k,
   k + k + k + k + k can be written as (TIMSS, 1999):
   a. k + 5
   b. 5k
   c. k^5
   d. 5(k + 1)

13.1   Questions for Discussion

1. What is 'the concept of variable'?
2. What is the difference between an unknown and a variable?

13.1   Children's Solutions and Discussion of Problems and Exercises

1. In $A = \pi r^2$, the symbol π is a constant, and A, and r are variables. In $E = mc^2$ (the speed of light) c is a constant and E (Energy) and m (mass) are variables.
3. This is an example of generalizing an operation.
4. Nationally, 15% of fourth graders gave the correct answer (NAEP, 1990).
5. In the United States, 73.7% of girls and 71.0% of boys in fourth grade had the correct solution (TIMSS, 2003).
6. In the United States, 86.1% of girls and 82% of boys correctly selected the answer (TIMSS, 2003).
7. Nationally, 61% of fourth graders chose correctly (NAEP, 2005).
8. In the United States, only 25.5% of eighth graders could give the correct representation (TIMSS, 2003).
9. In the United States, only 46% of eighth graders indicated the correct representation (TIMSS, 1999).

13.2 Algebraic Reasoning: Generalizing

When preservice teachers are asked, "What is algebra?" many might respond, "solving equations". This view can be described as symbolic manipulation and may also include factoring, combining like terms, and simplifying expressions. This understanding of algebra is **not** the algebra that elementary school children typically study. Algebra as symbolic manipulation or as a symbol system is very important but more appropriate for the secondary level. Even though children may be introduced to simple equations such as $2N + 1 = 7$, they typically do not solve them by using inverse or undoing operations. They typically use trial and error (National Research Council, 2001). A trial and error method is unproductive in solving more advanced mathematical equations.

Algebraic reasoning at the elementary level primarily focuses on algebra as a way of expressing generality or **algebra as generalized arithmetic**. Arithmetic involves working and operating with specifics, e.g., adding two numbers, whereas algebraic thinking entails operating with generalizations or representations of numbers, e.g., it does not matter which order two numbers are added, the result is always the same. Here is a more explicit distinction between arithmetic and algebra: arithmetic is adding $7 + 8$; algebraic reasoning is realizing that $7 + 8 = 8 + 7$ and that this property will hold for any two numbers, not just 7 and 8. Further we might express this relationship of adding any two numbers as: $a + b = b + a$.

Generalizing a Specific Problem

An example of how children might be encouraged to think algebraically in elementary school is through the generalization of a problem. Consider the following examples:

A typical elementary school math problem:

> Gina has 5 puppies. How many ears and tails do the puppies have?

How might a second grade child solve this problem?

Extensions of the problem:

> Gina has 6 puppies. How many ears and tails do the puppies have?
> Gina has 7 puppies. How many ears and tails do the puppies have?
> Gina has 10 puppies. How many ears and tails do the puppies have?

Algebraic extension of the problem:

> What if we do not know how many puppies Gina has? Is there any way you could describe how many ears and tails the puppies would have?

Any problem that requires children to extend the problem to the general case where the exact number is not known or given encourages them to think algebraically. This is an example an "algebrafied" task (Soares, Blanton, & Kaput, 2006) as children are looking for general relationships.

Generalizing Patterns

A common approach to developing algebraic reasoning is through the use of patterns which develops algebraic reasoning by generalizing a specific problem. Two kinds of patterns that can lead to the development of algebraic thinking are <u>number patterns</u> and <u>geometric patterns</u>.

The primary educational purposes of numeric pattern problems are to practice computation, to develop number relationships, and to engage in problem solving. A secondary educational purpose in using these problems is the development of algebraic reasoning.

<u>Number Patterns</u>

Consider these two patterns:

1.   ___ ___ 24 33 ___ ___ 60 ___
   What is the Rule? _____

2.   ___ 14 ___ ___ 32 ___ ___ 50
   What is the Rule? _____

When children are finding the rule and expressing it, they are doing algebraic thinking. For the first example, "+ 9" or "add 9" are typical solutions given by children that describe the first rule. Children may give the rule as "N + 9", but it is <u>not</u> likely and <u>not</u> necessary. These are differences in notation not understanding. The mental activity of finding the rule and expressing it symbolically are both examples of algebraic thinking.

Numeric patterns like these can be very challenging activities for children! The most common strategy that children use to solve pattern problems is "Trial and Error". A few children may use an averaging strategy, such as (32-14) ÷3 in the second problem, but most will not (see chapter 11 on how children find averages). In the second problem, can you explain why one divides by 3 when there are only two numbers in between?

<u>Geometric Patterns</u>

Geometric patterns encourage children to use both geometric thinking and their problem solving skills. The extension of these activities is also intended to help children develop algebraic thinking and the concept of variable.

Consider the following geometric pattern:

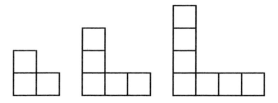

Initially, children are directed to draw the next one, two or three shapes in the sequence.

Next, in a subsequent lesson, children are asked to find out how many squares or objects will be in the 10th shape, the 20th, or 40th shape.

Finally, maybe several lessons later, children are asked how many squares will be in the nth shape. Can they give a rule or mathematical expression that expresses this pattern for the nth shape?

You will find below the first geometric pattern with the next two shapes drawn with shading added to one of the squares in each of the shapes. Notice that we could describe each shape as beginning with a shaded square with 2 squares added for each subsequent shape.

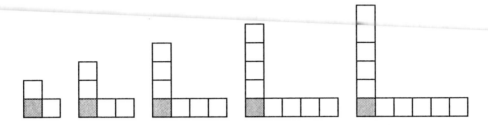

The pattern could be described as $2n + 1$ with 1 being the beginning shaded shape and 2 the number of squares added each time. Going from one shape to the next, children are adding 2 squares each time. Children will want to include + 2 in the expression, and it is probably a large leap to explain why it is $2n$ rather than + 2.

The geometric pattern can be expressed by the following numeric pattern as well:

$$3, 5, 7, 9, 11, \ldots$$

One aspect that may be confusing to children as they begin to describe both number and geometric patterns for the nth shape or term is that patterns can be described recursively or in closed form. For example, in the above geometric pattern the number of squares increases by 2 each time, if this pattern were numeric it would be +2. These are recursive descriptions. We can also describe the rule for the nth term as $2n + 1$. This is a closed form description of the pattern.

Generalizing a General Principle or Property

We now consider another example of algebraic reasoning in elementary school. In the following case, children are generalizing a principle. Certain ways of thinking mathematically are conducive to the development of algebraic reasoning such as the development of **number sense** or **relational thinking.** For instance, how might a child solve: 5 + 6 =? (See Chapter 3 for a more thorough discussion.) If he or she does not know the fact directly, but does know that 5 + 5 = 10, a natural way for the child to reason may be as follows: "5 + 5 = 10, then 5 + 6 must be one more than 10, so the answer is 11." If this double is the only one that the child knows or uses to solve this type of problem then the child is still exhibiting arithmetical thinking. However, if the child generalizes and is capable of applying a <u>doubles plus one strategy</u> to other combinations then he or she is exhibiting algebraic thinking.

We can express such thinking algebraically as:

If, $x + x = N$,
then $x + (x + 1) = N + 1$.

Even though children would likely not use an "x" or an "N" to describe their thinking, their thinking is still algebraic because one can think algebraically without using written symbols.

Similar strategies, which also demonstrate algebraic thinking include:

Doubles minus 1
Doubles plus 2
Doubles minus 2

This rule can be generalized even more by finding the nearest double and then adding or subtracting the difference between the double and the number. This rule allows for flexibility in thinking. Consider, for example, how one child solved $16 + 17 = $? *I know that 15 + 15 = 30 and 1 + 2 = 3, so 30 + 3 = 33.* Note that this child must also have a good concept of ten in order to decompose and then recompose the numbers.

Other strategies that illustrate algebraic thinking include using numerical relationships to solve arithmetical problems. Such strategies are a precursor to the type of thinking that children will be using in algebra.

For example, to add $99 + 99 = $? a student may add $100 + 100 = 200$, and subtract 2, $(200 - 2 = 198)$. While this type of thinking may be more difficult to express algebraically, it can be thought of algebraic thinking as long as students are able to generalize it. Remember, expressing the relationship symbolically is not the goal here.

Other examples involving the use of numerical relationships include using the top number fact to find the ones below it:

$1,000 + 1,000 = \underline{2,000}$ $25 \times 20 = \underline{500}$

$999 + 999 \quad = $ _____ $25 \times 19 = $ _____

$998 + 997 \quad = $ _____ $25 \times 18 = $ _____

Children who can generalize these arithmetical computations are thinking algebraically. Developing number sense or number relations like these helps children think algebraically. **A flexible proficiency and fluency with arithmetic is essential in order for children to develop algebraic thinking.** In the previous examples, note how children must know their doubles first; they must be able to mentally compute $1,000 + 1,000$ and 25×20, and they must be able to do these things without a great deal of thought so that they can begin to think about the related algebraic ideas. If children are taught arithmetic conceptually, these understandings may serve as a foundation for learning algebra in a conceptual manner.

Children who know that $3 + 4 = 4 + 3$ and $47 + 76 = 76 + 47$ and who believe that this will work for any two numbers are developing algebraic reasoning. Key questions to test for this development include:

- Is this rule true for all numbers?
- How do you know it will always be true?

It is not important that children can name the property, which is the commutative property of addition, but that they are developing an intuitive sense of these properties.

Other generalizations of principles of elementary school children might include:

- Any number added to zero is the number: $a + 0 = 0$.
- Any number times one is the number: $a \times 1 = a$.
- When a number and its opposite are added the result is always zero; $a + (-a) = 0$.
- When adding three or more numbers the order in which the numbers are added does not matter: $a + (b + c) = (a + b) + c$.

13.2   Problems and Exercises

<u>Solve the problems first</u> and then consider some data on how children solved the problems found in the **Children's Solutions and Discussion of Problems and Exercises** section.

1.   a.   Is $4 \times 7 = 3 \times 7 + 7$?   Why or why not?
      b.   Is $9 \times 6 = 10 \times 6 - 6$? Why or why not?

2. $37 \times \square = 703$.
      What is the value of $37 \times \square + 6$ (TIMSS, 2003)?

3.   ___ ___ 52 45 ___ ___ 24 ___

      What is the Rule? _____

4.   ___ 11 ___ ___ 23 ___ ___ 35 ____

      What is the Rule? _____

5.   Draw the next two shapes in the pattern. If you count the shaded square too, how many squares will be in the 10th shape. In the 25th shape? How many squares will be in the nth shape?

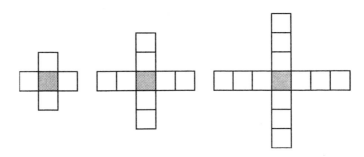

6.   How many squares are in a '2 by 2' square, a '3 by 3' square, and an 'n by n' square?

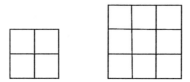

7.   A bus stops at the bus stop every 20 minutes, and the first bus arrives at 6:00 AM. It is a little after 3:00 PM. When will the next bus arrive? How did you figure this out? Describe a rule for when a bus will arrive.

8.   Peter wrote down a pattern of A's and B's that repeats in groups of 3. Here is the beginning of his pattern with some of the letters erased. Fill in the missing letters. (NAEP, 2003)

A B __ A __ B __ __ __

9.   (NAEP, 2003)

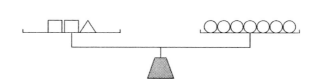

The objects on the scale above make it balance exactly. According to this scale, if △ balances with ◯◯◯, then ☐ balances with which of the following?

A) ◯
B) ◯◯
C) ◯◯◯
D) ◯◯◯◯

10.   The table below shows how the chirping of a cricket is related to the temperature outside. For example, a cricket chirps 144 times each minute when the temperature is $76°$.

Number of Chirps Per Minute	Temperature
144	$76°$
152	$78°$
160	$80°$
168	$82°$
176	$84°$

What would be the number of chirps per minute when the temperature outside is $90°$ if this pattern stays the same? (NAEP, 2003)

Answer: _____   Explain how you figured out your answer.

11.   John records the weight of his puppy every month in a chart like the one shown below. If the pattern of the puppy's weight gain continues, how many pounds will the puppy weigh at 5 months? (NAEP, 1992)

Puppy's Age	Puppy's Weight
1 month	10 lbs
2 months	15 lbs
3 months	19 lbs
4 months	22 lbs
5 months	?

A) 30   B) 27   C) 25   D) 24

12.   Children's pictures are to be hung in a line as shown in the figure below. Pictures that are hung next to each other share a tack. How many tacks are needed to hang 18 pictures in this way (NAEP, 1992)?

Answer: _____ tacks   Explain how you arrived at your answer.

13.   If the pattern shown below continues, could 375 be one of the products in this pattern? (NAEP, 1992)

$$2 \times 2 = 4$$
$$2 \times 2 \times 2 = 8$$
$$2 \times 2 \times 2 \times 2 = 16$$
$$2 \times 2 \times 2 \times 2 \times 2 = 32$$

Answer: _____   Explain why or why not.

14.   Use the table below to do parts a. and b. (NAEP, 1992)

Column A	Column B
12 →	3
16 →	4
24 →	6
40 →	10

a. What is the rule used in the table to get the numbers in column B from the numbers in column A?

   A) Divide the number in column A by 4.
   B) Multiply the number in column A by 4.
   C) Subtract 9 from the number in column A.
   D) Add 9 to the number in column A.

b. Suppose 120 is a number in column A of the table. Use the same rule to fill in the number in Column B.

Column A	Column B
120 →	

15.   In Toshi's class there were twice as many girls as boys. There are 8 boys in the class. What is the total number of boys and girls in the class (TIMSS, 2003)?
   a. 12
   b. 16
   c. 20
   d. 24

16.   Here is the beginning of a pattern of tiles. If the pattern continues, how many tiles will be in Figure 6 (TIMSS, 1995)?
   a. 12
   b. 15
   c. 18
   d. 21

Figure 1   Figure 2   Figure 3

13.2   Questions for Discussion

1.   How is a thorough understanding of arithmetic invaluable in helping children develop algebraic reasoning?
2.   How is knowing and using the fact that 5×99 is the same as $(5 \times 100) - 5$ an indication of algebraic thinking?
3.   Give some examples of how generalizing arithmetic is algebraic reasoning. Why is generalizing an important concept for children to learn?
4.   What is the **difference** between arithmetic and algebra?
5.   Why are the properties commutative, associative, and distributive important in algebra?
6.   What parts of Problems #3 and #4 might be considered algebraic reasoning? Why?
7.   How is the solving of Problem #7 an example of algebraic reasoning?

13.2   Children's Solutions and Discussion of Problems and Exercises

2.   Only 7.1% of fourth graders in the United States indicated the correct solution (TIMSS, 2003).
8.   Nationally, 52% of fourth graders gave the correct pattern. One incorrect response was ABCACBABA. Explain how you think the child arrived at this incorrect answer?
9.   Nationally, only 39% of fourth graders gave the correct answer.
10.   Nationally, only 3% of fourth graders gave the extended (correct) response with the answer and with a correct explanation that for every $2°$ the number of chirps increases by 8, or a ratio of $2°$ to 8 chirps; only 6% gave a satisfactory response with an answer of $86°$ (184 chirps) or $88°$ (192 chirps). Some didn't carry out the process far enough, yet they had an explanation that correctly described the ratio. Others correctly answered 200 with no explanation or an explanation that was not stated well. Still others gave a clear description of the ratio with a minor computational error (e.g., adding incorrectly). 13% gave partially correct answers

(e.g., they gave answers between 176 and 208 with explanations that stated that the chirps increase as temperature increases.). What follows are some solutions from fourth grade children.

<u>Extended (Correct) Response:</u>

Answer: 200 chirps

Explain how you figured out your answer.

Well each 2° it goes 8 more chips
86° it would be 184 chirps 88° it would
be 192 chirps 90° it would be 200 chirps

<u>Satisfactory Response:</u>

Answer: 200

Explain how you figured out your answer.

I got my answer by contine-
ing the graph until I got
to 90°f Then I did the same
on the other side

If you need more room for your work, use the space below.

184
192
86
88
90
20

<u>Partial Response:</u>

Answer: 194

Explain how you figured out your answer.

I went up 8 chirps each 2°

Minimal Response:

Answer. 140

Explain how you figured out your answer.

you just figure. the number. and it will work you just add them together

Incorrect Response:

Answer.   2

Explain how you figured out your answer.

They are counting backwards and forwards from 2.

11.   Nationally, 32% of fourth graders gave the correct response.
12.   Nationally, 25% of fourth graders gave the correct response.
13.   Nationally, 27% of fourth graders gave the correct response.
14.   a. Nationally, 42% of fourth graders gave the correct response.
       b. Nationally, 24% of fourth graders gave the correct response.
15.   In the United States, 54.3% of fourth graders correctly answered (TIMSS, 2003).
16.   Internationally, 52% of third grades and 63% of fourth graders correctly figured the number of tiles in the sixth figure (TIMSS, 1995).

13.3   Generalizing with Two Variables - Functions

The concept of function is an extremely important concept of advanced mathematics. Children are often introduced to functions through the context of a machine that has an input number and an output number. A simple function involves two variables and a relationship between the two variables. In algebra two variables are extremely important in connecting algebra, geometry, graphing, and the concept of function. Consider how the idea of two or multiple variables might be introduced to children in elementary school through the following activities.

Lima Bean Toss

This activity is from *Math Their Way* (1976) and is often used in Kindergarten through second grade. In this activity, children use lima beans with one side painted green and the other side painted white, and a sheet with the number of lima beans they are using drawn in boxes. Children roll their lima beans and color in the number that is painted that matches their roll. As they progress, they do the same activity and write a number sentence that matches their roll. For example, if they roll 7 lima beans and 4 come up green and 3 white then they might write the number sentence 4 + 3 = 7 and color in 4 of the 7 lima beans on the sheet.

The same ideas can be addressed using different contexts and problems:

- **Two Colored Counters**: Children toss two colored counters, usually red and yellow, and record and/or determine the possible outcomes.
- **Mice in Connected Big and Small Cages** (Carpenter et al. 2003): In this context a mouse might be half in each cage or in between. Children determine how many different combinations of mice could be in each cage, e.g., if you have 7 mice, where could they be?
- **How Many Chips are Under a Cup?** In this activity from the NCTM Investigations Series, children have chips or counters lying on the ground and then cover some of the chips with a cup, leaving some outside and some inside. The thrust of the activity is that children must determine all the different combinations of chips in and outside the cup.
- **Double Decker Bus:** In this Dutch activity people enter a bus. Some sit on the upper level and some on the lower level. Children must determine all the possible ways the passengers could be seated on the upper or lower levels.

These activities are typically used to help children develop the concept of number, especially in the lower grades, K-1. With some slight modifications, these activities can also be used to help children develop algebraic thinking and the beginning of the function concept.

To develop algebraic reasoning, require or ask children to:

- Find all the ways that the objects can be arranged.
- Explain how can we make sure we have found all the ways.

These important questions can lead to a discussion of algebraic ideas.

The solutions to the previously described activities can also be represented graphically. Such representations are similar to finding values for x and y or the coordinates to graph the equation: $x + y = 7$. Here x might represent the number of green beans and y the number of white beans.

These activities are similar to a function machine where children feed an input number into a machine and obtain an output number. Their task is discover what numbers fit the variables of the machine's inputs and outputs.

Remember that in both of these activities algebraic notation is not important in the initial explorations. Children are exploring the concept of two variables and function without expressing them as such. Only later does algebraic notation become important and even essential.

13.3   <u>Problems and Exercises</u>

1.
$$2 \times 4 = 3^2 - 1$$
$$4 \times 6 = 5^2 - 1$$
$$8 \times 10 = \underline{\quad} - 1$$
$$99 \times 101 = \underline{\quad} - 1$$

a. Fill in the blanks.

b. Give your own example.

c. Can you solve these number sentences mentally?

d. What generalization or conjecture can you make in words?

e. How would you express this pattern algebraically?

2. Nine mice are in connected small and large cages. What are all the possible ways the mice could be in the two cages?

3. Sam, a third grader, says that the number of possibilities is always one more than the number of mice, so in Problem #2 there are 10 possibilities. Will Sam's rule always work? Why?

4. Adam, a fifth grader, insists that for the equation $x + y = 8$, x and y cannot both be 4. Why does he think so? Is he right?

5. If you add three odd numbers, what kind of number will you answer always be? Can you explain why?

6. Every time Susan goes to the library, she checks out 5 books and returns 3. If Susan has 7 library books at home, how many books will she have the next time she goes to the library? What if we do not know how many books Susan has, can we say anything about the number of books she will have the next time she goes to the library?

7. A rabbit and a tortoise ran a race. If the rabbit runs at 8 mph and the tortoise runs at 2 mph, how far ahead of the tortoise will the rabbit be after 3 hours? After 8 hours? After 'n' hours?

8. If $\square$ represents the number of newspapers that Lee delivers each day, which of the following represents the total number of newspapers that Lee delivers in 5 days (NAEP, 1992)?

a. $5 + \square$

b. $5 \times \square$

c. $\square \div 5$

d. $(\square + \square) \times 5$

9.   A number machine takes a number and operates on it. When the Input Number is 5, the Output Number is 9, as shown below. When the Input Number is 7, which of these is the Output Number (TIMSS, 2003)?

   a. 11
   b. 13
   c. 14
   d. 25

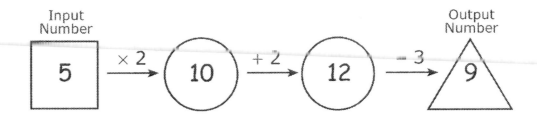

10.   What do you do to each number in Column A to get the number next to it in Column B (TIMSS, 1995)?

Column A	Column B
10	2
15	3
25	5
50	10

   a.   Add 8 to the number in Column A.
   b.   Subtract 8 from the number in Column A.
   c.   Multiply the number in Column A by 5.
   d.   Divide the number in Column A by 5

13.3   Questions for Discussion

   1.   How is understanding the pattern in Problem #1 an example of algebraic reasoning?
   2.   How is the solving of Problem #2 an example of algebraic reasoning?
   3.   How is the solving of Problem #7 an example of algebraic reasoning?

13.3   Children's Solutions and Discussion of Problems and Exercises

   8.   Nationally, 48% of fourth graders gave the correct response (NAEP, 1992).
   9.   In the United States, 48.4% of fourth graders had the correct solution (TIMSS, 2003).
   10.   Internationally, 27% of third graders and 39% of fourth graders had the correct solution (TIMSS, 1995).

13.4   Graphing: Coordinate Geometry

In the elementary grades, children typically do some simple graphing in coordinate geometry, but, more importantly they develop underlying arithmetical and geometrical concepts. One underlying concept is spatial orientation or knowing where one is and how to move around in that space. Developing map skills with children is one way of laying the foundation for graphing. Children and adults do not have mental maps in their heads, but rather they have specific knowledge that is usually not quantifiable and can put them into several frames of reference (Clements, 2003). For example, a child may know that she walks so far down one street and then turns at the large orange house to get to her home. However, the child may not be able to tell another how far down the street she walks. One's spatial orientation is personal knowledge containing both landmarks and reference points and is not a quantifiable understanding of distance.

In the early grades, children learn about the directions right, left, up, and down, and in later grades they learn about east, west, north, and south. These understandings are necessary in building and understanding graphs.

These concepts can serve as a foundation for children's understanding of both statistical graphs (see chapter 11) and coordinate graphs. One excellent way of introducing coordinate graphs and the graph of lines and curves is to have children graph the growth of plants. The skills necessary for this activity include many of the same skills as making a coordinate graph.

Typically, young children do not do well with double coordinate graphs. Even on a one-dimensional graph such as the number line, some children may use different scales for the positive and negative numbers (Clements, 2003). In general, children have shown that they are capable of locating points in one dimension in Grade 1, in two dimensions by Grade 4, and in three dimensions in Grade 6 (Clements, 2003).   With graph paper, scale is not typically a factor or perhaps children's understanding of scale is masked. However, with graphing calculators, scales are easily changed and some children have difficulty recognizing these changes in scale (Kieran & Chalouh, 1993).

Children have difficulty with the notion that the graph of a function (e.g., lines) is continuous (Kieran & Chalouh, 1993). For elementary school children, the variables x and y, in the equation $x + y = 7$ probably do not represent an infinite number of solutions. For $x + y = 7$, there are eight pairs of whole number solutions: 0,7; 1,6; 2,5; 3,4; 4,3; 5,2; 6,1; and 7,0. Elementary school children typically would not consider solutions containing decimals and fractions such as 2.5, 4.5; or 6½, ½. When they plot the points such as (3,4) and (4,3), they may likely be just 'connecting the dots' and not realizing that there are an infinite number of solutions between these two points alone. For many children, solutions exist only at the intersection of whole (and perhaps negative) numbers, e.g., (4,3), (5,2), (6,1), etc.

Graphing is more than a skill or a product! Graphing is a tool for communicating meaning or information, and it is a way to represent one's mathematical thinking.

13.4   Problems and Exercises

1.   For Problem #2, 13.3, graph all the ways the nine mice can be in a large and small cage on a coordinate system with one axis being the number in the small cage and the other axis being the number in the large cage.

2.   From the starting point of a family vacation, it is 60 miles to New Haven and 240 miles to South Bend. How far will you have to travel until you are half way between New Haven and South Bend?

3.   A point is shown on the grid below. The coordinates of the point are (2,5). On the same grid draw the point with coordinates (4,7) and the point with coordinates (8,0) (NAEP, 2003).

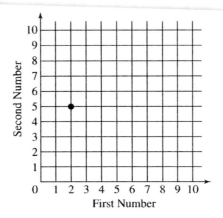

4.   On the grid below, the dot at (4,4) is circled. Circle two other dots where the first number is equal to the second number (NAEP, 1992).

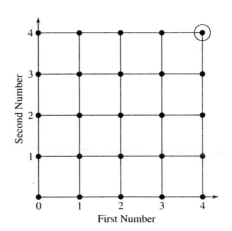

5.   Locate the points: (5,1), (2,4), (5,7), and (8,4) on a grid. Connect the points in the order that they were given. What shape did you make?

6.   The two lines below are the same length. What is the difference between these two lines?

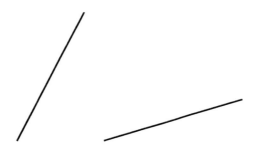

7.   This map shows city blocks with a delivery truck at one corner. The driver of the delivery truck starts at corner X. He goes 3 blocks east and 2 blocks north to get to the school. On what corner is the school located (TIMSS, 1995)?
a. A
b. B
c. C
d. D
e. E

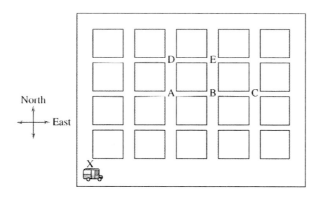

8.   On this grid, find the dot with the circle around it. We can describe where this dot is by saying it is at First Number 1, Second Number 3. Now find the dot with the triangle around it. Describe where the dot is on the grid in the same way. Fill in the numbers we would use:

First Number _____ Second Number _____

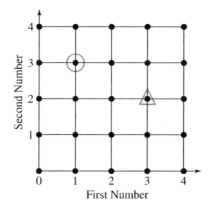

13.4   Questions for Discussion

1.   How is the game "Battleship" similar to graphing in the coordinate plane?
2.   How could graphing in a coordinate plane be used to answer the question in problem 6?
3.   What difficulties do young children sometimes have with graphs? How could you respond to these difficulties?

13.4   Children's Solutions and Discussion of Problems and Exercises

3.   Nationally, 44% of fourth graders had both points correctly drawn; 28% had only one of the two points correctly drawn.
4.   Nationally, 38% of fourth, graders correctly circled two (or more) of the correct dots and no others; 11% correctly circled one correct dot and no incorrect dot(s) circled.
7.   Internationally, 43% of third graders and 54% of fourth grade had the correct solution (TIMSS, 1995).
8.   Internationally, 30% of third graders and 42% of fourth grade indicated the coordinates of the dot (TIMSS, 1995).

13.5   The Concept of Equality

Equality is an important concept in algebra. If children understand equality, they will be able to use this concept to solve algebraic equations later in their schooling.

Consider how children might respond to this problem: Solve. $8 + 4 = \square + 5$.

Estimate what percent of children you think would give the following responses for each combined grade levels indicated:

Grade	7	12	17	12 and 17
1 & 2				
3 & 4				
5 & 6				

A child who has 12 as his/her answer may be thinking, "The answer comes after the equal sign." Children typically interpret the equal sign to mean: "do something" or "give the answer" rather than interpreting the sign as describing a relationship between numbers. A child may see the + sign and think "I add the 8 and 4 to get 12."

A child may see the 5 as an extra number, like extra information in a word problem that they need not use. However, a child with 17 as his/her answer may be thinking, "I need to add all the numbers in the problem."

Some children look at the equation as number sentences strung together, so they first have $8 + 4 = 12$ and then look at it as $12 + 5 = 17$. These children will put 12 in the box, but tell you the answer is 17.

Below are research results (Falkner, Levi & Carpenter, 1999) from 30 classrooms:

Grade	7	12	17	12 and 17
1 & 2	5%	58%	13%	8%
3 & 4	9%	49%	25%	10%
5 & 6	2%	76%	21%	2%

What do these results suggest about children's understanding of equality? These misconceptions center on children's understandings of symbols not mathematical relationships. Misconceptions, like those with the equal sign, can be difficult to alter.

Below are some common practices that contribute to children's misunderstanding of equality (Falkner, Levi & Carpenter, 1999).

- Sometimes equal signs are strung together as below.
  For the problem: What is 7 plus 3, plus 5, take away 4? Children might write:

  $7 + 3 = 10 + 5 = 15 - 4 = 11$

  However, 7 plus 3 is not equal to 11, $(7 + 3 \neq 11)$

- An equal sign means that the two entities are the same. Frequently equal signs are used to show a characteristic of one of the entities, for example, the age of a person. If Mary is 10 years old, this idea is sometimes written as Mary = 10. This expression does not convey equality; Mary is not the same as 10, her age is!

- Likewise an equal sign should not be used to convey the number of objects in a group. The group of stars is not the same thing as 5. The number of stars is 5.

13.5   Problems and Exercises

1.   What solutions might children have for the following equation? Why?

$$15 - 7 = \square + 2$$

2.   Farmer Brown's favorite hen laid 4 eggs Monday, 5 eggs Tuesday, 7 eggs Wednesday, 3 eggs Thursday, and 1 egg on Friday. How many eggs did the hen lay? Write a mathematical number sentence or sentences for this problem.

3.   What are all whole numbers that make $8 - \square > 3$ true? (NAEP, 2003)
a.0,1,2,3,4,5
b. 0,1,2,3,4
c. 0,1,2
d. 5

Why might a child give the answer d?

13.5   Questions for Discussion

1.   Why do you think it is challenging to change children's misconceptions about the symbol =, the equal sign?
2.   For Problem #2, why wouldn't you write the following as an answer:
$$4 + 5 = 9 + 7 = 16 + 3 = 19 + 1 = 20$$
What if a child wrote his or her solution this way? What would you ask the child?

13.5   Children's Solutions and Discussion of Problems and Exercises

1.   Some solutions children may give are: 8, 10, and 6.
3.   Nationally, 48% of fourth graders gave the correct response (NAEP, 2003).

Chapter 13: References

Baratta-Lorton, M. (1976). *Mathematics their way*. Menlo Park: Addison-Wesley.

Carpenter, T., Franke, M., & Levi, L. (2003). *Thinking Mathematically: Integrating Arithmetic & Algebra in Elementary School*. Heinemann: Portsmouth, NH

Clements, D. (2003). Teaching and learning geometry. In J. Kilpatrick, G. Martin, & D. Schifter (Eds.), *A research companion to the principles and standards for school mathematics*. 151-178. Reston, VA: NCTM.

Kieran, C. & Chalouh, L. (1993) Prealgebra: The transition from arithmetic to algebra. In D. T. Owens (Ed.) *Research Ideas for the classroom: Middle grades mathematics*. 179-198. Reston, VA: NCTM.

National Research Council. (2001). *Adding it up: Helping children learn mathematics*. J. Kilpatrick, J. Swafford, and B. Findell (Eds.). Mathematics Learning Study Committee, Center for Education, Division of Behavioral and Social Sciences and Education. Washington DC: National Academy Press.

Soares, J., Blanton, M. L., & Kaput, J. (2006). Thinking algebraically across the elementary school curriculum. *Teaching Children Mathematics, 12*, 228-235

Answers to Problems and Exercises

Chapter 1

1.1

Section A

1. 500,500
2. $1.10 compass and $1.90 protractor
3. 12 boys and 12 dogs
4. 5 inches
5. 220 posts
6. 32 days
7. Answers may vary
8. 45 rectangles

Section B

1. 6 horses and 12 turkeys
2. 15¢ pencil and 25¢ pen
3a. 156
3b. 192
4. 6
5. 60 pencils
6. 11
7. Answers may vary
8. 7

1.2

1. ABB
2. AABC
3. ABABBABBBABBBB
4. 2, 8, 14, 20, 23, 29
5. The perimeter doubles
6. The area quadruples
7. 1 5 10 10 5 1; 1 6 15 20 15 6 1
8. 13, 11, 6
9. a. 3, 97, 4

1.3

1. 9
2. 13 blocks
3. Answers may vary
4. 36
5. 15
6. More than 170 seconds
7. 8
8. 13 buses

Chapter 2

2.1

1-4. Answers may vary
5. 8 floors

2.2

1. Answers may vary
2. 15 is in the left region, 18 is in the center, and 20 is in the right region
3. Answers may vary
4. a. 2

Chapter 3

3.1

1. 8813200023188; 24 times
2a. 3
2b. 543
3. Answers may vary
4. Answers may vary
5. 5. 170
6. 5 358
7. c. 9635 and 9735

3.2

1. Answers may vary
2. 15; take-away
3. 15; compare
4. c. 32
5. b. 296
6. c. 3631
7. 227

3.3

1a. 135
1b. 128
1c. 920
2. Answers may vary
3. Answers may vary
4. d. 3
5. Answers may vary
6. answers may vary
7. $4 \times 5 = 20$ or $5 \times 4 = 20$
8. 2
9. c. 10
10. c. 4032
11a. 51
11b. d. $204 \div 4$

3.4

    1&2. Answers may vary

    3. 0

    4. a. ☐ x 7

    5. a. 370 x 1000

3.5

    1-15. Answers may vary

3.6

    1-7. Answers may vary

    8. Cheeseburger and Yogurt

    9. c. 60 + 60 + 60

    10. c. 80 x 60

    11a. c. 350,000

    11b. 135 cm and 144 cm

    12. b. 18

Chapter 4

4.1

    1-3. Answers may vary

    4. 3, 6, 9, 12, 15, and 18

    5. six; 1,2,3,4, 6, 12

    6. 40

4.2

    1&2. Answers may vary

    3. 2 and 8

    4. d. 265

    5. c. 21,567

    6&7. Answers may vary

4.3

    1. No

    2. False

    3. 25 primes

    4. 21 primes

4.4

    1-3. Answers may vary

    4. 12:00 PM

    5. 1, 4, 9, 16, 25, 36, …

    6. 12, 24, 36, 48

    7. 30 days

    8. b. 48

    9. 14 x 9 or 18 x 7

    10. a. 15

    11. 24

    12. 55

Chapter 5

5.1

    1. 14, 5, -1; Rule -3

    2. >

    3. <

    4. >

    5. <

    6. 7

    7. Answers may vary

5.2

    1. -16

    2. 7

    3. 6

    4. -12

    5. 50

    6. -125

    7. 175

    8. Susan is ahead, Jack is behind

    9. d. 8 degrees

    10. 10 degrees

5.3

    1. 10 yards

    2. 80 feet back

    3. 75 feet ahead

    4. Answers may vary

    5. 35

    6. e. 9

    7. c. 3- n

    8. a. 11

Chapter 6

6.1

    Set B

    1. 1/5

    2. 1/20

    3. 1/10

    4. 1/20

    5. 1/50

    6. 50¢

    7. $1.00

    8. one-tenth

    9. same

    10a. 50¢

    10b. 662/3¢

    11. No the child receiving piece B will get more.

    12. three-tenth of his money

13a. 1/6
13b. 1/18
13c. 1/36
13d. 1/9
14&15. Answers may vary
16. Snake woman
17. Answers may vary
18. ½ > 3/7; ½ < 5/8;
   therefore, 3/7 < 5/8
19. Answers may vary
20I. C
20II. C
20III. Answers may vary
21. 4
22. a. 1 and 2
23. d. 10
24. Yes

6.2
1. Answers may vary
2. ½ and 1/6
3. Answers may vary
4. Answers may vary
5. Answers may vary
6. b. 3/6
7. d. none
8. b. 2/5

6.3
1. 3/8
2-5. Answers may vary
6a. 8/13 meter
6b. 8 boxes
7. c. 6
8. b. 4
9. 200 red balls
10I. e. 17/25
10II. 10/11
10III. A. ½
10IV. $0.90

6.4
1. Answers may vary
2. 'picture solution not provided'
3. c. Kim said, "because 4/5 is closer
than 2/3 to 1."
4,5. Answers may vary

Chapter 7
7.1
1. 263 pennies
2. 324
3. 23
4. b. 170
5. 53
6. 239
7. 57,821
8. 999,995
9. Answers may vary
10. 1,349
11. b. 40
12. d. 78.24
13. a 0.233, 0.3, 0.32, 0.332
14. b 0.04
15. c. 0.0055

7.2
1-4. Answers may vary
5. 34.56
6. 30.00
7. 0.53
8. Answers may vary
9. b 0.0075
10. b. 108,000,000 km
11. c. 5 + 6 + 6 = 17
12. c. 0.2
13. b. four tenths
14. c. 0.7

7.3
1. 0.10, 0.13, 0.19, 0.25, 0.31
2-4. Answers may vary
5. c. $5.22
6. $120.15
7. $3.42
8a. $13.37
8b. Forgot the decimal point
10. compare
11. 10. 9 bills
12. b. 6.3
13. e. 2.88
14. 63.2 cm
15. e. 5150

7.4
1. 6 butterflies
2. 30 leaves

3. 3.6 miles
4. $16.00
5. girls
6a. 224
6b. 20 miles
6c. 30 chairs
6d. 70 tables
6e. 40
6f. 9 hours
6g. 573.2 parts oil
6h. 21 donuts
6i. 21 girls
7. 11.2 lbs.
8. 250 boys; 150 girls
9. 30 pupils
10. d. 27

7.5
1. Answers may vary
2. Yes
3. This is to be expected for;20% per day
4. $24.00
5. d. 99
6. c. 15% of $67; 20% of $80
7. c. 960 zeds
8. a. 12%
9a. 12.5%
9b. 25%
9c. 30%

Chapter 8
8.1
1. yes
2. a, b, c, d
3. c, d
4. Answers may vary
5. 12 pieces
6. Answers may vary
7. c. Park and Taylor
8. d. N
9. a
10. d
11. Answers may vary
8.2
1-3. Answers may vary
4. a, c
5. No.
6. 5

7. Answers may vary
8. Answers may vary
9. d
10. Answers may vary
11. d. isosceles
12. Answers may vary
13. Answers may vary
8.3
1. a.
2. a, b, d, e
3-10. Answers may vary
11. c.
12. c. Two
13. 60°
14. 60°
8.4
1-4. Answers may vary
5. b. 82°
6. b. ΔGHI and ΔGHF are congruent
7. a. GH = AB
8. e. The diagonals are perpendicular.
8.5
1& 2. Answers may vary
3. 0
4. 0
5. 0
6. -2
7. -4
8. Answers may vary
9. c. A basketball
10. a. A
11. b.
12. A
13. C. 12

Chapter 9
9.1
1. Translation
2. c and d
3a. translation
3b. rotation
3c. reflection
4. Answers may vary
5. d.
6. e.
7. c. 60
8. d. 80°

9. 9. b. <3 and <6
10. c. S

9.2

1&2. Answers may vary
3. c. 60°

9.3

1. b.
2-4. Answers may vary
5. c.
6&7. Answers may vary
8. c. 60°

9.4

1. 45, 15, 75
2. 4, 12½
3. Triangles 1 and 3
4. D
5. d. 50 km
6. c. I and IV
7. b. 4.5cm

Chapter 10

10.1

Set A. Answers may vary
Set B
1. 5 feet
2. 2. d. 5 kilometers
3. c. The length of a car
4. b. 10
5. 82°
6. Answers may vary
7. 1 and 3
8. 8. the length of a swimming pool
9. c. 60 kg
10. c. grams
11. a. The amount of water in a cup

10.2

1. 2½ inches
2-9. Answers may vary
10. b. Michael
11. Carlos
12. Answers may vary
12. c. 7 cm

10.3

1a. 10
1b. 10
1c. 10

1d. 14
1e. 9
1f. 8
1g. 9
1h. 4
1i. 12
1j. 6
1k. 10
1l. 8
1m. 5
1n. 8
1o. 9
1p. 4
1q. 9
1r. 3
1s. 4
1t. 7
1u. 5 ½
2. Answers may vary
3. a. 23
4. They are the same area.
5. Answers may vary
6. c. 36
7. 40.2 inches
8. b. 5
9. d. 54
10. C
11. Answers may vary
12. b. 11 square centimeters
13. d. 6 + 4 + 6 + 4
14. Answers may vary
15. b. 6 centimeters
16. 14 tiles

10.4

1. b. 8
2. a. The box with the tennis balls
3. d. 50 cubes
4. A

10.5

1. 9:59
2. 1:00 and 10:00
3. c. 3½
4. a. 2 miles
5. b. Half an hour
6. b. a 102 minute film
7. b. 20 hours

8. 7:25

Chapter 11
11.1
1. Answers may vary
2. Answers may vary
3. c. 1,300
4. d. rock
5. b. 8
6. 128
7. Answers may vary
8. N
9. c. most are 9 or older
10. 100
11. Answers may vary

11.2
1. B.
2. Answers may vary

11.3
1. Answers may vary
2. 155
3. 5
4. 170
5. Answers may vary
6. Answers may vary
7. Answers may vary but some may use the mean 7.6, or the median 7
8. c. Both averages were the same
9. b. $1.43
10. 69

11.4
1. They are the same; 20.
2. #1 – 6; #2 - 20
3. SD #1 = 2.0; SD #2 = 7.4
4. a. Monday

11.5
1. Answers may vary
2. b. The cafeteria
3. b. 20
4. Answers may vary

Chapter 12
12.1
1. 1/6; 0
2. Bag A
3. 3/11
4. a. Red

5. c. 3 out of 5
6. Answers may vary
7. Answers may vary
8. RR, RB, BR, BB
9. a. The bag with 10 marbles
10. a. 1 out of 4
11. b. 11/26

12.2
1. e. All results are equally likely
2. ½
3. ¼
4. No
5. no 8/28
6. {(1,1), (1,2), (1,3), (2,1), (2,2), (2,3), (3,1), 3,2),(3,3)}

Chapter 13
13.1
1. 'A' and 'r' are variables
   E and m are variables
2. □ is 3, ○ is 6, ▲ is 8
3. multiply the numbers & subtract 3
4. $67 = (8 \times 8) + 3$
5. $6 \times □$
6. $50 - □ = 20$
7. $N \times 7$
8. $4x + 6$
9. $5k$

13.2
1. Yes, these are both examples of the distributive property
2. 709
3. 66, 59, 52, 45, 38, 31, 24, 17
   The rule is; -7
4. 7, 11, 15, 19, 23, 27, 31, 35, 39
   The rule is: +4
5. 10th, 41; 25th, 101; nth, $4n + 1$
6. 4, 9, n^2
7. 3:20 PM, Answers may vary
8. ABBABBABB
9. B.
10. 200 chirps
11. D) 24
12. 19
13. No

14. A. Divide the number in column A
    by 4

14b. 30

15. d. 24

16. c. 18 tiles

13.3

1. 9^2 and 100^2; Answers may vary

2. 9,0; 8,1; 7,2; 6,3; 5,4, 4,5; 3,6;
   2,7; 1,8; 0,9

3. Yes

4. Answers may vary

5. An odd number

6. 9; Answers may vary

7. 3 hrs, 18 mi; 8 hrs, 48 mi;
   n hours, 6n

8. b. $\square \div 5$

9. b. 13

10. d. divide the number in Column
    A by 5

13.4

1. Graphical solutions not included

2. 150 miles

3. Graphical solutions not included

4. Graphical solutions not included

5. Square

6. Answers may vary

7. b. B

8. (3,2)

13.5

1. Answers may vary

2. 20 eggs

3. b. 0,1,2,3,4,

Index